lonely planet

KOREAN

Travel Phrasebook & Dictionary

Credits

Production Editor Aileen Cudmore

Language Writers Minkyoung Kim, Jonathan Hilts-Park

Thanks

Sofie Andersen, Marc Backwell, Fergal Condon, Gwen Cotter, Soyi Kim, Kellie Langdon, Saralinda Turner, Charles Usher, Clifton Wilkinson

Published by Lonely Planet Global Limited
CRN 554153

Digital Depot, Roe Lane off Thomas Street, Dublin
D08 TCV4, Ireland (EU authorised representative)

9th Edition – Oct 2026
ISBN 978 1 80653 180 6

Printed in Malaysia 10 9 8 7 6 5 4 3 2 1

Contact lonelyplanet.com/contact

Look out for the following icons throughout the book:

'Shortcut' Phrase
Easy-to-remember alternative to the full phrase

Q&A Pair
'Question-and-answer' pair – we suggest a response to the question asked

Look for
Phrases you may see on signs, menus etc

Listen for
Phrases you may hear from officials, locals etc

LANGUAGE TIP

An insight into the Korean language

CULTURE TIP

An insight into the local culture

How to read the phrases:

- Coloured words and phrases throughout the book are phonetic guides to help you pronounce Korean.
- Lists of phrases with tinted background are options you can choose to complete the phrase above them.

These abbreviations will help you choose the right words and phrases in this book:

f	feminine	m	masculine	sg	singular
inf	informal	pl	plural		
lit	literal	pol	polite		

CONTENTS

INTRO

Korean

한국어 han·gu·gŏ

Who Speaks Korean?

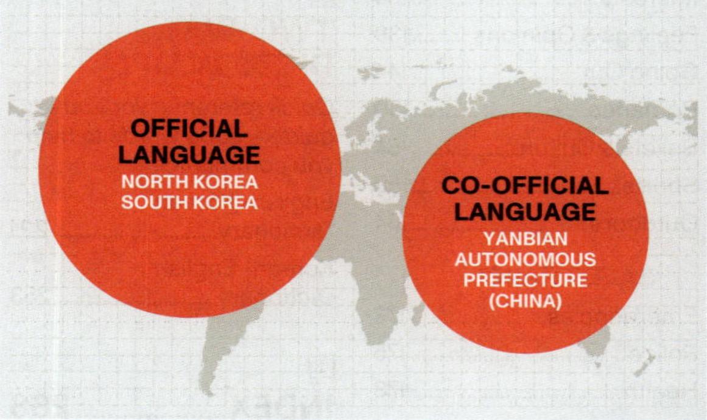

Why Bother

To understand what makes Koreans tick, you should know something about harmony and hierarchy, highly valued principles that draw on Confucian ideals. Start with the language: the Korean greeting an·nyŏng ha·se·yo 안녕하세요? (How are you?) is literally translated as 'Are you peaceful?'.

Distinctive Sounds

Korean distinguishes between 'aspirated' consonants (pronounced with a puff of air) and 'unaspirated' ones.

80 MILLION
speak Korean as their first language

10 MILLION
speak Korean as their second language

Korean Script

Korean script, Hangul, is simple and accessible. Each character represents a sound of its own. The emphasis is on the formation of syllables: eg 한 (the syllable han) is formed by an h (ㅎ), an a (ㅏ) and an n (ㄴ) in a syllabic 'box'. These 'boxes' are strung together to form words.

Korean Lexicon

Two sets of numbers are used: 'pure' Korean and 'Sino-Korean' (Korean pronunciation of words of Chinese origin). Each system has cardinal and ordinal numbers, but each is used for counting different types of things. Koreans will be forgiving if you mix them up!

Borrowings from English

Korean has borrowed many words from English, often combining them in a way that makes sense to Korean ears – eg won·num 원룸, from 'one room', is a studio apartment.

Language Family

Ural-Altaic – Manchu and Mongolian are listed as close relatives, though many scholars consider Korean a 'language isolate'.

Must-Know Grammar

Pronouns are generally not used in Korean. Instead, people are referred to by their name, title or relationship to the speaker. This book uses the so-called 'familiar polite form', a practical middle ground suitable for most situations.

Donations to English

Not many – you may recognise *kimchi, mukbang* or *taekwondo.*

5 Phrases TO LEARN BEFORE YOU GO

01 Do you have a Western-style room?

서양식 방 있나요? sŏ·yang·shik bang in·na·yo

Smaller lodgings may only have Korean-style rooms (with floor mattresses). If you want a 'proper' bed, check ahead.

02 Please bring a fork/knife.

포크/나이프 가져다 주세요.

p'o·k'ŭ/na·i·p'ŭ ga·jŏ·da ju·se·yo

In Korean restaurants the spoon is meant for rice and soup, and chopsticks are for everything else; ask if you need other utensils.

03 Can you make it less spicy?

덜 맵게 해 주시겠어요?

dŏl maep·gé hae·ju·shi·gess·ŏ·yo

Korean food is an enthusiastic assault on the senses, often spicy enough to trigger sweat or tears – you may want to play it safe.

04 Where can I find a sauna?

찜질방 어디에 있나요? jjim·jil·bang ŏ·di·é in·na·yo

Generally open 24 hours, these facilities with public baths are perfect when you need some down time – whether to watch TV, read, just relax or even sleep overnight.

05 Please call the tourist interpreting service.

통역 서비스에 전화해 주세요.

t'ong·yŏk sŏ·bi·sŭ·é jŏn·hwa·hae·ju·se·yo

To ensure that you get to the right place, Korean taxi drivers have a number to call to hook you up with someone who will translate directions for you.

10 Phrases TO SOUND LIKE A LOCAL

Hey!	여기요!	yŏ·gi·yo
Great!	좋아요!	jo·a·yo
Sure!	물론이죠!	mul·lo·ni·jyo
Maybe.	아마도요.	a·ma·do·yo
No way!	안 돼요!	an·dwae·yo
Just a minute.	잠시만요.	jam·shi·man·nyo
Just joking.	농담이에요.	nong·da·mi·e·yo
Never mind.	괜찮아요.	gwaen·cha·na·yo
No problem.	문제 없어요.	mun·jé ŏp·sŏ·yo
OK!	그렇게 해요.	gŭ·rŏ·k'é hae·yo

KOREAN

Pronunciation

Korean pronunciation should be pretty straightforward for English speakers, as most sounds are also found in English or have a close approximation. If you follow the coloured pronunciation guides we provide, you'll be able to produce the correct sounds, or at least come very close.

There are a number of competing Romanisation systems in use today for Hangul (the Korean script), and opinions differ greatly on which system is best suited to represent it. One of the most widely used is the McCune-Reischauer system (M–R), developed in the 1930s by two academics in Korea – George McCune and Edwin Reischauer.

In late 2000, however, a South Korean government agency unilaterally decreed that M–R would henceforth be scrapped in favour of a 'new' system (which is actually based on an older system) – the Revised Romanisation. The government has been changing road signs to reflect the 'new' Romanisation system, so you may encounter signs, maps and tourist literature with at least two different Romanisation systems. North Korea, however, officially tends to use a form of M–R.

In this book we've used a Romanisation system closely modelled on the South Korean government's pre-2000 version of M–R. It's been our experience that this system is easy for Korean-language newbies to use for pronouncing Korean words.

VOWEL SOUNDS

Korean has six basic vowels, all of which are found in English. The difference between the two 'combination vowels' (ae and e) is very subtle, and younger Koreans often don't make the distinction in their speech.

LETTER	ENGLISH EQUIVALENT	ENGLISH SOUND	KOREAN EXAMPLE	TRANSLITERATION
ㅏ	a	father	가수	ga·su
ㅓ	ŏ	son	서울	sŏ·ul
ㅗ	o	go	오빠	op·pa
ㅜ	u	nude	우리	u·ri
ㅣ	i	keen	시작	shi·jak
ㅡ	ŭ	put	그림	gŭ·rim
ㅐ	ae	bag	배우	bae·u
ㅔ	e/é	net	게시판	ge·shi·p'an
ㅢ	ŭi	as in 'uh each'	의사	ŭi·sa
ㅑ	ya	yahoo	야구	ya·gu
ㅕ	yŏ	young	여행	yŏ·haeng
ㅛ	yo	yoghurt	효도	hyo·do
ㅠ	yu	you	유학	yu·hak
ㅒ	yae	yank	얘기	yae·gi
ㅖ	ye	yet	예절	ye·jŏl
ㅘ	wa	wander	과일	gwa·il
ㅝ	wŏ	wonder	원숭이	wŏn·sung·i
ㅚ	oé	wet	외삼촌	oé·sam·ch'on
ㅟ	wi	week	귀신	gwi·shin
ㅙ	wae	wag	쾌락	k'wae·rak
ㅞ	we	wet	궤도	gwe·do

Note that when e appears at the end of a syllable we've used the symbol é to avoid mispronunciation.

The two other 'combination vowels' (oé and ŭi) are usually pronounced as two separate syllables. The first part is briefer than when it's an independent simple vowel, so that it almost sounds like a 'w'. When ŭi is preceded by a consonant, the ŭ is dropped, and only i is pronounced – eg 희망 hi·mang, not hŭi·mang (hope/desire).

WORD STRESS

Syllables are pronounced with fairly even emphasis in Korean, so we haven't indicated stressed syllables in this book.

CONSONANT SOUNDS

Most Korean consonant sounds are pretty close to their English counterparts. However, sometimes consonants are pronounced differently depending on their position within a word, or on the letters adjacent to them. You don't have to worry about these rules, though, as our pronunciation guides throughout this book give the correct pronunciation in the context of each phrase. If you'd like to learn more about forming syllables and sound changes in Korean, see **making syllables** (p14) and **consonant sound changes** (p14).

Korean distinguishes between aspirated consonants (formed by making a puff of air as they're pronounced) and unaspirated ones (pronounced without a puff of air). When Romanised, aspirated consonants (except for s and h) are immediately followed by an apostrophe. Some consonants can also be doubled to produce a tensed, unaspirated sound. Note, as shown in the following table, that s is pronounced sh when followed by the vowel i.

LETTER	ENGLISH EQUIVALENT	ENGLISH SOUND	KOREAN EXAMPLE	TRANSLITERATION
ㄱ	g	go	고구마	go·gu·ma
ㅋ	k'	king (aspirated)	콩나물	k'ong·na·mul
ㄲ	kk	skill	까치	kka·chi
ㄴ	n	nature	나눔	na·num
ㄷ	d	dog	어디	ŏ·di
ㅌ	t'	talk (aspirated)	탈춤	t'al·ch'um
ㄸ	tt	star	떡국	ttŏk·guk
ㄹ	l/r	lot/rod	몰라요/ 알아요	mol·la·yo/ a·ra·yo
ㅁ	m	marry	마음	ma·ŭm
ㅂ	b	bed	바보	ba·bo
ㅍ	p'	petal (aspirated)	포도	p'o·do
ㅃ	pp	spa	빨리	ppa·lli
ㅅ	s/ sh (before i)	sad/shot	선생님/ 심리학	sŏn·saeng·nim/ shim·ni·hak
ㅆ	ss	soul	쌀	ssal
ㅈ	j	jam	지도	ji·do
ㅊ	ch'	change (aspirated)	치마	ch'i·ma
ㅉ	jj	match	찌개	jjigae
ㅇ	ng at end of syllable/ silent at beginning of syllable	ring	은행	ŭn·haeng
ㅎ	h	happy (aspirated)	학교	hak·gyo

Making Syllables

In Korean, a syllable always consists of at least one vowel preceded by a consonant. Some syllables also have a consonant following the vowel. All basic vowels are either vertical (ㅏ, ㅑ, ㅓ, ㅕ and ㅣ) or horizontal (ㅗ, ㅛ, ㅜ, ㅠ and ㅡ). Combination vowels are vertical or horizontal, depending on the leftmost vowel of the combination. Vertical combination vowels are ㅐ ae, ㅔ e/é, ㅒ yae and ㅖ ye, and horizontal combination vowels are ㅚ oé, ㅢ ŭi, ㅘ wa, ㅙ wae, ㅞ we, ㅟ wi and ㅝ wŏ.

The initial position of a consonant is always to the left of a vertical vowel or above a horizontal vowel, as in ㅁ m, 마 ma, 모 mo, 미 mi, 무 mu, 매 mae or 뭐 mwŏ. Consonants following the vowel always go below the vowel, whether it's vertical or horizontal – eg 몸 mom and 맘 mam. Consonants preceding or following vertical or horizontal combination vowels follow the same positioning rules.

You might notice that the spaces between words in our coloured pronunciation guides don't always match the spacing in the Korean script. That's because the official rules for writing Korean are sometimes quite different from how words are coupled or divided in speech. Our pronunciation guides show you how to say the words in order to sound as natural as possible and be understood.

Consonant Sound Changes

Aspirated & Unaspirated Consonants

The unaspirated consonants are sometimes pronounced differently depending on their position within a word, as shown below:

LETTER	INITIAL/MIDDLE SOUND	FINAL SOUND
ㄱ	g	k
ㄷ	d	t
ㅂ	b	p
ㅈ	j	t
ㄹ	r/l	l

The -l at the end of a syllable or word sounds like a cross between an English 'l' and 'rl' in 'girl' or 'curl'. An unaspirated consonant, when preceded by h ㅎ as the final consonant of the previous syllable, becomes aspirated – compare 안다 an·da (to hug/embrace) and 않다 an·t'a (to not do something).

Double Consonants

Four unaspirated consonants (ㄱ, ㄷ, ㅂ, ㅈ) can be used to make double consonants. At the start of a word, they're pronounced more quickly and forcefully than their corresponding letters in English. As a general rule, in the middle of a word they're pronounced twice and are separated with a dot (eg k·k, p·p, t·t) in our pronunciation guides to indicate this.

The sound s (ㅅ) is the fifth consonant that can be turned into a double consonant, but represents a 'stronger' sound, rather than a sound pronounced twice. Therefore it's usually not separated with a dot (ie ss) in our pronunciation guides – with some exceptions, when it should actually be said twice (ie s·s). Similarly, two r (ㄹ) sounds representing the final consonant of one syllable and the first consonant of the following syllable are pronounced as l, eg mo·rae 모래 (sand), with one ㄹ, and mol·lae 몰래 (secretly), with two ㄹ. The double consonants are also pronounced differently depending on their position within a word:

LETTER	INITIAL SOUND	MIDDLE SOUND	FINAL SOUND
ㄲ	gg	kk	k
ㄸ	dd	tt	–
ㅃ	bb	pp	–
ㅆ	ss	ss	t
ㅉ	jj	tch	–

The 'Vowel Consonant'

The 'vowel consonant' ㅇ can be silent or pronounced, depending on its position within a syllable. At the beginning of a syllable it's silent (it serves as a place holder for a consonant in syllables that begin with a vowel sound). However, at the end of a syllable it's pronounced ng. Thus the two ㅇ characters found in the syllable 앙 ang, as in jung·ang 중앙 (central), sound completely different: the first one is silent, but the second one is pronounced ng.

If the 'vowel consonant' is immediately preceded by a consonant, the pronunciation of that consonant sound is 'moved' to the position of the 'vowel consonant'. For example, 작아요 (it's small), looks like it should be pronounced jag·a·yo, but it is actually pronounced ja·ga·yo.

Final Sound Changes

Five consonants are pronounced like a t sound when they're at the end of a word: ㅊ ch', ㅈ j, ㅅ s, ㅌ t' and ㄷ d.

Complex Consonants

There are 11 complex consonants, composed of two regular consonants. These are always at the end of a syllable. Their pronunciation depends on whether the following syllable starts with a vowel or not. Most of these complex consonants aren't common, so we won't go into them here.

Other Consonant Changes

While the pronunciation of a consonant changes according to its position within a word, it can also change depending on the consonant that immediately precedes or follows it. These sound changes are mostly the result of the tongue's position in the mouth. They occur especially when k/g ㄱ, p/b ㅂ and t/d ㄷ are followed by r/l ㄹ, n ㄴ or m ㅁ.

For example, if it's hard to pronounce the sound k followed by the sound m, the k will change to a sound that's closer to the m and easier to pronounce in conjunction with the m, eg 중국말 jung·guk + mal ('Chinese language', lit: China + talk). The k/g ㄱ followed by m ㅁ changes into ng + m, with the result being jung·gung·mal. Here are some more examples:

WORD	APPARENT PRONUNCIATION	ACTUAL PRONUNCIATION
입니다 (am/is/are pol)	ib·ni·da	im·ni·da
있는 (being/having)	it·nŭn	in·nŭn

THE HANGUL ALPHABET

Each of the letters of Hangul (the Korean alphabet) represents a distinct sound. Ten of the letters represent vowel sounds and 14 represent consonant sounds. As the vowel sounds table on page 11 shows, there are also 11 symbols representing the combination vowels formed from the original basic vowels. Add to that the symbols for the five double consonants, and you have an alphabet of 40 characters which is quite simple to learn. There are a further 11 letters for combined consonant sounds, but they follow the simple rules of the basic 14 consonants. The alphabet is given below, with the name of each letter.

KOREAN ALPHABET

		CONSONANTS			
ㄱ	gi·yŏk	ㅂ	bi·ŭp	ㅊ	ch'i·ŭt
ㄲ	ssang·gi·yŏk	ㅃ	ssang·bi·ŭp	ㅋ	k'i·ŭk
ㄴ	ni·ŭn	ㅅ	shi·ot	ㅌ	t'i·ŭt
ㄷ	di·gŭt	ㅆ	ssang·shi·ot	ㅍ	p'i·ŭp
ㄸ	ssang·di·gŭt	ㅇ	i·ŭng	ㅎ	hi·ŭt
ㄹ	ri·ŭl	ㅈ	ji·ŭt		
ㅁ	mi·ŭm	ㅉ	ssang·ji·ŭt		
		VOWELS			
ㅏ	a	ㅖ	yé	ㅝ	wŏ
ㅐ	ae	ㅗ	o	ㅞ	wé
ㅑ	ya	ㅘ	wa	ㅟ	wi
ㅒ	yae	ㅙ	wae	ㅠ	yu
ㅓ	ŏ	ㅚ	oé	ㅡ	ŭ
ㅔ	e/é	ㅛ	yo	ㅢ	ŭi
ㅕ	yŏ	ㅜ	u	ㅣ	i

KOREAN

Grammar

This chapter is designed to explain the main grammatical structures you need in order to make your own sentences. Look under each heading - listed in alphabetical order - for information on functions which these grammatical categories express in a sentence. For example, demonstratives are used for giving instructions, so you'll need them to tell the taxi driver where your hotel is, and so on.

ADJECTIVES & ADVERBS

Describing People/Things • Doing Things

Adjectives in Korean are very similar to verbs (see **verbs**, p31): they change following the same rules that depend on the final vowel of the stem and usually come at the end of a sentence. When translated into English, they include the word 'be'.

(be) high	높~ nop'~ (last vowel is o)
The mountain is high.	산이 높아요. (lit: mountain-i be-high) sa·ni no·p'a·yo (nop' + a·yo)
(be) big	크~ k'ŭ~ (last vowel is ŭ)

The park is big.	공원이 커요. (lit: park-i be-big) gong·wŏ·ni k'ŏ·yo (k'ŭ – ŭ + ŏ·yo)	

When an adjective comes before the noun, the ending ~ŭn ~은 (if the adjective ends in a consonant) or ~n ~ㄴ (if the adjective ends in a vowel) is added.

(be) high	높~ nop'~ (ends in a consonant)
This is a high mountain.	높은 산이에요. (lit: high mountain-be) no·p'ŭn sa·ni·e·yo
(be) big	크~ k'ŭ~ (ends in a vowel)
It's a big park.	큰 공원이에요. (lit: big park-be) k'ŭn gong·wo·ni·e·yo

Adverbs come before the verb they modify. See **verbs** (p31). They're usually made by adding ~gé/~ké ~게 to the adjective stem.

(be) safe	안전하~	an·jŏn·ha~
safely	안전하게	an·jŏn·ha·gé
drive safely	안전하게 운전해요 (lit: safely drive)	an·jŏn·ha·gé un·jŏn hae·yo

ARTICLES

Naming People/Things

Korean doesn't have an equivalent for 'a' and 'the'. The context will tell you whether something indefinite (corresponding to English 'a') or definite (corresponding to English 'the') is being referred to. A definite thing can be specified by the use of the demonstratives 'this' and 'that'. See **demonstratives** (p22).

BE

Describing People/Things • Making Statements

In Korean there are several verbs that translate as 'be'. To say that something or someone exists somewhere, iss·ŏ·yo 있어요 (there is/are) or ŏp·sŏ·yo 없어요 (there isn't/aren't) are used:

There's a book.	책이 있어요. (lit: book-i exist) ch'ae·gi iss·ŏ·yo
There aren't any books.	책이 없어요. (lit: book-i not-exist) ch'ae·gi ŏp·sŏ·yo

When 'be' combines with adjectives, the various forms of 'be' are built into the adjective itself (see **adjectives**, p18), but when you're talking about who you are, what you do or what something is, the verb to use is i·da 이다. Its polite familiar form is ~i·e·yo ~이에요 (if the preceding word ends in a consonant) or ~ye·yo ~예요 (if the preceding word ends in a vowel):

We're Australians.	우리는 호주사람이에요. (lit: we-nŭn Australia-people-be) u·ri·nŭn ho·ju·sa·ra·mi·e·yo
This is a university.	대학교예요. (lit: university-be) dae·hak·kyo·ye·yo

The negative of 'be' is a·ni·e·yo 아니에요, regardless of whether the previous word ends in a vowel or consonant.

This isn't our hotel.	우리 호텔이 아니에요. (lit: we hotel-i be-not) u·ri ho·t'e·ri a·ni·e·yo

The past tense of ~i·e·yo/~ye·yo is ~이었어요 ~i·ŏss·ŏ·yo, and the past tense of a·ni·e·yo is 아니었어요 a·ni·ŏss·ŏ·yo.

COUNTERS/CLASSIFIERS

Counting People/Things • Describing People/Things • Naming People/Things

When describing how many there are of an item, you use the 'pure Korean' number (see **numbers & amounts**, p38) and a specific marker (called a 'counter' or 'classifier') for that type of thing. The word order is: noun–number–classifier. Note that the 'pure Korean' words for one, two, three and four (ha·na, dul, set, net), and higher numbers ending in one, two, three or four, are shortened when followed by another word: they become 한~ han~, 두~ du~, 세~ se~, 네~ ne~.

For example, any flat pieces of paper, including tickets, are counted using the classifier ~jang ~장: han·jang (one ticket), tu·jang (two tickets), se·jang (three tickets) etc. When in doubt, it's acceptable for a foreigner to simply use the classifier ~gae ~개 for things in general, except for counting people. Here are other useful classifiers:

COMMON CLASSIFIERS

people pol	~ 분	~ bun
people pol & inf	~ 명	~ myŏng
animals	~ 마리	~ ma·ri
things in general	~ 개	~ gae
flat pieces of paper	~ 장	~ jang
books/notebooks	~ 권	~ gwŏn
cups/glasses	~ 잔	~ jan
bottles	~ 병	~ byŏng
vehicles	~ 대	~ dae

DEMONSTRATIVES

Giving Instructions • Indicating Location • Pointing Things Out

Three prefixes are used to indicate 'this' and 'that' in Korean: i~ 이~, gŭ~ 그~ and jŏ~ 저~. The prefix i~ (this) indicates something or someone close to the speaker:

this photo	이 사진	i·sa·jin

The prefix gŭ~ (that) is used to indicate something or someone close to the listener, or something previously mentioned:

that mobile phone	그 핸드폰	gŭ·haen·dŭ·p'on

The prefix jŏ~ (that over there) indicates someone or something away from both the speaker and the listener, but still visible:

that restaurant over there	저 식당	jŏ·shik·tang

HAVE

Possessing

To express possession in Korean, use the word iss·ŏ·yo (there is/are) for positive statements and ŏp·sŏ·yo (there isn't/aren't) for negative statements. The thing possessed is the subject of the sentence, while the possessor is the topic of the sentence (see **particles** for an explanation of these terms).

I have a car.	저는 차가 있어요. (lit: I-nŭn car-ga there-is) jŏ·nŭn ch'a·ga iss·ŏ·yo

I don't have a house.	저는 집이 없어요. (lit: I-nŭn house-i there-isn't) jŏ·nŭn ji·bi ŏp·sŏ·yo	

See also **be** (p20) and **possessives** (p29).

NEGATIVES

Negating

There are two simple ways to make a negative sentence in Korean. The difference between them is primarily a matter of preference. The first way is to precede the verb or adjective with an~ 안~, which functions as 'not':

It's not spicy.	안 매워요. (lit: not-spicy)	an·mae·wŏ·yo
I'm not going.	안 가요. (lit: not-go)	an·ga·yo

The second way of making a negative is by adding ~ji a·na·yo to the verb stem. See **verbs** (p31).

go	가~	ga~
I'm not going.	가지 않아요. (lit: go-ji a·na·yo)	ga·ji a·na·yo

See also **be** (p20) and **have** for the negative forms of these verbs.

PARTICLES

Doing Things • Giving Instructions • Indicating Location • Naming People/Things • Possessing

Korean nouns and pronouns are usually followed by a particle which shows the function of that noun or pronoun in the sentence (eg subject, direct object etc). Other particles act as prepositions (corresponding to the English 'at', 'to' etc), designating time, location, direction, destination and so on. In conversational speech, subject and direct object particles are often omitted, especially when the subject or object is clear.

Since particles are attached to the noun, they become part of the pronunciation of the noun itself. Which form of the particle is used often depends on whether the noun ends in a vowel or a consonant. In this book, for particles which have different forms, we give the form used if the noun ends in a consonant first, followed by the form used if the noun ends in a vowel.

Adding a particle may alter the pronunciation of the consonant that precedes it. For more on consonant changes, see **pronunciation** (p10). Below are the most common Korean particles.

Subject Particle

The subject particle ~i/~ga ~이/~가 (after a consonant/vowel respectively) is attached to the noun that functions as the subject of the sentence.

mountain(s)	산 san
The mountains are beautiful.	산이 아름다워요. (lit: mountain-i be-beautiful) sa·ni a·rŭm·da·wŏ·yo
I (as subject)	제 je
I will do it.	제가 하겠어요. (lit: I-ga do-will) je·ga ha·gess·ŏ·yo

Topic Particle

The topic particle ~ŭn/~nŭn ~은/~는 (after a consonant/vowel respectively) is used to show the subject of the sentence when you want to emphasise another part of the sentence besides the subject. A topic particle can be used to mention what the sentence is about. Topic particles tend to replace subject particles, and there's a subtle difference between the two, which may be difficult for an English speaker to catch.

Busan	부산 bu·san
Busan isn't cold.	부산은 춥지 않아요. (lit: Busan-ŭn cold-not – the emphasis is on 'not cold') bu·sa·nŭn ch'up·ji a·na·yo
I	저 jŏ
I'm a student.	저는 학생이에요. (lit: I-nŭn student-am – the emphasis is on 'student') jŏ·nŭn hak·saeng·i·e·yo

Direct Object Particle

The direct object particle ~ŭl/~rŭl ~을/~를 (after a consonant/vowel respectively) indicates the noun or pronoun that's affected by the verb.

book	책 ch'aek
My friend wants to buy a book.	제 친구가 책을 사고 싶어해요. (lit: my friend-ga book-ŭl buy want) jé ch'in·gu·ga ch'ae·gŭl sa·go shi·p'ŏ·hae·yo
bus	버스 bŏ·sŭ
I'm riding the bus.	버스를 타요. (lit: bus-rŭl ride) bŏ·sŭ·rŭl t'a·yo

Indirect Object Particle

The indirect object particles ~han·t'é ~한테 and ~e·gé ~에게 are used to show to whom something is given. There's no real difference between these two particles – the choice is one of personal preference.

that woman	그 여자 gŭ·yŏ·ja
I gave my ticket to that woman.	그 여자한테 표를 주었어요. (lit: that-woman-han·t'é ticket-rŭl gave) gŭ·yŏ·ja·han·t'é p'yo·rŭl ju·ŏss·ŏ·yo
child	어린이 ŏ·ri·ni
I gave the child a cookie.	어린이에게 과자를 주었어요. (lit: child-e·gé cookie-rŭl gave) ŏ·ri·ni·e·gé gwa·ja·rŭl ju·ŏss·ŏ·yo

Possessive Particle

The possessive particle in Korean is spelled ~ŭi ~의, but it's almost always pronounced ~é. It's used to indicate the possessor in the sentence, while the word following it shows what's possessed.

Mr Kim	미스터 김	mi·sŭ·t'ŏ gim
Mr Kim's car	미스터 김의 차 (lit: Mr Kim-é car)	mi·sŭ·t'ŏ gi·mé ch'a
Japan	일본	il·bon
the Japanese economy	일본의 경제 (lit: Japan-é economy)	il·bo·né gyŏng·jé

When the possession is clear, however, the possessive particle is often dropped. In a series of nouns, the subsequent noun (or nouns) are assumed to belong to the preceding noun. See also **possessives** (p29).

our school's car park	우리 학교 주차장 (lit: we school car park)	u·ri hak·kyo ju·ch'a·jang

Location Particle

The location particle ~é ~에 is used to indicate time, location or destination. Because of the context there's rarely any confusion about the meaning of this particle.

Wednesday	수요일	su·yo·il
on Wednesday	수요일에	su·yo·i·ré (su·yo·il + é)
four o'clock	네 시	ne·shi
at four o'clock	네 시에	ne·shi·é
Korea	한국	han·guk
in Korea	한국에	han·gu·gé (han·guk + é)
Seoul	서울	sŏ·ul
to Seoul	서울에	sŏ·u·ré (sŏ·ul + é)

PERSONAL PRONOUNS

Doing Things • Making Statements

Pronouns are generally not used in Korean, especially in the third person ('he/him', 'she/her' and 'they/them'). Instead, people are referred to by their name, their title, or especially their relationship to the speaker or listener, expressed in the form of speech. For more on this, see **titles & addressing people** (p123).

This book presents the so-called 'familiar polite form', a practical middle ground between the high form (characterised by the verb endings ~m·ni·da ~ㅂ니다 and ~m·nik·ka ~ㅂ니까) and lower forms of speech (characterised by reduced verb endings or no verb endings at all). The high form is appropriate on first meeting someone, but would sound awkward in everyday situations. On the other hand, using the low form for people you don't know could offend them. Some commonly used pronouns are shown in the table below. They can be used for both men and women.

	SINGULAR			PLURAL	
I inf/pol	내/제	nae/je	**we/us**	우리	u·ri
me inf/pol	나/저	na/jŏ			
you inf	너	nŏ	**you** inf	너희들	nŏ·hi·dŭl
you pol	당신	dang·shin	**you** pol	여러분	yŏ·rŏ·bun
she/her inf	그녀	gŭ·nyŏ	**they/them**	그들	gŭ·dŭl
he/him inf	그	gŭ			
she/her/he/him pol	그분	gŭ·bun			

Note that the third person is usually expressed by combining the words for 'this' and 'that' with the noun. See **demonstratives** (p22). The pronoun 'you' is often replaced by a third-person reference (ie a person's title or their name), especially when speaking to someone in a higher position.

PLURALS

Naming People/Things

Korean has a simple way of turning singular nouns into plurals by adding ~dŭl ~들, but this is usually omitted.

person/people	사람	sa·ram
people	사람들	sa·ram·dŭl

POSSESSIVES

Possessing

Possession is generally indicated through the use of the possessive particle. See **particles** (p23). However, special possessive adjectives for 'my' and 'your' have developed based on the possessive particle ~é.

POSSESSIVES

my inf	내	nae	from: na 나 (me inf) + é
my pol	제	jé	from: jŏ 저 (me pol) + é
your inf	네	né	from: nŏ 너 (you inf sg) + é
your pol	당신의	dang·shi·né	from: dang·shin 당신 (you pol sg) + é

In the case of 'your', nŏ·é 너의 (from nŏ + é) can also be used for clarity, since the pronunciation of nae (my inf) and né (your inf) are so similar. See also **have** (p22) and **personal pronouns** (p27).

QUESTIONS

Asking Questions

To ask about specific information, add one of the question words shown in the table on the next page just before the verb (usually towards the end of a sentence).

Where's the train station?	기차역이 어디예요? (lit: train-station-i where-is) gi·ch'a·yŏ·gi ŏ·di·ye·yo

QUESTION WORDS

how	어떻게	ŏt·tŏ·k'é
what (as subject)	뭐/뭐가	mwŏ/mwŏ·ga
what (as direct object)	뭘/무엇을	mwŏl/mu·ŏ·sŭl
when	언제	ŏn·jé
where	어디	ŏ·di
which	어느	ŏ·nŭ
who (as subject)	누가	nu·ga
who (as direct object)	누구를	nu·gu·rŭl
why	왜	wae

In the familiar polite form of speech, there's no difference in the word order or verb ending for statements and questions – a rising tone at the end indicates a question, as it can in English.

Answering questions in Korean and in English can be somewhat different. A Korean may answer 'yes' or 'no' depending on agreement or disagreement with the question. This can be confusing when the question is negative. For example, an English speaker might answer the question 'You're not a student?' with 'no' (ie 'No, I'm not') but a Korean might answer 'yes' (ie 'Yes, that's right'). The examples of these answers are given below.

yes	네	né
Yes, that's right.	네, 맞아요. (lit: yes be-right)	né ma·ja·yo
Yes, it is.	네, 그래요. (lit: yes be-like-that)	né gŭ·rae·yo
no	아니요	a·ni·yo
No, it's not.	아니요, 안 그래요. (lit: no be-like-that)	a·ni·yo an·gŭ·rae·yo

VERBS

Doing Things • Making Statements

In Korean, verbs go at the end of the sentence and don't change according to the subject. There are three basic tenses – past, present and future. In a Korean dictionary, verbs are always listed in their basic form, which is the verb stem plus the ending ~da/~ta ~다. You need to know the verb stem in order to use a verb in its past, present or future tense.

Verb endings are not used only to refer to past, present or future, but also to express the relationship between the speaker and the listener, or the speaker and the subject. See also **personal pronouns** (p27). In this phrasebook, including the dictionary, verbs are typically given in the 'familiar polite' form of speech (verb stem plus the ending ~yo ~요), which is appropriate for most situations you're likely to encounter.

Note that the pronunciation of consonants may change when endings are added. See **pronunciation** (p10) for more on consonant changes. In the following section, we have only presented regular verbs. An asterisk (*) indicates that the personal pronoun 'I' can be replaced by 'you', 'she', 'he', 'it', 'we' or 'they'.

Present

The present tense is usually formed by adding a 아 or ŏ 어 to the verb stem. To make the sentence polite, add ~yo ~요 as a final ending.

If the last vowel of the verb stem is a 아 or o 오, followed by a consonant, the verb ending for the present tense is ~a·yo:

look for	찾~	ch'aj~ (last vowel a)
I* look for	찾아요	ch'a·ja·yo (ch'aj + a·yo)
melt	녹~	nok~ (last vowel o)
it melts	녹아요	no·ga·yo (nok + a·yo)

If a verb stem ends in a 아 without a consonant following it, add ~yo instead of ~a·yo:

go	가~	ga~
I* go	가요	ga·yo (not ga·a·yo)

If a verb stem ends in o 오 without a consonant following it, ~o·a·yo at the end (the stem's o + a·yo) can change to ~wa·yo:

see	보~	bo~
I* see	봐요	bwa·yo (or bo·a·yo 보아요)

If the verb stem ends in ŭ 으, replace the ŭ with ~ŏ·yo:

use	쓰~	ssŭ~
I* use	써요	ssŏ·yo (ssŭ – ŭ + ŏ·yo)

If the last vowel of the verb stem is u, i or a combination vowel, add ~ŏ·yo to the stem:

eat	먹~	mŏg~
I* eat	먹어요	mŏ·gŏ·yo
bloom	피~	pi~
it* blooms	피어요	pi·ŏ·yo

If a verb stem ends in a ŏ 어 without a consonant following it, add ~yo instead of ~ŏ·yo:

stand	서~	sŏ~
I* stand	서요	sŏ·yo

If a verb stem ends in u 우 without a consonant following it, ~u·ŏ·yo at the end (the stem's u + ŏ·yo) can change to ~wŏ·yo:

learn	배우~	bae·u~
I* learn	배워요	bae·wŏ·yo (or bae·u·ŏ·yo 배우어요)

The common verbs ha 하~ (do) and dwoé 되~ (become) conjugate a bit differently. Instead of simply adding ~yo or ŏ-yo, change the stems to hae 해 and dwae 돼 and then add ~yo:

do	하~	ha~
I* do	해요	hae·yo
become	되~	dwoé
I* become	돼요	dwae-yo

Past

Forming the past tense is simple – the same rules apply as for the present, depending on the last vowel of the verb stem.

If the last vowel is a 아 or o 오, add ~ass·ŏ·yo or ~ssŏ·yo to the verb stem.

I* looked for	찾았어요	ch'a·jass·ŏ·yo (ch'aj + ass·ŏ·yo)
it melted	녹았어요	no·gass·ŏ·yo (nok + ass·ŏ·yo)
I* went	갔어요	gass·ŏ·yo (ga + ssŏ·yo)
I* saw	봤어요	bwass·ŏ·yo (bo + ass·ŏ·yo)

If the last vowel of the stem is ŭ 으, drop ŭ and add ~ŏss·ŏ·yo:

I* used	썼어요	ssŏss·ŏ·yo (ssŭ – ŭ + ŏss·ŏ·yo)

If the last vowel is ŏ, u, i or one of the combination vowels, the past tense ending will be ~ŏss·ŏ·yo:

I* learned	배웠어요	bae·wŏss·o·yo (bae·u + ŏss·ŏ·yo)

Future

If the verb stem ends with a consonant, just add ~ŭl gŏ·ye·yo ~을 거예요 to form the future tense. If the verb stem ends with a vowel, add ~l gŏ·ye·yo ~ㄹ 거예요. These can also appear as ~ŭlk·ke·yo ~을게요 and ~lk·ke·yo ~ㄹ게요, respectively.

look for	찾~	ch'aj~
I* will look for	찾을 거예요	ch'a·jŭl gŏ·ye·yo (ch'aj + ŭl gŏ·ye·yo)
go	가~	ga~
I* will go	갈 거예요	gal gŏ·ye·yo (ga + l gŏ·ye·yo)

Alternatively, regardless of whether the verb stem ends with a consonant or a vowel, ~gess·ŏ·yo ~겠어요 can be added in order to make future tense.

WORD ORDER

Making Statements

Korean word order differs from that of English: the typical order is subject–object–verb, rather than subject–verb–object. The subject is not always necessary.

I came from Australia.	(저는) 호주에서 왔어요. (lit: (I-nŭn) Australia-from came) (jŏ·nŭn) ho·ju·e·sŏ wass·ŏ·yo

See also **negatives** (p23) and **questions** (p29).

LANGUAGE TIP: VOWELS & CONSONANTS

Throughout this book, when two options are given to complete words in a follow-on list, the first one is for a word ending with a consonant, and the second one for a word ending with a vowel:

...이/가 ...·i/·ga	...과/와 ...·gwa/·wa
...은/는 ...·ŭn/·nŭn	...이에요/예요 ...·i·e·yo/·ye·yo
...을/를 ...·ŭl/·rŭl	...이요/요 ...·i·yo/·yo

In case of ...으로/로 ...·ŭ·ro/·ro, if the noun ends with the consonant l ㄹ, 로 (pronounced ·lo) should be added.

BASICS

Understanding

KEY PHRASES

Do you speak English?	영어 할 줄 아세요?	yŏng·ŏ hal jul a·se·yo?
I don't understand.	못 알아 들었어요.	mo·da·ra·dŭ·rŏss·ŏ·yo
What does … mean?	… 무슨 뜻이에요?	… mu·sŭn·ddŭ·shi·e·yo

Q **Do you speak (English)?**	(영어) 할 줄 아세요? (yŏng·ŏ) hal jul a·se·yo?
Q **Does anyone speak (English)?**	(영어) 하시는 분 있나요? (yŏng·ŏ) ha·shi·nŭn·bun in·na·yo
A **I speak (English).**	전 (영어) 해요. jŏn (yŏng·ŏ) hae·yo
A **I don't speak (Korean).**	전 (한국말) 못 해요. jŏn (han·gung·mal) mo·t'ae·yo
A **I speak a little.**	조금 할 줄 알아요. jo·gŭm hal·jul a·ra·yo
Q **Do you understand?**	알아 들으셨나요? a·ra·dŭ·rŭ·shŏn·na·yo
A **I understand.**	알아 들었어요. a·ra·dŭ·rŏss·ŏ·yo
A **I don't understand.**	못 알아 들었어요. mo·da·ra·dŭ·rŏss·ŏ·yo
I'd like to learn some Korean.	한국말 좀 배우고 싶어요. han·gung·mal jom bae·u·go shi·p'ŏ·yo

LANGUAGE TIP: KONGLISH

Koreans have borrowed many words from English. These 'Konglish' terms are often shorter versions of English words (eg a·p'a·t'ŭ 아파트 is 'apartment'), though some are made by combining English words (eg haen·dŭ·p'on 핸드폰 is 'mobile/cell phone', lit: 'hand phone'). However, the meanings of the English words and the Konglish terms don't always add up. A hat·do·gŭ 핫도그 (from 'hot dog'), for example, usually refers to a 'corn dog', and a k'on·do 콘도 (from 'condo') means 'time-share'.

What does ... mean?	… 무슨 뜻이에요? … mu·sŭn·ddŭ·shi·e·yo
What's this called in Korean?	한국말로 이걸 뭐라고 하나요? han·gung·mal·lo i·gŏl mwŏ·ra·go ha·na·yo
How do you say ... in Korean?	…이/가 한국말로 뭐예요? …·i/·ga han·gung·mal·lo mwŏ·ye·yo
How do you pronounce this?	이걸 어떻게 발음하나요? i·gŏl ŏt·tŏ·k'é ba·rŭm·ha·na·yo
How do you write ...?	… 어떻게 쓰나요? … ŏt·tŏ·k'é ssŭ·na·yo
Could you please repeat that?	다시 말씀해 주시겠어요? da·shi mal·ssŭm·hae ju·shi·gess·ŏ·yo
Could you please write it down?	적어 주시겠어요? jŏ·gŏ ju·shi·gess·ŏ·yo
Could you please speak more slowly?	천천히 말씀해 주시겠어요? ch'ŏn·ch'ŏn·hi mal·ssŭm·hae ju·shi·gess·ŏ·yo

Slowly, please! 천천히요! ch'ŏn·ch'ŏn·hi·yo

Numbers & Amounts

KEY PHRASES

How much (amount)?	얼만큼요?	ŏl·man·k'ŭm·myo
How many?	몇 개나요?	myŏk·kae·na·yo
a little/some	조금	jo·gŭm
a lot/many	많이	ma·ni

PURE KOREAN CARDINAL NUMBERS

Pure Korean numbers are used for expressing the hour when telling the time, for counting objects and people, and for expressing your age. They can only be written in Hangul or as digits, not in Chinese characters. From 100 on, however, Sino-Korean numbers take over (p40). Note also that there's no pure Korean word for 'zero'.

1	하나	ha·na
2	둘	dul
3	셋	set
4	넷	net
5	다섯	da·sŏt
6	여섯	yŏ·sŏt
7	일곱	il·gop
8	여덟	yŏ·dŏl
9	아홉	a·hop
10	열	yŏl
11	열하나	yŏl·ha·na
12	열둘	yŏl·dul

13	열셋	yŏl·set
14	열넷	yŏl·let
15	열다섯	yŏl·da·sŏt
16	열여섯	yŏl·yŏ·sŏt
17	열일곱	yŏl·il·gop
18	열여덟	yŏl·yŏ·dŏl
19	열아홉	yŏ·ra·hop
20	스물	sŭ·mul
21	스물하나	sŭ·mul·ha·na
22	스물둘	sŭ·mul·dul
30	서른	sŏ·rŭn
40	마흔	ma·hŭn
50	쉰	shwin
60	예순	ye·sun
70	일흔	il·hŭn
80	여든	yŏ·dŭn
90	아흔	a·hŭn

LANGUAGE TIP: 'PURE' & SINO-KOREAN NUMBERS

Two numbering systems are used in Korea: the 'pure Korean' words for numbers and those with 'Sino-Korean' pronunciation (the Korean pronunciation of numbers of Chinese origin).

Each system has both cardinal and ordinal numbers. Both pure Korean and Sino-Korean numbers are used to state quantities of things. Pure Korean numbers are also used as counters or classifiers (see **grammar**, p21). There's a clear separation between the types of things counted with each system, but Korean speakers will be forgiving if you mix up the two.

SINO-KOREAN CARDINAL NUMBERS

Sino-Korean numbers are used to express minutes when telling the time, as well as dates and months of the year. They're also used for addresses, phone numbers, amounts of money and floors of a building. From 100 on, they take over from pure Korean numbers. They may be written in Hangul, as digits, or in Chinese characters.

0	영/공	yŏng/gong
1	일	il
2	이	i
3	삼	sam
4	사	sa
5	오	o
6	육	yuk
7	칠	ch'il
8	팔	p'al
9	구	gu
10	십	ship
11	십일	shi·bil
12	십이	shi·bi
13	십삼	ship·sam
14	십사	ship·sa
15	십오	shi·bo
16	십육	shim·nyuk
17	십칠	ship·ch'il
18	십팔	ship·p'al
19	십구	ship·gu
20	이십	i·ship
21	이십일	i·shi·bil
22	이십이	i·shi·bi
30	삼십	sam·ship

40	사십	sa·ship
50	오십	o·ship
60	육십	yuk·ship
70	칠십	ch'il·ship
80	팔십	p'al·ship
90	구십	gu·ship
100	백	baek
200	이백	i·baek
1000	천	ch'ŏn
2000	이천	i·ch'ŏn
10,000	만	man
50,000	오만	o·man
100,000	십만	shim·man
800,000	팔십만	p'al·shim·man
1,000,000	백만	paeng·man
3,000,000	삼백만	sam·baeng·man

ORDINAL NUMBERS

Add the suffix ·jjae 째 to pure Korean cardinal numbers to create ordinals. Note that here, ha·na 하나 (one) has been replaced by a new word, ch'ŏt 첫. For two-digit ordinal numbers ending in 1 or 2, abbreviated forms are used (han 한 and tu 두).

1st	첫째	chŏt·jjae
2nd	둘째	dul·jjae
3rd	셋째	set·jjae
4th	넷째	net·jjae
5th	다섯째	da·sŏt·jjae

Unlike the cardinal numbers, pure Korean and Sino-Korean ordinal numbers are more easily interchangeable. The Sino-Korean method is to simply add the prefix je· before the Sino-Korean cardinal number.

1st	제일/제1	je·il
2nd	제이/제2	je·i
3rd	제삼/제3	je·sam

FRACTIONS & DECIMALS

Fractions use Sino-Korean numbers, but they're in reverse order from the words in English. Note that 'half' has its own Sino-Korean word, ban 반. When counting objects, 'half' comes after the counting marker (see the literal translations below).

a half	이분의 일/반	i·bu·ne·il/ban
two and a half (things)	두 개 반 (lit: two-gae-half)	du·gae·ban
a quarter	사분의 일	sa·bu·ne·il
a third	삼분의 일	sam·bu·ne·il
three-quarters	사분의 삼 (lit: four-divide-é-three)	sa·bu·ne·sam
all	다	da

Decimals are read using Sino-Korean numbers. The word for the decimal point itself is jŏm 점.

3.14	삼 점 일 사	sam·jŏ·mil·sa
4.2	사 점 이	sa·jŏ·mi

LANGUAGE TIP: COUNTERS/CLASSIFIERS

When describing how many there are of an item, you use the pure Korean number followed by a specific marker used to count that type of thing – a bit like saying 'three pairs of shoes' in English. For examples of counters (or 'classifiers') and how to use them, see **grammar** (p21).

LANGUAGE TIP: THE 1.5 GENERATION

The term used for ethnic Koreans born in Korea but raised elsewhere is il·jŏ·mo·sé 일 점 오세 (lit: 1.5 generation).

USEFUL AMOUNTS

How much (amount)?	얼만큼요? ŏl·man·k'ŭm·myo
How many?	몇 개나요? myŏk·kae·na·yo
Please give me ...	... 주세요. ... ju·se·yo

double	두 배	du·bae
triple	세 배	se·bae
10 times as much	열 배	yŏl·bae
enough ...	... 충분히	... ch'ung·bun·hi
a few	몇 개	myŏk·kae
less ...	... 덜	... dŏl
a little	조금	jo·gŭm
a lot	많이	ma·ni
many	많이	ma·ni
more ...	... 더	... dŏ
much	많이	ma·ni
some ...	... 조금	... jo·gŭm

CULTURE TIP: WEIGHTS & MEASURES

Korea generally employs the metric system. However, there are still some traditional measures for food (gŭn 근 and don 돈) and area (p'yŏng 평, most commonly used to measure floor space). In addition, Koreans still use the imperial system in some sports such as golf.

In 2006 the government set out to officially convert all nonmetric measurements in both the public and corporate sectors to metric, with threats of fines to back up the move. In particular, they're targeting traditional measures, but it's still not clear how well the new rules will be applied by Mr Cho hawking vegetables in the local market or Ms Park trying to sell that 30-*pyong* apartment.

Note that certain measures use pure Korean numbers, while others use Sino-Korean numbers:

Pure Korean numbers

한 돈	han·don	*don* (3.75g)
한 근	han·gŭn	*gun* (600g)
... 한 병	... han·byŏng	a bottle of ...
한 쌍	han·ssang	pair
한 조각	han·jo·gak	slice
한 캔	han·k'aen	tin (can)

Sino-Korean numbers

일 그램	il·gŭ·raem	gram
일 킬로그램	il·k'il·lo·gŭ·raem	kilogram
오백 시시	o·baek·shi·shi	half a litre (500 mL)
일 리터	il·li·tŏ	litre
일 평	il·p'yŏng	*pyong* (3.3 sq metres)
(만 원)어치 ...	(ma·nwŏn)·ŏ·ch'i ...	(10,000 won) worth of ...

Time & Dates

KEY PHRASES

What time is it?	몇 시예요?	myŏs·shi·ye·yo
At what time ...?	몇 시에 ...?	myŏs·shi·é ...
What date is it today?	오늘이 며칠이에요?	o·nŭ·ri myŏ·chi·ri·e·yo

TELLING THE TIME

In Korean, time is usually told using a 12-hour clock, but schedules for trains, buses, movies and so on typically use a 24-hour clock. Both the pure Korean and the Sino-Korean numbering systems are used (see **numbers & amounts**, p38). The hour is expressed with pure Korean cardinal numbers followed by ·shi 시 (hour), and the minutes are expressed with Sino-Korean cardinal numbers followed by ·bun 분 (minutes). The suffix ·ban 반 (half) can be used to indicate half past the hour. To describe a time before the hour, add ·jŏn 전 (before) to the number of minutes (in Sino-Korean cardinal numbers) before the hour.

Q **What time is it?**	몇 시예요? myŏs·shi·ye·yo
A **It's (one) o'clock.**	(한) 시요. (han)·shi·yo
A **It's (two) o'clock.**	(두) 시요. (du)·shi·yo
A **Five past (two).**	(두) 시 오 분이요. (du)·shi o·bu·ni·yo
A **Quarter past (two).**	(두) 시 십오 분이요. (du)·shi shi·bo·bu·ni·yo

Ⓐ **Half past (two).**	(두) 시 삼십 분이요. (du)·shi sam·ship·bu·ni·yo (두) 시 반이요. (du)·shi ba·ni·yo
Ⓐ **Quarter to (three).**	(세) 시 십오 분 전이요. (se)·shi shi·bo·bun jŏ·ni·yo
Ⓐ **Twenty to (three).**	(세) 시 이십 분 전이요. (se)·shi i·ship·bun jŏ·ni·yo
(9)am	오전 (아홉 시) o·jŏn (a·hop·shi)
(3)pm	오후 (세 시) o·hu (se·shi)
Ⓠ **At what time ...?**	몇 시에 ...? myŏs·shi·é ...
Ⓐ **At (five) o'clock.**	(다섯) 시에요. (da·sŏs)·shi·é·yo
Ⓐ **At (7.57pm).**	(오후 일곱 시 오십칠 분)에요. (o·hu il·gop·shi o·ship·ch'il·bun)·é·yo

dawn	새벽	sae·byŏk
sunrise	해돋이/일출	hae·do·ji/il·ch'ul
morning	아침	a·ch'im
day	낮	nat
noon	정오	jŏng·o
afternoon	오후	o·hu
evening	저녁	jŏ·nyŏk
night	밤	bam
sunset	해넘이/일몰	hae·nŏ·mi/il·mol
midnight	자정	ja·jŏng

THE CALENDAR

Like their English counterparts, the Korean words which represent the days of the week have a special meaning. Starting with Sunday, the names represent the sun, the moon, fire, water, trees, gold and land.

Monday	월요일	wŏ·ryo·il
Tuesday	화요일	hwa·yo·il
Wednesday	수요일	su·yo·il
Thursday	목요일	mo·gyo·il
Friday	금요일	gŭ·myo·il
Saturday	토요일	t'o·yo·il
Sunday	일요일	i·ryo·il

The word for each month is simply its corresponding Sino-Korean cardinal number followed by ·wŏl 월 (the Sino-Korean word for 'moon/month'). The only exceptions are that yuk 육 (six) becomes yu 유 and ship 십 (10) becomes shi 시. Lunar calendar dates use the same terminology, so Koreans may differentiate between the two by referring to yang·nyŏk 양력 (Western calendar) or ŭm·nyŏk 음력 (lunar calendar).

January	일월	i·rwŏl
February	이월	i·wŏl
March	삼월	sa·mwŏl
April	사월	sa·wŏl
May	오월	o·wŏl
June	유월	yu·wŏl
July	칠월	ch'i·rwŏl
August	팔월	p'a·rwŏl
September	구월	ku·wŏl
October	시월	shi·wŏl
November	십일월	shi·bi·rwŏl
December	십이월	shi·bi·wŏl

Dates are given from larger to smaller (ie year–month–date) using Sino-Korean cardinal numbers followed by ·nyŏn 년, ·wŏl 월 and ·il 일 to express the year, month and date respectively. For counting the actual number of days, see the box on page 49.

CULTURE TIP: THE LUNAR CALENDAR

The Western (Gregorian) calendar is used in Korea, but traditional holidays such as Chusok (which falls on the 15th day of the eighth lunar month), Buddha's Birthday and, of course, Lunar New Year (the first day of the first lunar month) are calculated according to the lunar calendar. Korean calendars often have lunar dates printed in small numbers at the bottom of each day. The lunar year starts in late January or in early February. Like the Gregorian calendar, the lunar calendar has 12 months. Most Koreans know their birth date in both calendars.

Q **What date is it today?**	오늘이 며칠이에요? o·nŭ·ri myŏ·chi·ri·e·yo
A **It's (13 October 2027).**	(이천이십칠년 시월 십삼일)이에요. (i·ch'ŏn·i·ship·chil·nyŏn shi·wŏl ship·sa·mir)·i·e·yo

The Korean calendar is divided into four seasons, each starting a few weeks earlier than its Western counterpart. Korean seasons are further divided into four periods corresponding roughly to that season starting, rising, falling and ending.

spring	봄	bom
summer	여름	yŏ·rŭm
autumn/fall	가을	ga·ŭl
winter	겨울	gyŏ·ul
summer solstice	하지	ha·ji
winter solstice	동지	dong·ji
rainy season	장마	jang·ma

PRESENT

(right) now	(바로) 지금	(ba·ro) ji·gŭm
today	오늘	o·nŭl

tonight	오늘 밤	o·nŭl·bam
for (two days)	(이틀) 동안	(i·t'ŭl)·dong·an
this morning	오늘 아침	o·nŭl a·ch'im
this afternoon	오늘 오후	o·nŭl o·hu
this week	이번 주	i·bŏn·ju
this month	이번 달	i·bŏn·dal
this year	올해	ol·hae

PAST

yesterday	어제	ŏ·jé
the day before yesterday	그저께	gŭ·jŏk·ké
since (May)	(오월)부터	(o·wŏl)·bu·t'ŏ
half an hour ago	삼십 분 전에	sam·ship·bun·jŏ·né
three days ago	사흘 전에	sa·hŭl·jŏ·né

☑ LANGUAGE TIP: COUNTING DAYS

Korean uses both a Sino-Korean and a pure Korean system of counting days. The first one is easy: you just combine Sino-Korean numbers with il 일, the Sino-Korean word for 'day':

one day	일일	i·ril
two days	이일	i·il
three days	삼일	sa·mil
four days	사일	sa·il
five days	오일	o·il
six days	육일	yu·gil

Pure Korean, however, has special words for 'one day' (ha·ru 하루), 'two days' (i·t'ŭl 이틀), 'three days' (sa·hŭl 사흘) and so on.

five years ago	오 년 전에	o·nyŏn·jŏ·né
a while ago	얼마 전에	ŏl·ma·jŏ·né
yesterday morning	어제 아침	ŏ·jé a·ch'im
yesterday afternoon	어제 오후	ŏ·jé o·hu
yesterday evening	어제 저녁	ŏ·jé jŏ·nyŏk
last night	어젯밤	ŏ·jép·pam
last week	지난주	ji·nan·ju
last month	지난달	ji·nan·dal
last year	작년	jang·nyŏn

FUTURE

tomorrow	내일	nae·il
the day after tomorrow	모레	mo·ré
until (June)	(유월)까지	(yu·wŏl)k·ka·ji
in five minutes	오 분 안에	o·bun a·né
in an hour	한 시간 안에	han·shi·gan a·né
in six days	엿새 안에	yŏs·sae a·né
in a month	한 달 안에	han·dal a·né
tomorrow morning	내일 아침	nae·il a·ch'im
tomorrow afternoon	내일 오후	nae·il o·hu
tomorrow evening	내일 저녁	nae·il jŏ·nyŏk
next week	다음 주	da·ŭm·ju
next month	다음 달	da·ŭm·dal
next year	내년	nae·nyŏn

PRACTICAL

Transport

KEY PHRASES

When's the next bus?	다음 버스 언제 있나요?	da·ŭm bŏ·sŭ ŏn·jé in·na·yo
A one-way ticket to ..., please.	... 편도 표 주세요.	... p'yŏn·do p'yo ju·se·yo
Please tell me when we get to ...	...에 도착하면 좀 알려주세요.	...·é do·ch'a·k'a·myŏn jom al·lyŏ·ju·se·yo
Please take me to ...	...으로 가 주세요.	...·ŭ·ro ga·ju·se·yo
I'd like to hire a car.	차 빌리고 싶어요.	ch'a bil·li·go shi·p'ŏ·yo

GETTING AROUND

Does this ... go to (Cheonan)?	이 ... (천안)에 가나요? i ... (ch'ŏ·nan)·é ga·na·yo
Which ... goes to (Myeongdong)?	어느 ...이/가 (명동)에 가나요? ŏ·nŭ ...·i/·ga (myŏng·dong)·é ga·na·yo

boat	배	bae
bus	버스	bŏ·sŭ
metro line	지하철 노선	ji·ha·ch'ŏl no·sŏn
train	기차	gi·ch'a

When's the first (bus)?	첫 (버스) 언제 있나요? ch'ŏt (bŏ·sŭ) ŏn·jé in·na·yo
When's the last (bus)?	마지막 (버스) 언제 있나요? ma·ji·mak (bŏ·sŭ) ŏn·jé in·na·yo
When's the next (bus)?	다음 (버스) 언제 있나요? da·ŭm (bŏ·sŭ) ŏn·jé in·na·yo
What time does it leave?	언제 떠나요? ŏn·jé dŏ·na·yo
What time does it get to (Busan)?	(부산)에 언제 도착하나요? (bu·san)·é ŏn·jé do·ch'a·k'a·na·yo
How long will it be delayed?	얼마나 연착되나요? ŏl·ma·na yŏn·ch'ak·doé·na·yo
Is this seat available?	여기 자리 있나요? yŏ·gi ja·ri in·na·yo

Is this seat free? 빈 자리예요? bin ja·ri·ye·yo

That's my seat.	제 자리예요. jé ja·ri·ye·yo
Please tell me when we get to (Daejeon).	(대전)에 도착하면 좀 알려주세요. (dae·jŏn)·é do·ch'a·k'a·myŏn jom al·lyŏ·ju·se·yo
How long do we stop here?	여기서 얼마 동안 서나요? yŏ·gi·sŏ ŏl·ma dong·an sŏ·na·yo
Can we get there by public transport?	대중교통으로 갈 수 있나요? dae·jung·gyo·t'ong·ŭ·ro gal·su in·na·yo
Let's walk there.	우리 걸어 가요. u·ri gŏ·rŏ·ga·yo

BUYING TICKETS

Where do I buy a ticket?	표 어디에서 사나요? p'yo ŏ·di·e·sŏ sa·na·yo
Do I need to book?	예약해야 하나요? ye·ya·k'ae·ya ha·na·yo
A ... ticket (to Daegu), please.	(대구 가는) ... 표 주세요. (dae·gu ga·nŭn) ... p'yo ju·se·yo

1st-class	일등석	il·dŭng·sŏk
child's	어린이	ŏ·ri·ni
one-way	편도	p'yŏn·do
return	왕복	wang·bok
standard class	일반석	il·ban·sŏk
standing room	입석	ip·sŏk
student	학생	hak·saeng

I'd like a/an ... seat.	... 주세요. ... ju·se·yo

aisle	내측 좌석	nae·ch'ŭk jwa·sŏk
window	창측 좌석	ch'ang·ch'ŭk jwa·sŏk

Is there a couchette/sleeper?	침대차 있나요? ch'im·dae·ch'a in·na·yo
Is there a toilet?	화장실 있나요? hwa·jang·shil in·na·yo
How long does the trip take?	얼마나 걸리나요? ŏl·ma·na gŏl·li·na·yo

Buying a Ticket

WHAT TIME IS THE NEXT ...?
다음 ... 언제 있나요?
da·ŭm ... ŏn·jé in·na·yo

BOAT
배
bae

BUS
버스
bŏ·sŭ

TRAIN
기차
ki·ch'a

ONE ... TICKET, PLEASE.
... 표 주세요.
... p'yo ju·se·yo

ONE-WAY
편도
p'yŏn·do

RETURN
왕복
wang·bok

I'D LIKE A/AN ... SEAT.
... 주세요.
... ju·se·yo

AISLE
내측 좌석
nae·ch'ŭk jwa·sŏk

WINDOW
창측 좌석
ch'ang·ch'ŭk jwa·sŏk

WHICH PLATFORM DOES IT DEPART FROM?
어느 승강장에서 출발하나요?
ŏ·nŭ sŭng·gang·jang·e·sŏ ch'ul·bal ha·na·yo

Is it a direct route?	직행 노선인가요? ji·k'aeng no·sŏ·nin·ga·yo
Can I get a stand-by ticket?	대기표를 살 수 있나요? dae·gi·p'yo·rŭl sal·su in·na·yo
What time should I check in?	체크인 몇 시예요? ch'e·k'ŭ·in myŏs·shi·ye·yo
I'd like to cancel my ticket.	표를 취소해 주세요. p'yo·rŭl ch'wi·so·hae ju·se·yo
I'd like to change my ticket.	표를 바꿔 주세요. p'yo·rŭl bak·kwŏ ju·se·yo
I'd like to collect my ticket.	표를 받으려고요. p'yo·rŭl ba·dŭ·ryŏ·go·yo
I'd like to confirm my ticket.	표 예약 확인 해 주세요. p'yo ye·yak hwa·gin hae·ju·se·yo

LUGGAGE

My luggage is damaged.	제 짐이 망가졌어요. jé ji·mi mang·ga·jŏss·ŏ·yo
My luggage is lost.	제 짐이 없어졌어요. jé ji·mi ŏp·sŏ·jŏss·ŏ·yo

LISTEN FOR

갈아타는 곳	ga·ra·t'a·nŭn·got	transfer point
종점	jong·jŏm	final stop
만석	man·sŏk	full
승강장	sŭng·gang·jang	platform
지연/연착	ji·yŏn/yŏn·ch'ak	delayed
취소/결항	ch'wi·so/gyŏl·hang	cancelled

LISTEN FOR

기내 반입 수하물	gi·nae ba·nip su·ha·mul	carry-on baggage
초과 수하물	ch'o·gwa su·ha·mul	excess baggage
탑승권	t'ap·sŭng·gwŏn	boarding pass
환승	hwan·sŭng	transit

My luggage has been stolen. 제 짐을 도둑 맞았어요. jé ji·mŭl do·dung·ma·jass·ŏ·yo

Where can I find a/the ...? … 어디에 있나요? ... ŏ·di·é in·na·yo

baggage claim	수하물 수취대	su·ha·mul su·ch'wi·dae
left-luggage office	분실 수하물 보관소	bun·shil su·ha·mul bo·gwan·so
luggage locker	짐 보관소	jim bo·gwan·so
trolley/cart	짐 카트	jim k'a·t'ŭ

PLANE

When does flight (OZ 603) arrive/depart? (OZ603)편 언제 도착하나요/ 출발하나요? (o·ji yuk·kong·sam)·p'yŏn ŏn·jé do·ch'a·k'a·na·yo/ ch'ul·bal·ha·na·yo

Where's (the) ...?	... 어디 있나요?	... ŏ·di in·na·yo

airport shuttle bus	공항 리무진 버스	gong·hang ri·mu·jin bŏ·sŭ
arrivals hall	입국장	ip·guk·jang
departures hall	출국장	ch'ul·guk·jang
duty-free shop	면세점	myŏn·se·jŏm
gate (20)	(이십)번 게이트	(i·ship)·bŏn ge·i·t'ŭ

BUS

Where's the bus stop?	버스 정류장이 어디예요?	bŏ·sŭ jŏng·nyu·jang·i ŏ·di·ye·yo
How often do buses come?	버스가 얼마나 자주 오나요?	bŏ·sŭ·ga ŏl·ma·na ja·ju o·na·yo
What's the next stop?	다음 정류장이 어디예요?	da·ŭm chŏng·nyu·jang·i ŏ·di·ye·yo
I'd like to get off at (Nadaemun).	(남대문)에서 내려요.	(nam·dae·mun)·e·sŏ nae·ryŏ·yo

LOOK FOR

노약자, 장애인, 임산부 좌석	no·yak·ja jang·ae·in im·san·bu jwa·sŏk	seats for seniors, the disabled, and pregnant women

... bus ... 버스
... bŏ·sŭ

1st-class city	좌석	jwa·sŏk
city	시내	shi·nae
city tour	시티투어	shi·t'i·t'u·ŏ
express	고속	go·sok
intercity	광역	gwang·yŏk
local	마을/지선	ma·ŭl/ji·sŏn
direct	직행	ji·k'aeng
shuttle	순환	sun·hwan
tourist	관광	gwan·gwang

METRO/SUBWAY

There's no difference in meaning between the terms jŏn·ch'ŏl 전철 (metro) and ji·ha·ch'ŏl 지하철 (subway) in Korean. The signs in all of the subway systems are bilingual (Korean and English) or even trilingual (with Chinese characters) and are colour-coordinated, so it's easy to get around.

Does this train go to (Incheon)?	이 기차 (인천) 가나요? i·gi·ch'a (in·ch'ŏn) ga·na·yo
Where's exit (1)?	(1)번 출구가 어디예요? (il)·bŏn ch'ul·gu·ga ŏ·di·ye·yo
Where do I go to transfer to ...?	...으로/로 갈아타려면 어디로 가야 해요? ...ŭ·ro/·ro ga·ra·t'a·ryŏ·myŏn ŏ·di·ro ga·ya hae·yo

TRAIN

What's the next station?	다음 역이 어디예요? da·ŭm yŏ·gi ŏ·di·ye·yo
Does it stop at (Gyeongju)?	(경주) 가나요? (gyŏng·ju) ga·na·yo
Do I need to change?	갈아타야 하나요? ga·ra·t'a·ya ha·na·yo
Is it direct?	직행 노선이에요? ji·k'aeng no·sŏ·ni·e·yo
I'd like (the) ...	... 주세요. ... ju·se·yo

1st class	특실	t'ŭk·shil
dining section	식당칸	shik·dang·k'an
KTX (bullet train) regular class	케이티엑스 일반실	k'e·i·t'i·ek·sŭ il·ban·shil
sleeping section	침대칸	ch'im·dae·k'an

CULTURE TIP: TRAIN TYPES

Train service in Korea varies according to the type of train you're on.

The sae·ma·ŭl 새마을 *(Saemaeul)* are comfortable express trains that hit only a few cities on their cross-country journey. These are cheaper than the KTX (bullet train), but take about twice as long to make the journey.

One notch lower still is the mu·gung·hwa 무궁화 *(Mugunghwa)*, which is cheaper and stops at even more stations.

LISTEN FOR

교통카드 충전소	gyo·t'ong k'a·dŭ ch'ung·jŏn·so place to add money to prepaid transit card
노선도	no·sŏn·do subway/railway line information
... 방면	... bang·myŏn (trains going) in the direction of ...
안내도	an·nae·do map with information about facilities
운임표	u·nim·p'yo list of fares
첫 차/막 차	ch'ŏt·ch'a/mak·ch'a first/last train (of the day)
현 위치	hyŏn wi·ch'i You are here.

BOAT

Where does the boat leave from?	배가 어디서 출발하나요? bae·ga ŏ·di·sŏ ch'ul·bal ha·na·yo
Is this a sightseeing boat?	이게 유람선인가요? i·gé yu·ram·sŏn·in·ga·yo
Can I take my car on the boat?	차를 배에 실을 수 있나요? ch'a·rŭl bae·é shi·rŭl·su in·na·yo
cabin	선실 sŏn·shil
deck	갑판 gap·p'an
high-speed ferry	쾌속선 k'wae·sok·sŏn
lifeboat	구명선 gu·myŏng·sŏn
life jacket	구명조끼 gu·myŏng·jok·ki

TAXI

To make communication easier between drivers and overseas visitors, taxi drivers who don't speak English have a number to call to hook you up with someone who will translate for you.

Where's the taxi rank?	택시 정류장이 어디예요? t'aek·shi jŏng·nyu·jang·i ŏ·di·ye·yo
deluxe taxi	모범 택시 mo·bŏm t'aek·shi
regular taxi	일반 택시 il·ban t'aek·shi
Is this taxi available?	이 택시 타도 되나요? i·t'aek·shi t'a·do doé·na·yo

Is this taxi free? 빈 차예요? bin ch'a·ye·yo

I'd like a taxi at (9am).	(오전 아홉시)에 택시 타려고요. (o·jŏn a·hop·shi)·é t'aek·shi t'a·ryŏ·go·yo
I'd like a taxi tomorrow.	내일 택시 타려고요. nae il t'aek·shi t'a·ryŏ·go·yo

CULTURE TIP: SHARING A RIDE

To make some extra money and to ease demand during busy times (especially after the subways and most buses stop running), regular taxis may double up on passengers, a practice called hap·sŭng 합승. Although technically illegal, hap·sŭng still happens. It offers no savings benefit for the passengers, but it can dramatically increase the likelihood of getting a taxi at busy times and is generally safe.

How much is the ...?	... 얼마예요? ... ŏl·ma·ye·yo	

call-out fee	호출료	ho·ch'ul·lyo
fare to (Gangnam station)	(강남역)까지 가는 요금	(gang·nam·nyŏk)·kka·ji ga·nŭn yo·gŭm
flag fall/hiring charge	기본 요금	gi·bon yo·gŭm
late-night surcharge	할증	hal·jŭng

Please put the meter on.	미터기 켜 주세요. mi·t'ŏ·gi k'yŏ·ju·se·yo
Please don't pick up another passenger.	합승하지 마세요. hap·sŭng ha·ji ma·se·yo
Please take me to (Insa-dong).	(인사동)으로 가 주세요. (in·sa·dong)·ŭ·ro ga·ju·se·yo

To ...	…이요/요.	...·i·yo/·yo

Please slow down.	천천히 가 주세요. ch'ŏn·ch'ŏn·hi ga·ju·se·yo
Please stop here.	여기 내릴게요. yŏ·gi nae·rilk·ke·yo
Please wait here.	여기서 기다려 주세요. yŏ·gi·sŏ gi·da·ryŏ·ju·se·yo

For other useful phrases, see **directions** (p71), and **money & banking** (p104).

CAR

I'd like to hire a/an ... … 빌리고 싶어요.
... bil·li·go shi·p'ŏ·yo

4WD	사륜구동	sa·ryun·gu·dong
automatic	오토매틱	o·t'o·mae·t'ik
car	차	ch'a
manual	수동	su·dong

with air conditioning/ a driver 에어컨/기사 있는
e·ŏ·k'ŏn/gi·sa in·nŭn

How much for daily/ weekly hire? 하루/한 주 렌트에 얼마예요?
ha·ru/han·ju ren·t'ŭ·é ŏl·ma·ye·yo

Do you have a road map/ atlas? 지도 있나요?
ji·do in·na·yo

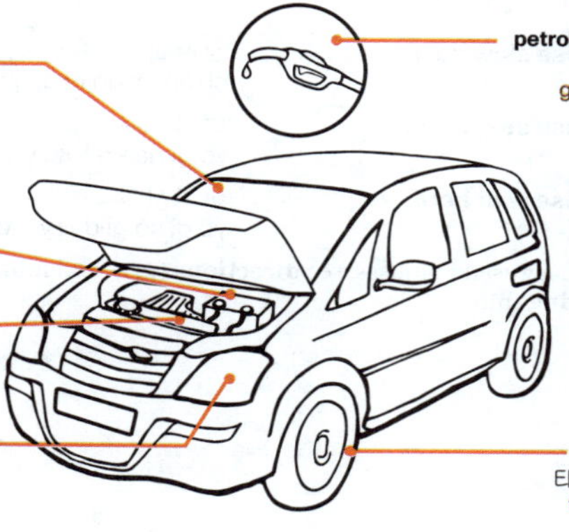

What's the speed limit?	제한 속도가 얼마예요? je·han·sok·do·ga ŏl·ma·ye·yo
Is this the road to (Donghae)?	이게 (동해) 가는 길인가요? i·gé (dong·hae) ga·nŭn gi·rin·ga·yo
Do you have a guide to the road rules (in English)?	(영어로 된) 교통법규 책자 있나요? (yŏng·ŏ·ro·doén) gyo·t'ong·bŏp·gyu ch'aek·ja in·na·yo
Where's a petrol/gas station?	주유소가 어디있나요? ju·yu·so·ga ŏ·di in·na·yo
Where's the LPG filling station?	엘피지 충전소가 어디 있나요? el·p'i·ji ch'ung·jŏn·so·ga ŏ·di in·na·yo
What kind of fuel does this take?	어떤 연료를 써요? ŏt·tŏn yŏl·lyo·rŭl ssŏ·yo
Please fill it up.	가득 채워주세요. ga·dŭk ch'ae·wŏ·ju·se·yo
I'd like (30,000) won worth of fuel, please.	(삼만) 원어치 넣어주세요. (sam·man)·wŏ·nŏ·ch'i nŏ·ŏ·ju·se·yo

LOOK FOR

경유	gyŏng·yu	diesel
디젤	di·jel	diesel
엘피지	el·p'i·ji	LPG
(무연) 휘발유	(mu·yŏn) hwi·bal·lyu	(unleaded) petrol/gas

LISTEN FOR

고속도로 요금	go·sok·do·ro yo·gŭm	expressway toll
과속 카메라	gwa·sok k'a·me·ra	speed camera
무료	mu·ryo	free
벌금	bŏl·gŭm	fine
안전벨트	an·jŏn·bel·t'ŭ	seat belt
운전면허증	un·jŏn·myŏn·hŏ·jŭng	driver's licence
터널 요금	t'ŏ·nŏl yo·gŭm	tunnel toll

(How long) Can I park here?	(얼마 동안) 여기 주차해도 되나요? (ŏl·ma·dong·an) yŏ·gi ju·ch'a·hae·do doé·na·yo
Do I have to pay?	돈 내야 하나요? don nae·ya ha·na·yo
Please check the engine oil.	엔진오일 체크해 주세요. en·jin o·il ch'e·k'ŭ·hae·ju·se·yo
Please check the tyre pressure.	타이어 공기압 체크해 주세요. t'a·i·ŏ gong·gi·ap ch'e·k'ŭ·hae·ju·se·yo
Please check the coolant.	냉각수 체크해 주세요. naeng·gak·su ch'e·k'ŭ·hae·ju·se·yo
I need a mechanic.	자동차정비사가 필요해요. ja·dong·ch'a jŏng·bi·sa·ga p'i·ryo·hae·yo
I've had an accident.	사고가 났어요. sa·go·ga nass·ŏ·yo
The car has broken down (at Jongno).	(종로에서) 차가 고장났어요. (jong·no·e·sŏ) ch'a·ga go·jang·nass·ŏ·yo

자전거 빌리려고요.
ja·jŏn·gŏ bil·li·ryŏ·go·yo
I'd like to hire a bicycle.

BICYCLE

I'd like my bicycle repaired.	자전거 고치려고요. ja·jŏn·gŏ go·ch'i·ryŏ·go·yo
I'd like to buy a bicycle.	자전거 사려고요. ja·jŏn·gŏ sa·ryŏ·go·yo
I'd like to hire a bicycle.	자전거 빌리려고요. ja·jŏn·gŏ bil·li·ryŏ·go·yo
Do I need a helmet?	헬멧 써야 하나요? hel·met ssŏ·ya ha·na·yo
Are there bicycle paths?	자전거 도로가 있나요? ja·jŏn·gŏ do·ro·ga in·na·yo
I have a puncture.	타이어에 펑크 났어요. t'a·i·ŏ·é p'ŏng·k'ŭ nass·ŏ·yo
How much is it per day/hour?	하루에/한 시간에 얼마예요? ha·ru·é/han·shi·ga·né ŏl·ma·ye·yo

LOOK FOR

견인지역	gyŏ·nin·ji·yŏk	Tow-away zone
고속도로	go·sok·do·ro	Expressway
낙석 지역	nak·sŏk ji·yŏk	Falling rocks
무료주차	mu·ryo·ju·ch'a	Free parking
버스전용차로	bŏ·sŭ·jŏ·nyong·ch'a·ro	Bus-only lane
보행금지	bo·haeng·gŭm·ji	Pedestrians prohibited
비보호	bi·bo·ho	Turn when safe
안개지역	an·gae·ji·yŏk	Fog zone
양보	yang·bo	Give way
어린이 보호 구역	ŏ·ri·ni bo·ho gu·yŏk	Watch for children
요금	yo·gŭm	Toll
우회	u·hoé	Detour
유료주차	yu·ryo·ju·ch'a	Pay parking
위험	wi·hŏm	Danger
일방통행	il·bang·t'ong·haeng	One way
입구	ip·gu	Entrance
정지	jŏng·ji	Stop
좌신호시	jwa·shin·ho·shi	On left turn arrow only
주차금지	ju·ch'a·gŭm·ji	No parking
진입금지	ji·nip·gŭm·ji	No entry
적신호시	jŏk·shin·ho·shi	On red light only
천천히	ch'ŏn·ch'ŏn·hi	Slow down
출구	ch'ul·gu	Exit

Border Crossing

KEY PHRASES

I'm here for ... days.	...일 동안 있을 거예요.	...il dong·an iss·ŭl·gŏ·ye·yo
I'm staying at ...	...에 묵어요.	...·é mu·gŏ·yo
I have nothing to declare.	신고할 것이 없습니다.	shin·go·hal gŏ·shi ŏp·sŭm·ni·da

PASSPORT CONTROL

I'm here in transit.	환승하려고요. hwan·sŭng ha·ryŏ·go·yo
I'm here for a holiday.	여행하러 왔어요. yŏ·haeng ha·rŏ wass·ŏ·yo
I'm here on business.	사업차 왔어요. sa·ŏp·ch'a wass·ŏ·yo
I'm here to study.	공부하러 왔어요. gong·bu ha·rŏ wass·ŏ·yo
I'm here for (two weeks).	(이 주) 동안 있을 거예요. i·ju dong·an iss·ŭl·gŏ·ye·yo

one day	하루	ha·ru
two days	이틀	i·t'ŭl
three days	사흘	sa·hŭl
(10) days	(십) 일	(shib)·il
(three) weeks	(삼) 주	(sam)·ju
(two) months	(두) 달	(du)·dal

I'm going to (Gwangju).	(광주)에 가요. (gwang·ju)·é ga·yo

I'm staying at the (Balhae Hotel).	(발해 호텔)에 묵어요. (bal·hae ho·t'er)·é mu·gŏ·yo

AT CUSTOMS

I have nothing/something to declare.	신고할 것이 없습니다/있습니다. shin·go·hal gŏ·shi ŏp·sŭm·ni·da/iss·sŭm·ni·da
Do I have to declare this?	이거 신고해야 하나요? i·gŏ shin·go hae·ya ha·na·yo
I didn't know I had to declare it.	신고해야 하는 줄 몰랐습니다. shin·go hae·ya ha·nŭn·jul mol·lass·sŭm·ni·da
That's mine.	그건 제 거예요. gŭ·gŏn jék·kŏ·ye·yo
That's not mine.	그건 제 것이 아닌데요. gŭ·gŏn jek·kŏ·shi a·nin·de·yo
I need an (English) interpreter.	(영어) 통역이 필요한데요. (yŏng·ŏ) t'ong·yŏ·gi p'i·ryo·han·de·yo
Do you have this form in (English)?	(영어)로 된 서류 있나요? (yŏng·ŏ)·ro doén sŏ·ryu in·na·yo

For payments and receipts, see **money & banking** (p104).

LOOK FOR

검역 심사	gŏ·myŏk shim·sa	Quarantine screening
면세점	myŏn·se·jŏm	Duty-free shop
세관 신고	se·gwan shin·go	Customs
외국인 심사대	oé·gu·gin shim·sa·dae	Inspection for visitors
입국 심사	ip·guk shim·sa	Immigration

Directions

KEY PHRASES

Where is ...?	... 어디 있나요?	... ŏ·di in·na·yo
What's the address?	주소가 뭐예요?	ju·so·ga mwŏ·ye·yo
How far is it?	얼마나 먼가요?	ŏl·ma·na mŏn·ga·yo

Ⓠ **Where's a bank?**	은행 어디 있나요? ŭn·haeng ŏ·di in·na·yo
Ⓠ **Where's the market?**	시장 어디 있나요? shi·jang ŏ·di in·na·yo
Ⓐ **It's ...**	... 에 있어요. ...·é iss·ŏ·yo
What's the address?	주소가 뭐예요? ju·so·ga mwŏ·ye·yo
How do I get there?	거기에 어떻게 가나요? gŏ·gi·é ŏt·tŏ·k'é ga·na·yo
How far is it?	얼마나 먼가요? ŏl·ma·na mŏn·ga·yo
Please show me (on the map).	(지도에서) 어디인지 가르쳐 주세요. (ji·do·e·sŏ) ŏ·di·in·ji ga·rŭ·ch'ŏ ju·se·yo

LISTEN FOR

Koreans often arrange to meet at a local landmark, like a subway exit, a fast-food joint or the entrance to a department store. When you ask for directions, don't be surprised if total strangers go out of their way to take you to exactly where you're going instead of just explaining it. Businesses often give out cards that include not just their address, but also a small map, called yak·do 약도, which indicates their location in relation to a subway station or a well-known structure.

... 뒤에	... dwi·é	behind ...
여기	yŏ·gi	here
... 앞에	... a·p'é	in front of ...
... 가까이에	... gak·ka·i·é	near ...
... 옆에	... yŏ·p'é	next to ...
모퉁이에	mo·t'ung·i·é	on the corner
... 반대편에	... ban·dae·p'yŏ·né	opposite ...
저기	jŏ·gi	over there
정면에	jŏng·myŏ·né	straight ahead

가까워요.	gak·ka·wŏ·yo It's near.
멀어요.	mŏ·rŏ·yo It's far.
좌회전 하세요.	jwa·hoé·jŏn ha·se·yo Turn left.
우회전 하세요.	u·hoé·jŏn ha·se·yo Turn right.
(다음) 모퉁이에서 도세요.	(da·ŭm) mo·t'ung·i·e·sŏ do·se·yo Turn at the (next) corner.
횡단보도에서 도세요.	hoéng·dan·bo·do·e·sŏ do·se·yo Turn at the pedestrian crossing.

by bus	버스로 bŏ·sŭ·ro
by subway	지하철로 chi·ha·ch'ŏl·lo
by taxi	택시로 t'aek·shi·ro
by train	기차로 gi·ch'a·ro
on foot	걸어서 gŏ·rŏ·sŏ

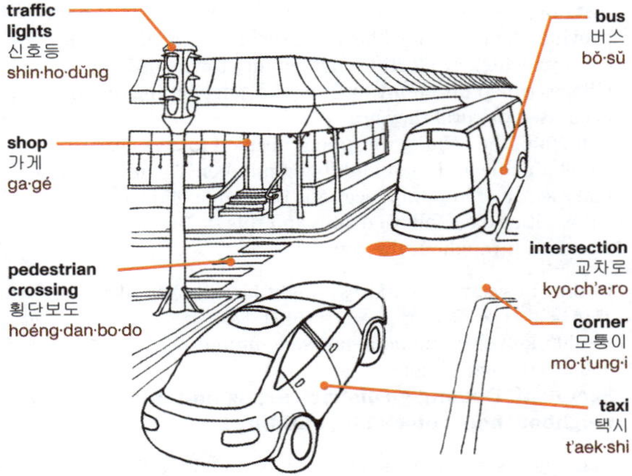

☑ CULTURE TIP: WRITING ADDRESSES

Postal addresses, or jhu·so 주소, are written in reverse order from those in the West: they go from the largest to the smallest administrative unit, with the block and house or apartment number last. When writing an address in English, however, it's acceptable to write it as you would in the West, from local to national.

The largest unit is do 도 (lit: province), gwang·yŏk·shi 광역시 (lit: wide-area city, meaning 'metropolitan prefecture') or t'ŭk·byŏl·shi 특별시 (lit: special city, only used for Seoul). The urban parts of provinces are usually divided into shi 시 (lit: city), which are then divided into ·gu 구 (urban district) and dong 동 (neighbourhood), or just dong, depending on their size. The rural parts of both provinces and gwang·yŏk·shi are divided into gun 군 (lit: county), which are further divided into townships and villages called ŭp 읍, myŏn 면 or ri 리, depending on how urbanised or rural they are.

In 2006, the Seoul government decided to give every street a name and each building a number. The idea was to make sense of building locations through a logical system. Other cities have followed suit, and this system is now standard throughout the country.

In the old system, an address might have looked like this:
서울특별시 도봉구 쌍문동 150번지 1호
sŏ·ul·t'ŭk·byŏl·shi do·bong·gu ssang·mun·dong bae·go·ship·bŏn·ji il·ho
Seoul-shi, Dobong-gu district, Ssangmun-dong neighbourhood, block 150, building 1

In the new system, the same address would read:
서울특별시 도봉구 정의4길 21번
sŏ·ul·t'ŭk·byŏl·shi do·bong·gu jŏng·i sa·gil i·shi·bil·bŏn
Seoul-shi, Dobong-gu district, Chŏngi-4-gil street, number 21

Accommodation

KEY PHRASES

Where's a hotel?	호텔 어디있어요?	ho·t'el ŏ·di iss·ŏ·yo
Do you have a double room?	더블 룸 있나요?	dŏ·bŭl rum in·na·yo
How much is it per night?	하룻밤에 얼마예요?	ha·rup·pa·mé ŏl·ma·ye·yo
Is breakfast included?	아침 포함인가요?	a·ch'im p'o·ha·min·ga·yo
What time is checkout?	체크아웃 언제예요?	ch'e·k'ŭ·a·ut ŏn·je·ye·yo

FINDING ACCOMMODATION

Where's a ...? ... 어디있어요? ... ŏ·di iss·ŏ·yo

campsite	야영장	ya·yŏng·jang
guesthouse	민박집	min·bak·jip
hotel	호텔	ho·t'el
motel	여관/여인숙	yŏ·gwan/yŏ·in·suk
mountain hut	산장	san·jang
temple to stay at	템플 스테이	t'em·p'ŭl sŭ·t'e·i
traditional house	한옥	ha·nok
youth hostel	유스 호스텔	yu·sŭ ho·sŭ·t'el

Can you recommend somewhere ...? ... 숙소 추천해 주세요. ... suk·so ch'u·ch'ŏn hae·ju·se·yo

cheap	싼	ssan
clean	깨끗한	ggaek·kŭ·t'an
good	좋은	cho·ŭn
nearby	가까운	gak·ka·un
safe for women	여자가 있기에 안전한	yŏ·ja·ga ik·ki·é an·jŏn·han

I want something near the ... ...에서 가까우면 좋겠어요. ...·e·sŏ gak·ka·u·myŏn jo·k'ess·ŏ·yo

beach	해변	hae·byŏn
city centre	시내	shi·nae
mountains	산	san
metro station	지하철역	ji·ha·ch'ŏl·yŏk
train station	기차역	gi·ch'a·yŏk

BOOKING AHEAD & CHECKING IN

I'd like to book a room, please. 방 예약하려고 하는데요. bang ye·ya·k'a·ryŏ·go ha·nŭn·de·yo

Are there rooms?	방 있나요?	bang in·na·yo

I have a reservation. 예약했어요. ye·ya·k'aess·ŏ·yo

For (three) nights/weeks. (삼) 박이요/주요. (sam)·ba·gi·yo/·ju·yo

From (2 July) to (6 July).	(칠월 이일)부터 (칠월 육일)까지요. (ch'i·rwŏl i·il)·bu·t'ŏ (ch'i·rwŏl yu·gil)k·ka·ji·yo
Do you have a single room?	싱글 룸 있나요? shing·gŭl rum in·na·yo
Do you have a double room?	더블 룸 있나요? dŏ·bŭl rum in·na·yo
Do you have a twin room?	트윈 룸 있나요? t'ŭ·win rum in·na·yo
I want a room with (a/an) ...	... 방으로 할게요. ... bang·ŭ·ro halk·ke·yo

bathroom	욕실 있는	yok·shi·rin·nŭn
cable TV	케이블 나오는	k'e·i·bŭl na·o·nŭn
internet connection	인터넷 되는	in·t'ŏ·net doé·nŭn
view	전망 좋은	jŏn·mang jo·ŭn

How much per night?	하룻밤에 얼마예요? ha·rup·pam·é ŏl·ma·ye·yo
How much per person?	한 명에 얼마예요? han·myŏng·é ŏl·ma·ye·yo
Is breakfast included?	아침 포함인가요? a·ch'im p'o·ha·min·ga·yo
Is there anything cheaper?	더 싼 건 없나요? dŏ·ssan·gŏn ŏm·na·yo
Can I see it?	좀 볼 수 있나요? jom bol·su in·na·yo
I'll take it.	이 방으로 할게요. i·bang·ŭ·ro halk·ke·yo

For methods of payment, see **money & banking** (p104).

REQUESTS & QUERIES

When/Where is breakfast served?	아침은 언제/어디서 먹나요? a·ch'i·mŭn ŏn·jé/ŏ·di·sŏ mŏng·na·yo
Is there hot water all day?	온수 하루 종일 나오나요? on·su ha·ru·jong·il na·o·na·yo
When is the hot water on?	온수 언제 나오나요? on·su ŏn·jé na·o·na·yo
Please wake me at (seven).	(일곱) 시에 깨워주세요. (il·gop)·shi·é kkae·wŏ·ju·se·yo
Can I use the internet?	인터넷 써도 되나요? in·t'ŏ·net ssŏ·do doé·na·yo
Can I use the kitchen?	주방 써도 되나요? ju·bang ssŏ·do doé·na·yo
Is there a/an ...?	... 있나요? ... in·na·yo

lift/elevator	엘리베이터	el·li·be·i·t'ŏ
laundry service	세탁 서비스	se·t'ak sŏ·bi·sŭ
message board	메모 남길 알림판	me·mo·nam·gil al·lim·p'an
safe	금고	gŭm·go
swimming pool	수영장	su·yŏng·jang

Can I have an extra blanket, please?	이불 더 주실 수 있나요? i·bul dŏ ju·shil·su in·na·yo
Can I have my key, please?	열쇠 주실 수 있나요? yŏl·soé ju·shil·su in·na·yo

i

Finding a Room

DO YOU HAVE A ... ROOM?
... 룸 있나요?
... rum in·na·yo

DOUBLE
더블
dŏ·bŭl

SINGLE
싱글
shing·gŭl

HOW MUCH IS IT PER ...?
...에 얼마예요?
...·é ŏl·ma·ye·yo

NIGHT
하룻밤
ha·rup·pam

PERSON
한 명
han·myŏng

IS BREAKFAST INCLUDED?
아침 포함인가요?
a·ch'im p'o·ha·min·ga·yo

CAN I SEE THE ROOM?
좀 볼 수 있나요?
jom bol·su in·na·yo

I'LL TAKE IT.
이 방으로 할게요.
i·bang·ŭ·ro halk·ke·yo

I WON'T TAKE IT.
이 방은 안 할래요.
i·bang·ŭn an·hal·lae·yo

CULTURE TIP: ROOM TYPES

Large hotels have 'Western-style' rooms (chim-dae-bang 침대방), with beds in every room, but smaller places may only have 'Korean-style' rooms (on-dol-bang 온돌방), offering yo 요 (floor mattresses) instead. These are very comfortable in the winter, when the on·dol 온돌 (floor-heating systems) are turned on.

I'm locked out of my room.	열쇠를 방에 두고 나와 버렸어요. yŏl·soé·rŭl bang·é du·go na·wa·bŏ·ryŏss·ŏ·yo
Do you arrange tours here?	여행 주선 해주시나요? yŏ·haeng·ju·sŏn hae·ju·shi·na·yo
Do you change money here?	여기서 환전할 수 있나요? yŏ·gi·sŏ hwan·jŏn hal·su in·na·yo
Is there a message for me?	저한테 온 메시지 없나요? jŏ·han·t'é on·me·shi·ji ŏm·na·yo
Can I leave a message for someone?	메시지 남길 수 있나요? me·shi·ji nam·gil·su in·na·yo

LISTEN FOR

몇 박이요?	myŏp·pa·gi·yo	How many nights?
신분증	shin·bun·jŭng	identification
전용 욕실	jŏ·nyong yok·shil	private bathroom
공용 욕실	gong·yong yok·shil	shared bathroom
열쇠	yŏl·soé	key
프런트	p'u·rŏn·t'ŭ	reception

COMPLAINTS

It's too ... 너무 ... nŏ·mu ...

bright	밝아요	bal·ga·yo
cold	추워요	ch'u·wŏ·yo
dark	어두워요	ŏ·du·wŏ·yo
dirty	지저분해요	ji·jŏ·bun·hae·yo
noisy	시끄러워요	shik·kŭ·rŏ·wŏ·yo
small	작아요	ja·ga·yo

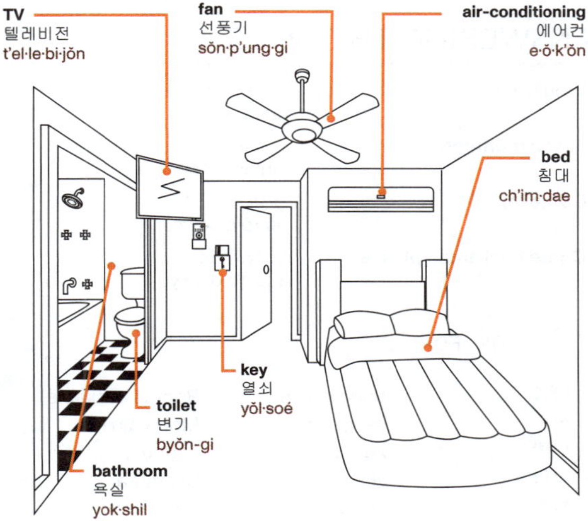

The air-conditioning doesn't work.	에어컨이 안 돼요. e·ŏ·k'ŏ·ni an·dwae·yo
The toilet won't flush.	변기가 막혔어요. byŏn·gi·ga ma·k'yŏss·ŏ·yo
There's no hot water.	온수가 안 나와요. on·su·ga an·na·wa·yo
This (pillow) isn't clean.	이 (베개) 깨끗하지 않은데요. i (be·gae) ggaek·ku·t'a·ji a·nŭn·de·yo
Please change the sheets.	시트 갈아 주세요. shi·t'ŭ ga·ra·ju·se·yo
Please clean the room.	방 청소 해 주세요. bang ch'ŏng·so hae·ju·se·yo

ANSWERING THE DOOR

Who is it?	누구세요? nu·gu·se·yo
Just a moment.	잠시만요. jam·shi·man·nyo
Come in.	들어오세요. dŭ·rŏ·o·se·yo
Come back later, please.	이따가 오세요. it·ta·ga o·se·yo

LOOK FOR

방 있음	bang·iss·ŭm	Rooms available
산장	san·jang	Mountain hut
세탁	se·t'ak	Laundry
식당	shik·tang	Restaurant
욕실	yok·shil	Bathroom

CHECKING OUT

What time is checkout?	체크아웃 언제예요? ch'e·k'ŭ·a·ut ŏn·je·ye·yo
Can I have a late checkout?	체크아웃 좀 늦게 해도 되나요? ch'e·k'ŭ·a·ut jom nŭk·ké hae·do doé·na·yo
Can you call a taxi for me (for 11 o'clock)?	(열한 시까지) 택시 불러 주시겠어요? (yŏl·han·shik·ka·ji) t'aek·shi bul·lŏ·ju·shi·gess·ŏ·yo
Can I leave my (backpack) here?	(배낭) 여기 두고 가도 되나요? (bae·nang) yŏ·gi·du·go ga·do·doé·na·yo
Can I have my deposit, please?	보증금 돌려 주시겠어요? bo·jŭng·gŭm tol·lyŏ ju·shi·gess·ŏ·yo
Can I have my passport, please?	여권 돌려 주시겠어요? yŏk·kwŏn dol·lyŏ ju·shi·gess·ŏ·yo
Can I have my valuables, please?	귀중품 돌려 주시겠어요? gwi·jung·p'um dol·lyŏ ju·shi·gess·ŏ·yo
I'm leaving now.	지금 가요. ji·gŭm ga·yo
I'll be back in (three) days.	(삼) 일 안에 돌아올게요. (sam)·i·ra·né do·ra·olk·ke·yo
I'll be back on (Tuesday).	(화요일)에 돌아올게요. (hwa·yo·ir)·é do·ra·olk·ke·yo
Thank you for all your help.	여러가지로 고맙습니다. yŏ·rŏ·ga·ji·ro go·map·sŭm·ni·da

CAMPING

Is there a campsite nearby?	근처에 야영장 있나요? gŭn·ch'ŏ·é ya·yŏng·jang in·na·yo
Does this temple offer sleeping accommodation?	여기서 템플 스테이 할 수 있나요? yŏ·gi·sŏ t'em·p'ŭl sŭ·t'e·i hal·su in·na·yo
Where can we get permits for camping?	야영하려면 어디서 허락 받나요? ya·yŏng ha·ryŏ·myŏn ŏ·di·sŏ hŏ·rak ban·na·yo
Do you have ...?	... 있나요? ... in·na·yo

electricity	전기 시설	jŏn·gi shi·sŏl
a laundry	세탁할 곳	se·t'a·k'al·got
shower facilities	샤워 시설	sha·wŏ shi·sŏl
tents for hire	빌릴 텐트	bil·lil t'en·t'ŭ

How much per person?	일인당 얼마예요? i·rin·dang ŏl·ma·ye·yo
How much per tent?	텐트당 얼마예요? t'en·t'ŭ·dang ŏl·ma·ye·yo
How much per vehicle?	한 차당 얼마예요? han·ch'a·dang ŏl·ma·ye·yo
Is the water drinkable?	마셔도 되는 물인가요? ma·shŏ·do doé·nŭn mu·rin·ga·yo
Can I camp here?	여기서 야영해도 되나요? yŏ·gi·sŏ ya·yŏng·hae·do doé·na·yo
Could I borrow ...?	... 빌릴 수 있나요? ... bil·lil·su in·na·yo

예약했어요.
ye·ya·k'aess·ŏ·yo
I have a reservation.

RENTING

Renting apartments or houses for short-term stays is almost unheard of in Korea. Renting rooms in boarding houses, however, is quite common, and can be arranged through bu·dong·san 부동산 (real estate agencies) for a small fee.

Do you have a/an ... for rent?	... 빌릴 수 있나요? ... bil·lil·su in·na·yo	

apartment	아파트	a·p'a·t'ŭ
cabin	펜션	pen·syŏn
house	집	jip
room	방	bang

I'd like to rent it for (one) month.	(한) 달 동안 빌릴게요. (han)·dal·dong·an bil·lilk·ke·yo
Is there a deposit?	보증금 내야 하나요? bo·jŭng·gŭm nae·ya ha·na·yo
How much is the deposit?	보증금이 얼마예요? bo·jŭng·gŭm·i ŏl·ma·ye·yo
Are bills extra?	공공요금은 따로 내나요? gong·gong yo·gŭ·mŭn dda·ro nae·na·yo

STAYING WITH LOCALS

Can I stay at your place?	당신 집에서 지내도 될까요? dang·shin ji·be·sŏ ji·nae·do doélk·ka·yo
I have my own floor mattress.	제 요 있어요. jé yo iss·ŏ·yo
I have my own sleeping bag.	제 침낭 있어요. jé ch'im·nang iss·ŏ·yo
Is there anything I can do to help?	뭐 도와드릴 것 없나요? mwŏ do·wa·du·ril·gŏt ŏm·na·yo
Can I bring anything for the meal?	먹을 것 가져갈까요? mŏ·gŭl·gŏt ga·jŏ galk·ka·yo
Can I do the dishes?	설거지 할까요? sŏl·gŏ·ji halk·ka·yo
Can I set/clear the table?	상을 차릴까요/치울까요? sang·ŭl ch'a·rilk·ka·yo/ch'i·ulk·ka·yo
Can I take out the rubbish?	쓰레기 버릴까요? ssŭ·re·gi bŏ·rilk·ka·yo
Thank you for your hospitality.	환대해 주셔서 고맙습니다. hwan·dae hae·ju·shŏ·sŏ go·map·sŭm·ni·da

To compliment your hosts' cooking, see **compliments & complaints** (p198).

Shopping

KEY PHRASES

Do you have ...?	... 있나요?	... in·na·yo
Can I look at it?	보여 주시겠어요?	bo·yŏ ju·shi·gess·ŏ·yo
Can I try it on?	입어봐도 되나요?	i·bŏ·bwa·do doé·na·yo
How much is it?	얼마예요?	ŏl·ma·ye·yo
That's too expensive.	너무 비싸요.	nŏ·mu bi·ssa·yo

LOOKING FOR ...

What hours are shops open?	영업 시간이 언제예요? yŏng·ŏp shi·ga·ni ŏn·je·ye·yo
Where can I buy (a padlock)?	(자물쇠) 어디서 살 수 있나요? (ja·mul·soé) ŏ·di·sŏ sal·su in·na·yo
Where's the nearest ...?	제일 가까운 ...이/가 어디 있나요? jé·il gak·ka·un ...·i/·ga ŏ·di in·na·yo

big discount store	대형할인점	dae·hyŏng ha·rin·jŏm
convenience store	편의점	p'yŏ·ni·jŏm
department store	백화점	bae·k'wa·jŏm
supermarket	슈퍼마켓	shu·p'ŏ·ma·k'et
market	시장	shi·jang

For more items and shopping locations, see the **dictionary** (p221).

MAKING A PURCHASE

I'm just looking.	그냥 구경할게요. gŭ·nyang gu·gyŏng halk·ke·yo
Do you have (tissues)?	(휴지) 있나요? (hyu·ji) in·na·yo
Can I look at it?	보여 주시겠어요? bo·yŏ ju·shi·gess·ŏ·yo
Do you have any others?	다른 건 없나요? da·rŭn·gŏn ŏm·na·yo
How much is it?	얼마예요? ŏl·ma·ye·yo
I'd like a bag, please.	봉투 주세요. bong·t'u ju·se·yo
Does it have a guarantee?	품질 보증 되나요? p'um·jil bo·jŭng doé·na·yo
Can you order it for me?	주문해 주실 수 있나요? ju·mun·hae ju·shil·su in·na·yo
Can I pick it up later?	나중에 가져 가도 되나요? na·jung·é ga·jŏ·ga·do doé·na·yo

LISTEN FOR

도와 드릴까요?	do·wa dŭ·rilk·ka·yo Can I help you?
뭐 드릴까요?	mwŏ dŭ·rilk·ka·yo What would you like?
다른 것 도와 드릴 것 없나요?	da·rŭn·gŏt do·wa dŭ·ril·gŏt ŏm·na·yo Anything else?
없는데요.	ŏm·nŭn·de·yo No, we don't have any.

CULTURE TIP: SUPERSTITIONS

Koreans don't mind if you just browse, but if you're the first customer of the day in a small shop, the just might press you to buy something – superstition dictates you'll set the pace for the rest of the day.

Could I have it wrapped?	포장해 주시겠어요? p'o·jang·hae ju·shi·gess·ŏ·yo
The quality isn't good.	품질이 안 좋아요. p'um·ji·ri an·jo·a·yo
It's faulty.	불량이에요. bul·lyang·i·e·yo
I'd like to return this, please.	반품하고 싶습니다. ban·p'um ha·go ship·sŭm·ni·da
I'd like my change, please.	잔돈 주세요. jan·don ju·se·yo
I'd like a refund, please.	환불하고 싶습니다. hwan·bul ha·go ship·sŭm·ni·da
Could I have a receipt, please?	영수증 주시겠어요? yŏng·su·jŭng ju·shi·gess·ŏ·yo

Receipt, please.	영수증 주세요.	yŏng·su·jŭng ju·se·yo

BARGAINING

Bargaining is still done in small shops and with street vendors, but it's gradually falling out of favour. A good rule of thumb is that if something has a price tag on it, that price should be considered nonnegotiable.

That's too expensive.	너무 비싸요. nŏ·mu bi·ssa·yo

LISTEN FOR

흥정	hŭng·jŏng	bargain
판매	p'an·mae	for sale
바가지	ba·ga·ji	rip-off n
세일	se·il	sale n
매진	mae·jin	sold out
특가 상품	t'ŭk·ka sang·p'um	specially priced item

Do you have something cheaper?	더 싼 것 있나요? dŏ·ssan·gŏt in·na·yo
Please give me a discount.	깎아 주세요. ggak·ka·ju·se·yo
What's your final price?	얼마까지 해 주실 수 있나요? ŏl·mak·ka·ji hae·ju·shil·su in·na·yo
No more than (20,000 won).	(이만 원) 이상은 안 돼요. (i·man·wŏn) i·sang·ŭn an·dwae·yo
I'll give you (90,000 won).	(구만 원) 드릴게요. (gu·man·wŏn) dŭ·rilk·ke·yo

BOOKS & READING

Is there a/an ...?	... 있나요? ... in·na·yo

bookshop	서점	sŏ·jŏm
dictionary	사전	sa·jŏn
newspaper (in English)	(영자) 신문	(yŏng·ja) shin·mun
(English-language) section	(영어 책) 코너	(yŏng·ŏ ch'aek) k'o·nŏ

Making a Purchase

I'D LIKE TO BUY...
…을/를 사고 싶어요.
...·ŭl/·rŭl sa·go shi·p'ŏ·yo

HOW MUCH IS IT?
얼마예요?
ŏl·ma·ye·yo

OR

CAN YOU WRITE DOWN THE PRICE?
가격을 써 주시겠어요?
ga·gyŏ·gŭl ssŏ ju·shi·gess·ŏ·yo

DO YOU ACCEPT CREDIT CARDS?
신용카드 받으시나요?
shi·nyong k'a·dŭ ba·dŭ·shi·na·yo

COULD I HAVE A ..., PLEASE?
… 주세요.
... ju·se·yo

RECEIPT
영수증
yŏng·su·jŭng

BAG
봉투
bong·t'u

Can you recommend a book for me?	책 추천 해 주시겠어요? ch'aek ch'u·ch'ŏn hae·ju·shi·gess·ŏ·yo
Do you have any books in English by (Hyon Hui)?	영어로 된 (현희)의 책 있나요? yŏng·ŏ·ro·doén (hyŏn·hi)·é ch'aek in·na·yo

CLOTHES

My size is ...	제 사이즈는 ... 이에요/예요. jé sa·i·jŭ·nŭn ... ·i·e·yo/·ye·yo

(40)	(사십)	(sa·ship)
small	스몰	sŭ·mol
medium	미디엄	mi·di·ŏm
large	라지	ra·ji

Can I try it on?	입어봐도 되나요? i·bŏ·bwa·do doé·na·yo
It doesn't fit.	안 맞아요. an·ma·ja·yo

VIDEO & PHOTOGRAPHY

Can you ...?	... 수 있나요?	... su in·na·yo

print digital photos	디지털 사진 인쇄할	di·ji·t'ŏl sa·jin in·swae·hal
recharge the battery for my digital camera	디카 배터리 충전할	di·k'a bae·t'ŏ·ri ch'ung·jŏn·hal
transfer photos from my camera to USB	디카 안의 사진을 유에스비로 옮길	di·k'a a·né sa·ji·nŭl yu·esŭ·bi·ro om·gil

Do you have (a) ... for this camera?	이 카메라용 ... 있나요?	i·k'a·me·ra·yong ... in·na·yo

batteries	배터리	bae·t'ŏ·ri
flash	플래시	p'ŭl·lae·shi
(zoom) lens	(줌) 렌즈	(jum) ren·jŭ
light meter	조명 측정기	jo·myŏng ch'ŭk·jŏng·gi
memory cards	메모리 카드	me·mo·ri k'a·dŭ

I need a cable to recharge this battery.	충전용 케이블이 필요해요. ch'ung·jŏn·nyong k'e·i·bŭ·ri p'i·ryo·hae·yo
... camera	... 카메라 ... k'a·me·ra

digital	디지털	di·ji·t'ŏl
disposable	일회용	il·hoé·yong
underwater	수중	su·jung

REPAIRS

Can I have my ... repaired here? ... 고칠 수 있나요?
... go·ch'il·su in·na·yo

backpack	배낭	bae·nang
bag	가방	ga·bang
camera	카메라	k'a·me·ra
shoes	신발	shin·bal
sunglasses	선글라스	sŏn·gŭl·la·sŭ

When will it be ready? 언제 다 되나요?
ŏn·jé da·doé·na·yo

얼마예요?
ŏl·ma·ye·yo
How much is it?

☑ CULTURE TIP: HOLIDAYS & FESTIVALS

Cherry Blossom Festivals (April)	벚꽃 축제 bŏk·kot ch'uk·ché
Chusok (Harvest Moon Festival)	추석 ch'u·sŏk
Hangul Day (9 October)	한글날 han·gŭl·lal
Lunar New Year	구정/설날 ku·jŏng/sŏl·lal
National Foundation Day (3 October)	개천절 gae·ch'ŏn·jŏl

SOUVENIRS

embroidery	자수품 ja·su·p'um
lacquerware	나전칠기 na·jŏn·ch'il·gi
pottery	도자기 do·ja·gi
traditional Korean clothing	한복 han·bok
traditional Korean paper	한지 han·ji
traditional stone figures of Jejudo	하르방 ha·rŭ·bang

Communications

KEY PHRASES

What's the wi-fi password?	와이파이 비밀번호가 뭐예요?	wa·i·pa·i bi·mil·bŏn·ho·ga mwŏ·ye·yo
I want to send a parcel.	소포 부치려고요.	so·p'o bu·ch'i·ryŏ·go·yo
I want to make a call.	전화하고 싶어요.	chŏn·hwa·ha·go shi·p'ŏ·yo

THE INTERNET

Is there a PC-room nearby?	주변에 피시방 있나요? chu·byŏ·né p'i·shi·bang in·na·yo
Do you have internet access here?	여기 와이파이 되나요? yŏ·gi in·t'ŏ·net yŏn·gyŏl doé·na·yo
Is there wi-fi access here?	여기 무선 인터넷 되나요? yŏ·gi wa·i·pa·i doé·na·yo
Can I connect my laptop here?	여기 노트북 연결해도 되나요? yŏ·gi no·t'ŭ·buk yŏn·gyŏl hae·do doé·na·yo

I'd like to ...

download my photos	사진 다운 받으려고요.	sa·jin da·un ba·dŭ·ryŏ·go·yo
use a printer/ scanner	프린터/스캐너 쓰려고요.	p'ŭ·rin·t'ŏ/ sŭ·k'ae·nŏ ssŭ·ryŏ·go·yo
rent a portable wi-fi hotspot	포켓 와이파이 빌리려고요.	po·ket wa·i·pa·i bil·li·ryŏ·go·yo

Do you have headphones (with a microphone)?
(마이크 달린) 헤드폰 있나요?
(ma·i·k'ŭ dal·lin) he·dŭ·pon in·na·yo

Can I connect my ... to this computer?
제 ...을/를 이 컴퓨터에 연결해도 되나요?
jé ...·ŭl/·rŭl i·k'ŏm·pyu·t'ŏ·é yŏn·gyŏl hae·do doé·na·yo

camera	카메라	k'a·me·ra
portable hard drive	외장 하드	oé·jang ha·dŭ
USB flash drive	유에스비	yu·e·sŭ·bi

How much per hour?
시간당 얼마예요?
shi·gan dang ŏl·ma·ye·yo

How much per page?
페이지당 얼마예요?
p'e·i·ji dang ŏl·ma·ye·yo

How do I log in?
로그인 어떻게 하나요?
ro·gŭ·in ŏt·tŏ·k'é ha·na·yo

What's the password?
비밀번호가 뭐예요?
bi·mil·bŏn·ho·ga mwŏ·ye·yo

CULTURE TIP: PC-ROOMS

In Korea, you can take advantage of cheap high-speed connections at home or in 24-hour p'i·shi·bang 피시방 (lit: PC-room). These are the Korean equivalent of internet cafes, and can be found even in the most out-of-the-way towns.

It's crashed.	얼었어요. ŏ·rŏss·ŏ·yo
I've finished.	다 했어요. da haess·ŏ·yo

MOBILE/CELL PHONE

I'd like a charger for my phone.	휴대폰 충전기 주세요. hyu·dae·p'on ch'ung·jŏn·gi ju·se·yo
I'd like a SIM card for hire.	심 카드 빌리려고요. shim ka·dŭ bil·li·ryŏ·go·yo
Where can I charge my phone?	휴대폰 어디서 충전할 수 있어요? hyu·dae·pon ŏ·di·sŏ chung·jŏn·hal su iss·ŏ·yo

LISTEN FOR

일 분당 (육십) 원이요.	il·bun·dang (yuk·shib)·wŏ·ni·yo	(60) won per minute.

PHONE

Q What's your phone number?	전화번호가 뭐예요? jŏn·hwa·bŏn·ho·ga mwŏ·ye·yo
A The number is ...	번호는 ... 이에요/예요. bŏn·ho·nŭn ... ·i·e·yo/·ye·yo
What's the area/country code for ...?	... 지역/국가 번호가 뭐예요? ... ji·yŏk/guk·ka bŏn·ho·ga mwŏ·ye·yo

LISTEN FOR

잘못 거셨습니다.	jal·mot gŏ·shŏss·sŭm·ni·da Wrong number.
누구신데요?	nu·gu·shin·de·yo Who's calling?
누구 바꿔 드릴까요?	nu·gu bak·kwŏ dŭ·rilk·ka·yo Who do you want to speak to?
잠시만요.	jam·shi·man·nyo One moment, please.
지금 없는데요.	ji·gŭm ŏm·nŭn·de·yo He/She isn't here.

I want to ...	... 싶어요. ... shi·p'ŏ·yo

call (Singapore)	(싱가포르)에 전화하고	(shing·ga·p'o·rŭ)·é jŏn·hwa·ha·go
make a (local) call	(시내) 전화하고	(shi·nae) jŏn·hwa·ha·go

It's engaged.	통화 중이에요. t'ong·hwa·jung·i·e·yo
I've been cut off.	전화가 끊겼어요. jŏn·hwa·ga ggŭn·k'yŏss·ŏ·yo
The connection's bad.	연결 상태가 나빠요. yŏn·gyŏl sang·t'ae·ga nap·pa·yo

LANGUAGE TIP: SAYING PHONE NUMBERS

In Korean, phone numbers are read in the following order: first the area code, followed by é 에, then the three- or four-digit prefix, followed by é, and at the end the last four digits – eg gong·il·gong·é sa·mo·gu·ch'i·ré i·gong·o·gu 공일공에 삼오구칠에 이공오구 (010 3597 2059). Note that in Seoul the 02 area code is often dropped.

Hello.	여보세요. yŏ·bo·se·yo
It's ...	...인데요. ...·in·de·yo
Can I speak to (Eunjeong)? (name ends in a consonant)	(은정)이 있어요? (ŭn·jŏng)·i iss·ŏ·yo
Can I speak to (Hyemi)? (name ends in a vowel)	(혜미) 있어요? (hye·mi) iss·ŏ·yo
Please tell him/her I called.	제가 전화했다고 전해 주세요. je·ga jŏn·hwa haet·ta·go jŏn·hae ju·se·yo
Can I leave a message?	메시지 남길 수 있나요? me·shi·ji nam·gil·su in·na·yo
I don't have a contact number.	전 연락처가 없어요. jŏn yŏl·lak·ch'ŏ·ga ŏp·sŏ·yo
I'll call back later.	제가 다시 전화할게요. je·ga da·shi jŏn·hwa halk·ke·yo
Is there a mobile phone number I can reach him/her at?	연락 가능한 휴대폰 번호 알 수 있나요? yŏl·lak ga·nŭng·han hyu·dae·p'on bŏn·ho al·su in·na·yo

What time should I call?	언제 전화하면 돼요? ŏn·jé jŏn·hwa ha·myŏn dwae·yo	

For telephone numbers, see **numbers & amounts** (p38).

POST OFFICE

I want to send a letter.	편지 부치려고요. p'yŏn·ji bu·ch'i·ryŏ·go·yo
I want to send a parcel.	소포 부치려고요. so·p'o bu·ch'i·ryŏ·go·yo
I want to send a postcard.	엽서 부치려고요. yŏp·sŏ bu·ch'i·ryŏ·go·yo
I want to buy an envelope.	봉투 사려고 하는데요. bong·t'u sa·ryŏ·go ha·nŭn·de·yo
I want to buy a stamp.	우표 사려고 하는데요. u·p'yo sa·ryŏ·go ha·nŭn·de·yo
Can you send it by express mail?	빠른 우편으로 보낼 수 있나요? bba·rŭn u·p'yŏ·nŭ·ro bo·nael·su in·na·yo
Please send it by air/ surface mail to (Australia).	(호주)에 항공편으로/ 선편으로 보내주세요. (ho·ju)·é hang·gong·p'yŏ·nŭ·ro/ sŏn·p'yŏ·nŭ·ro bo·nae ju·se·yo

LISTEN FOR

항공 우편	hang·gong u·p'yŏn	airmail
국내	gung·nae	domestic
빠른 우편	bba·rŭn u·p'yŏn	express mail
파손주의	p'a·son·ju·i	fragile
국제	guk·je	international
등기우편	dŭng·gi u·p'yŏn	registered mail
선편 우편	sŏn·p'yŏn u·p'yŏn	surface (sea) mail

Money & Banking

KEY PHRASES

How much is this?	이거 얼마예요?	i·gŏ ŏl·ma·ye·yo
What's the exchange rate?	환율이 얼마예요?	hwa·nyul·i ŏl·ma·ye·yo
Where's an ATM?	현금 인출기 어디 있어요?	hyŏn·gŭm in·ch'ul·gi ŏ·di iss·ŏ·yo
I'd like to change money.	환전해 주세요.	hwan·jŏn hae·ju·se·yo
I'd like to get change for this note.	작은 돈으로 바꿔주세요.	ja·gŭn do·nŭ·ro bak·kwŏ·ju·se·yo

PAYING THE BILL

Q **How much is this?**	이거 얼마예요? i·gŏ ŏl·ma·ye·yo
A **It's (1000) won.**	(천) 원이에요. (ch'on)·wŏ·ni·e·yo
A **It's free.**	무료예요/서비스예요. mu·ryo·ye·yo/sŏ·bi·sŭ·ye·yo
Please write down the price.	가격을 적어주세요. ga·gyŏ·gŭl jŏ·gŏ·ju·se·yo
There's a mistake in the bill.	계산서가 잘못 되었네요. gye·san·sŏ·ga jal·mot doe·ŏt·ne·yo

Do you accept credit cards?	신용카드 받으시나요? shi·nyong·k'a·dŭ ba·dŭ·shi·na·yo
Do you accept debit cards?	체크카드 받으시나요? ch'e·k'ŭ·k'a·dŭ ba·dŭ·shi·na·yo
Do you accept dollars/yen?	달러/엔 받으시나요? dal·lŏ/en ba·dŭ·shi·na·yo
I'd like my change, please.	거스름돈 주세요. gŏ·sŭ·rŭm·don ju·se·yo
I'd like a receipt, please.	영수증 주세요. yŏng·su·jŭng ju·se·yo
I'd like a refund, please.	환불하고 싶습니다. hwan·bul ha·go ship·sŭm·ni·da

BANKING

What time does the bank open/close?	은행 문 언제 여나요/닫나요? ŭn·haeng mun ŏn·jé yŏ·na·yo/dan·na·yo
What days is the bank open?	무슨 요일에 문 여나요? mu·sŭn yo·i·ré mun yŏ·na·yo

☑ CULTURE TIP: KOREAN CURRENCY

The standard unit of currency in South Korea is the won. It's symbolised by a ₩ and is sometimes written 'KRW'. The largest paper denomination is ₩50,000. The country's economy is becoming increasingly cashless, however, and it's common to pay for even the smallest purchases digitally or by card. Still, it's a good idea to carry some cash with you to use at street stalls and in traditional markets, which sometimes don't accept other forms of payment.

Where's a bank?	은행 어디 있어요? ŭn·haeng ŏ·di iss·ŏ·yo
Where's an ATM?	현금인출기 어디 있어요? hyŏn·gŭm in·ch'ul·gi ŏ·di iss·ŏ·yo
Where's a foreign exchange office?	환전소 어디 있어요? hwan·jŏn·so ŏ·di iss·ŏ·yo
I'd like to change money.	환전해 주세요. hwan·jŏn hae·ju·se·yo
I'd like to get a cash advance.	현금서비스 받으려고요. hyŏn·gŭm sŏ·bi·sŭ ba·dŭ·ryŏ·go·yo
I'd like to get change for this note.	작은 돈으로 바꿔주세요. ja·gŭn do·nŭ·ro bak·kwŏ·ju·se·yo
I'd like to withdraw money.	현금 인출 하려고요. hyŏn·gŭm in·ch'ul ha·ryŏ·go·yo
What's the charge for that?	수수료가 얼마예요? su·su·ryo·ga ŏl·ma·ye·yo
What's the exchange rate?	환율이 얼마예요? hwa·nyul·i ŏl·ma·ye·yo
I've forgotten my PIN.	핀 넘버를 잊어 버렸어요. p'in nŏm·bŏ·rŭl i·jŏ·bŏ·ryŏss·ŏ·yo

LISTEN FOR

수수료	su·su·ryo commission/fee
신분증	shin·bun·jŭng identification
문제가 있어요.	mun·je·ga iss·ŏ·yo There's a problem.
잔고가 없어요.	jan·go·ga ŏp·sŏ·yo You have no funds left.
그건 안 되는데요.	gŭ·gŏn an·doé·nŭn·de·yo We can't do that.
여기 서명하세요/ 사인하세요.	yŏ·gi sŏ·myŏng·ha·se·yo/ sa·in·ha·se·yo Sign here.

The ATM took my card.	현금인출기가 카드를 먹었어요. hyŏn·gŭm in·ch'ul·gi·ga k'a·dŭ·rŭl mŏ·gŏss·ŏ·yo
Can I use my credit card to withdraw money?	신용카드로 현금인출 할 수 있나요? shi·nyong·k'a·dŭ·ro hyŏn·gŭ·min·ch'ul hal·su in·na·yo
Can I transfer money overseas?	해외 송금 할 수 있나요? hae·oé song·gŭm hal·su in·na·yo

Business

KEY PHRASES

I'm attending a conference.	회의에 참가하러 왔어요.	hoé·i·é ch'am·ga ha·rŏ wass·ŏ·yo
I have an appointment with ...	...과/와 약속이 있어요.	...·gwa/·wa yak·so·gi iss·ŏ·yo
Can I have your business card?	명함 좀 부탁드립니다.	myŏng·ham jom bu·t'ak dŭ·rim·ni·da

Where's the business centre?	비즈니스 센터 어디있나요? bi·jŭ·ni·sŭ sen·t'ŏ ŏ·di in·na·yo
Where's the conference/ meeting?	회의장 어디있나요? hoé·i·jang ŏ·di in·na·yo
I'm attending a ...	...에 참가하러 왔어요. ...·é ch'am·ga ha·rŏ wass·ŏ·yo

conference	회의	hoé·i
course	강의	gang·i
meeting	회의	hoé·i
trade fair	무역 박람회	mu·yŏk bang·nam·hoé

I'm with (the UN).	(유엔) 일 때문에 왔어요. (yu·en)·ilt· tae·mu·né wass·ŏ·yo
I'm with my colleague(s).	동료와/동료들과 같이 왔어요. dong·nyo·wa/dong·nyo·dŭl·gwa ga·ch'i wass·ŏ·yo

I'm with (two) others.	다른 (두) 명과 같이 왔어요.	da·rŭn (du)·myŏng·gwa ga·ch'i wass·ŏ·yo
I'm alone.	혼자예요.	hon·ja·ye·yo
I have an appointment with ...	...과/와 약속이 있어요.	...·gwa/·wa yak·so·gi iss·ŏ·yo
Q Can I have your business card?	명함 좀 부탁드립니다?	myŏng·ham jom bu·t'ak dŭ·rim·ni·da
A Here's my business card.	제 명함입니다.	jé myŏng·ham im·ni·da
I need (a/an) ...	...이/가 필요해요.	...·i/·ga p'i·ryo·hae·yo

business card	명함	myŏng·ham
computer	컴퓨터	k'ŏm·p'yu·t'ŏ
internet connection	인터넷 접속	in·t'ŏ·net jŏp·sok
interpreter who speaks (English)	(영어) 통역	(yŏng·ŏ) t'ong·yŏk

That went very well.	잘 되었어요.	jal doé·ŏss·ŏ·yo
Thank you for your time.	시간 내 주셔서 고맙습니다.	shi·gan nae·ju·shŏ·sŏ go·map·sŭm·ni·da
Shall we go for a drink?	술 마시러 갈까요?	sul ma·shi·rŏ galk·ka·yo
Shall we go for a meal?	밥 먹으러 갈까요?	bap·mŏ·gŭ·rŏ galk·ka·yo

Sightseeing

KEY PHRASES

I'd like a guide.	여행안내서 주세요.	yŏ·haeng an·nae·sŏ ju·se·yo
Can I take a photo?	사진 찍어도 될까요?	sa·jin jji·gŏ·do doélk·ka·yo
When's the museum open?	박물관 문 언제 여나요?	bang·mul·gwan mun ŏn·jé yŏ·na·yo
I'm interested in ...	...을/를 좋아해요.	...·ŭl/·rŭl jo·a·hae·yo
When's the next tour?	다음 투어 언제예요?	da·ŭm t'u·ŏ ŏn·je·ye·yo

REQUESTS & QUERIES

I'd like a/an ...
... 주세요.
... ju·se·yo

audio guide	음성 안내 세트	ŭm·sŏng an·nae se·t'ŭ
catalogue	안내 책자	an·nae ch'aek·ja
guide (in English)	(영어로 된) 여행안내서	(yŏng·ŏ·ro·doén) yŏ·haeng an·nae·sŏ
map	지도	ji·do

I'd like to go somewhere off the beaten track.
흔하지 않은 새로운 곳에 가고 싶어요.
hŭn·ha·ji a·nŭn sae·ro·un·go·sé ga·go shi·p'ŏ·yo

Do you have information on ... sights?	... 관광지 정보 있나요? ... gwan·gwang·ji jŏng·bo in·na·yo

cultural	문화에 관련된	mun·hwa·é gwal·lyŏn·doén
historical	역사에 관련된	yŏk·sa·é gwal·lyŏn·doén
natural	자연이 있는	ja·yŏ·ni in·nŭn
religious	종교에 관련된	jong·gyo·é gwal·lyŏn·doén

I'd like to see ...	... 보고 싶어요. ... bo·go shi·p'ŏ·yo
What's that?	저게 뭐예요? jŏ·gé mŏ·ye·yo
How old is it?	얼마나 오래 되었나요? ŏl·ma·na o·rae doé·ŏn·na·yo
Who built/made it?	누가 지었나요/만들었나요? nu·ga ji·ŏn·na·yo/man·dŭ·rŏn·na·yo
Could you take a photo of me/us?	제/우리 사진 좀 찍어 주시겠어요? jé/u·ri sa·jin jom jji·gŏ ju·shi·gess·ŏ·yo
Can I take a photo (of you)?	(당신) 사진 찍어도 될까요? (dang·shin) sa·jin jji·gŏ·do doélk·ka·yo

GETTING IN

What time does it open/close?	언제 여나요/닫나요? ŏn·jé yŏn·na·yo/dan·na·yo
What's the admission charge?	입장료 얼마예요? ip·jang·nyo ŏl·ma·ye·yo

Is there a discount for ...?	... 할인 있나요? ... ha·rin in·na·yo

children	어린이	ŏ·ri·ni
families	가족	ga·jok
groups	단체	dan·ch'é
senior citizens	경로	gyŏng·no
students	학생	hak·saeng

GALLERIES & MUSEUMS

When's the gallery/ museum open?	미술관/박물관 문 언제 여나요? mi·sul·gwan/bang·mul·gwan mun ŏn·jé yŏ·na·yo
Q **What kind of art are you interested in?**	어떤 종류의 미술을 좋아하세요? ŏt·tŏn jong·nyu·é mi·su·rŭl jo·a·ha·se·yo
A **I'm interested in ...**	...을/를 좋아해요 ...·ŭl/·rŭl jo·a·hae·yo
Q **What's in the collection?**	어떤 전시회예요? ŏt·tŏn jŏn·shi·hoé·ye·yo
A **It's an exhibition of ...**	... 전시회예요. ... jŏn·shi·hoé·ye·yo
Q **What do you think of ...?**	...에 대해 어떻게 생각하세요? ...·é dae·hae ŏt·tŏ·k'é saeng·ga·k'a·se·yo
A **It reminds me of ...**	... 생각이 나게 하네요. ... saeng·ga·gi na·gé ha·ne·yo

TOURS

Can you recommend a ...?	... 추천해 주시겠어요? ... ch'u·ch'ŏn·hae ju·shi·gess·ŏ·yo

When's the next boat trip?	다음 선박 여행 언제예요? da·ŭm sŏn·bak yŏ·haeng ŏn·je·ye·yo
When's the next day trip?	다음 일일 여행 언제예요? da·ŭm i·ril yŏ·haeng ŏn·je·ye·yo
When's the next (sightseeing) tour?	다음 (관광) 투어 언제예요? da·ŭm (gwan·gwang) t'u·ŏ ŏn·je·ye·yo
Is accommodation included?	숙박 포함인가요? suk·bak p'o·ha·min·ga·yo
Is food included?	음식 포함인가요? ŭm·shik p'o·ha·min·ga·yo
Is transport included?	교통비 포함인가요? gyo·t'ong·bi p'o·ha·min·ga·yo

사진 찍어도 될까요?
sa·jin jji·gŏ·do doélk·ka·yo
Can I take a photo?

LOOK FOR

휴무	hyu·mu	Closed
비상구	bi·sang·gu	Emergency exit
무료 입장	mu·ryo ip·jang	Free admission
안내	an·nae	Information
신사용	shin·sa·yong	Men
출입 금지	ch'u·rip gŭm·ji	No entry
금연 구역	gŭ·myŏn gu·yŏk	No smoking area
영업 중	yŏng·ŏp·jung	Open
사진 촬영 금지	sa·jin ch'wa·ryŏng gŭm·ji	Photography prohibited
... 금지	... gŭm·ji	... prohibited
예약	ye·yak	Reserved
흡연 구역	hŭ·byŏn gu·yŏk	Smoking area
화장실	hwa·jang·shil	Toilets
숙녀용	sung·nyŏ·yong	Women

I'd like to hire a local guide.
현지 가이드가 있었으면 해요.
hyŏn·ji ga·i·dŭ·ga iss·ŏss·ŭ·myŏn hae·yo

How long is the tour?
투어가 얼마나 걸리나요?
t'u·ŏ·ga ŏl·ma·na gŏl·li·na·yo

What time should we be back?
언제까지 돌아와야 되나요?
ŏn·jek·ka·ji do·ra·wa·ya doé·na·yo

I've lost my group.
우리 그룹을 놓쳐 버렸어요.
u·ri gŭ·ru·bŭl no·ch'ŏ·bŏ·ryŏss·ŏ·yo

I'm with them.
저 팀이랑 같이 왔어요.
jŏ t'i·mi·rang ga·ch'i wass·ŏ·yo

Accessible Travel

KEY PHRASES

I need assistance.	도움이 필요해요.	do·u·mi p'i·ryo·hae·yo
Is there wheelchair access?	휠체어 출입구가 있나요?	hwil·ch'e·ŏ ch'u·rip·gu·ga in·na·yo
Are there toilets for people with a disability?	장애인 전용 화장실 있나요?	jang·ae·in jŏ·nyong hwa·jang·shil in·na·yo

I have a disability.	전 장애인인데요. jŏn jang·ae·in in·de·yo
I need assistance.	도움이 필요해요. do·u·mi p'i·ryo·hae·yo
What facilities do you have for people with a disability?	장애인 시설이 뭐가 있나요? jang·ae·in shi·sŏ·ri mwŏ·ga in·na·yo
Are guide dogs permitted?	맹인 안내견 출입 가능한가요? maeng·in an·nae·gyŏn ch'u·rip ga·nŭng·han·ga·yo
Are there parking spaces for people with a disability?	장애인 전용 주차 공간이 있나요? jang·ae·in jŏ·nyong ju·ch'a·gong·ga·ni in·na·yo
Is there wheelchair access?	휠체어 출입구가 있나요? hwil·ch'e·ŏ ch'u·rip·gu·ga in·na·yo

How wide is the entrance?	입구가 얼마나 넓은가요? ip·gu·ga ŏl·ma·na nŏl·bŭn·ga·yo
How many steps are there?	계단이 몇 개인가요? gye·da·ni myŏk·kae in·ga·yo
Is there a lift/elevator?	엘리베이터 있나요? el·li·be·i·t'ŏ in·na·yo
Are there toilets for people with a disability?	장애인 전용 화장실 있나요? jang·ae·in jŏ·nyong hwa·jang·shil in·na·yo
Are there rails in the bathroom?	욕실에 핸드레일 있나요? yok·shi·ré haen·dŭ·re·il in·na·yo
Please call me a taxi for people with a disability.	장애인용 택시 불러 주세요. jang·ae·in·nyong t'aek·shi bul·lŏ ju·se·yo
Could you help me cross the street safely?	길 건너는 데 좀 도와주시겠어요? gil gŏn·nŏ·nŭn·dé jom do·wa·ju·shi·gess·ŏ·yo
Is there somewhere I can sit down?	앉을 수 있는 곳 있나요? an·jŭl·su in·nŭn·got in·na·yo
guide dog	맹인 안내견 maeng·in an·nae·gyŏn
person with a disability	장애인 jang·ae·in
ramp	램프 raem·p'ŭ
walking frame	보행기/워커 bo·haeng·gi/wŏ·k'ŏ
walking stick	지팡이 ji·p'ang·i
wheelchair	휠체어 hwil·ch'é·ŏ

Travel with Children

KEY PHRASES

Are children allowed?	어린이 입장 할 수 있나요?	ŏ·ri·ni ip·jang hal·su in·na·yo
Is there a discount for children?	어린이 할인 있나요?	ŏ·ri·ni ha·rin in·na·yo
Is there a baby change room?	기저귀 가는 곳 있나요?	gi·jŏ·gwi ga·nŭn·got in·na·yo

Is there a ...? ... 있나요? ... in·na·yo

baby change room	기저귀 가는 곳	gi·jŏ·gwi ga·nŭn·got
child-minding service	아기 맡기는 곳	a·gi mak·ki·nŭn·got
children's menu	어린이 메뉴	ŏ·ri·ni me·nyu
discount for children	어린이 할인	ŏ·ri·ni ha·rin

I need a/an ... ...이/가 필요해요. ...·i/·ga p'i·ryo·hae·yo

baby seat	어린이 좌석	ŏ·ri·ni jwa·sŏk
cot	아기 침대	a·gi ch'im·dae
highchair	유아용 높은 의자	yu·a·yong no·p'ŭn ŭi·ja
pram/stroller	유모차	yu·mo·ch'a

Do you sell ...?	... 있나요? ... in·na·yo	
baby wipes	아기용 물티슈	a·gi·yong mul·t'i·shyu
disposable nappies/diapers	일회용 기저귀	il·hoé·yong gi·jŏ·gwi
painkillers for infants	어린이용 진통제	ŏ·ri·ni·yong jin·t'ong·jé
tissues	티슈	t'i·shyu

Are there any good places to take children around here?	주위에 아이들 데려 가기 좋은 곳 있나요? ju·wi·é a·i·dŭl de·ryŏ·ga·gi jo·ŭn·got in·na·yo
Are children allowed?	어린이 입장 할 수 있나요? ŏ·ri·ni ip·jang hal·su in·na·yo
Do you mind if I breastfeed here?	여기서 모유 줘도 될까요? yŏ·gi·sŏ mo·yu·jwŏ·do doélk·ka·yo
Is this suitable for (six)-year-old children?	(여섯) 살에게 적당한가요? (yŏ·sŏs)·sa·re·gé jŏk·tang·han·ga·yo
Is there a doctor who is good with children?	아이들 잘 다루는 의사 있나요? a·i·dŭl jal da·ru·nŭn ŭi·sa in·na·yo
Is there a dentist who is good with children?	아이들 잘 다루는 치과의사 있나요? a·i·dŭl jal da·ru·nŭn ch'i·gwa·ŭi·sa in·na·yo

If your child is sick, see **health** (p178).

SOCIAL

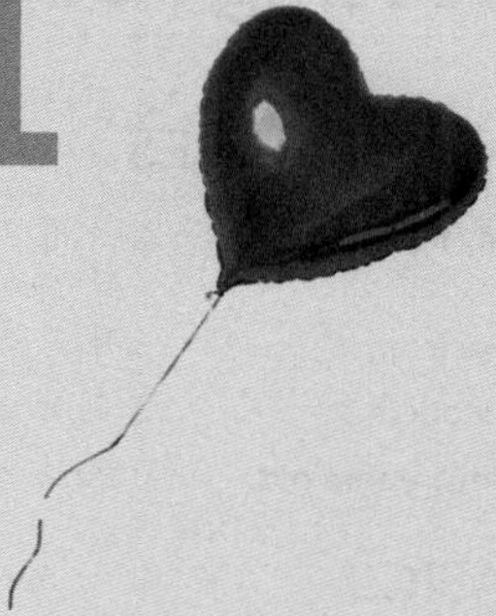

Meeting People

KEY PHRASES

My name is...	제 이름은 ...입니다.	je i·rŭ·mŭn ...·im·ni·da
I'm from ...	...에서 왔어요.	...·e·sŏ wass·ŏ·yo
I work in ...	... 에서 일을 해요.	... e·sŏ i·rŭl hae·yo
I'm ... years old.	저는 ... 살이에요.	jŏ·nŭn ... sa·ri·e·yo

BASICS

In Korean society a person with seniority or of higher age is accorded greater respect, which is demonstrated through language. A simple way to avoid offence, especially when speaking to older Koreans, is to add the polite ending ~yo ~요 to the end of your sentences, even if it's a one-word sentence!

Even when speaking to someone younger or with less seniority than yourself, it's considered good manners to use the polite forms. With the less formal younger generation, though, informal expressions are perfectly acceptable.

Yes.	네./예. né/yé
No.	아니요. a·ni·yo
Thank you. pol	고맙습니다. go·map·sŭm·ni·da 감사합니다. gam·sa·ham·ni·da
Many thanks. pol	정말 고맙습니다. jŏng·mal go·map·sŭm·ni·da
You're welcome. pol	괜찮아요 gwaen·cha·na·yo

You're welcome. inf	아니에요./뭘요. a·ni·e·yo/mwŏl·yo
Excuse me. pol **(to get attention)**	실례합니다. shil·lé·ham·ni·da
Excuse me. pol **(to get past)**	잠시만요. jam·shi·man·nyo
Sorry. pol	죄송합니다./ 미안합니다. choé·song ham·ni·da/ mi·an·ham·ni·da
May I?	해도 되나요? hae·do doé·na·yo

GREETINGS & GOODBYES

At all times of the day, the greeting an·nyŏng ha·se·yo 안녕하세요 (hello) is appropriate. However, at lunchtime, dinnertime or immediately afterward, Koreans often greet someone they know by asking shik·sa ha·shŏss·ŏ·yo 식사 하셨어요? (Did you have a meal?). So ingrained is this habit that many Koreans will ask non-Koreans the same question in English. A simple né 네 (yes) is all that's expected in reply.

Hello. pol	안녕하세요. an·nyŏng ha·se·yo
Hi. inf	안녕. an·nyŏng
Ⓠ **How are you?**	안녕하세요? (lit: Are you well?) an·nyŏng ha·se·yo
Ⓐ **Fine, thanks. And you?**	네. 안녕하세요? (lit: Yes. Are you well?) ne an·nyŏng ha·se·yo
Ⓠ **What's your name?**	성함이 어떻게 되세요? sŏng·ha·mi ŏt·tŏ·k'é doe·se·yo?
Ⓐ **My name is ...**	제 이름은 ...입니다. je i·rŭ·mŭn ...·im·ni·da

When introducing people, the phrase i·bu·nŭn 이 분은 (lit: this person) may be omitted, but the introduction should be accompanied with an open palm gesturing toward the person being introduced.

I'd like to introduce you to (Park Sujin).	이 분은 (박수진) 씨예요.	i·bu·nŭn (bak·su·jin)·shi·ye·yo
This is ...	…이에요/예요.	...·i·e·yo/·ye·yo
This is my ...	(이 분은) 제 … 이에요/예요.	(i·bu·nŭn) jé ... ·i·e·yo/·ye·yo

child	아이	a·i
colleague	동료	dong·nyo
friend	친구	ch'in·gu
partner	파트너	p'a·tŭ·nŏ

I'm pleased to meet you. pol	만나서 반갑습니다.	man·na·sŏ ban·gap·sŭm·ni·da
See you later.	다음에 봬요.	da·ŭ·mé bwae·yo
Goodbye. (when leaving) pol	안녕히 계세요.	an·nyŏng·hee gye·se·yo
Goodbye. (when staying) pol	안녕히 가세요.	an·nyŏng·hee ga·se·yo
Bye. inf	안녕..	an·nyŏng
Have a nice day!	좋은 하루 보내세요!	jo·ŭn ha·ru bo·nae·se·yo
Bon voyage!	즐거운 여행 하세요!	jŭl·gŏ·un yŏ·haeng ha·se·yo

☑ LANGUAGE TIP: SAYING 'PLEASE' & 'SORRY'

To ask someone to do something, combine the main verb with ju·se·yo 주세요 (give). To offer something to someone, use the 'high form' of the verb 'receive' – ba·dŭ·se·yo 받으세요. When offering food or drink, though, dŭ·se·yo 드세요 (lit: eat this) or ma·ni dŭ·se·yo 많이 드세요 (lit: eat a lot) are more appropriate expressions. The word 'please' is rarely used on its own to reinforce a request. Actually, je·bal 제발 (lit: please) sounds like desperate pleading in Korean. Avoid using it, unless you desperately require someone's assistance.

In Korea people will rarely say anything when they bump into someone on the street. The expression joé·song ham·ni·da 죄송합니다 (sorry) is generally reserved for apologising for a more serious issue.

TITLES & ADDRESSING PEOPLE

Traditional forms of address are still the norm in Korea. They almost always follow the person's name. The less familiar you are with the speaker, the more likely it is you'll address that person by his or her surname. You'd never refer to a much older person by his or her given name.

Mr/Mrs/Miss	... 씨 ...·shi/·ssi
Mr Donghun (first name)	동헌 씨 dong·hŏn·shi
Ms Taegyong (first name)	태경 씨 t'ae·gyŏng·shi
Mr Yang Donghun	양동헌 씨 yang·dong·hŏn·shi
Ms Kim Taegyong	김태경 씨 kim·t'ae·gyŏng·shi

When addressing or calling a child or a close friend (someone with similar social status), you can simply add a 아 (if the name ends in a consonant) or ya 야 (if the name ends in a vowel).

Jong-un!	정은아! jŏng·ŭ·na
Sangmi!	상미야! sang·mi·ya

There are also special forms of addressing people, such as sŏn·bae·nim 선배님 (a person in your group older than you, or at a higher social level), hu·bae 후배 (a person in your group younger than you, or at a lower social level). You can also use the following:

Chairman (Kang)	(강) 사장님 (gang)·sa·jang·nim
Dr (Cho)	(조) 박사님 (jo)·bak·sa·nim
Professor (Lee)	(이) 교수님 (i)·gyo·su·nim
Teacher (Jonathan)	(조나단) 선생님 (jo·na·dan)·sŏn·saeng·nim

☑ LANGUAGE TIP: 'THAT' PERSON

The title sŏn·saeng·nim 선생님 (meaning 'teacher' or 'higher person') is very useful if you're not sure how to address someone. Not knowing the relative position of an overseas 'guest', many Koreans will refer to him or her simply as sŏn·saeng·nim. If a traveller looks sufficiently young or not businesslike, they may be referred to simply as hak·saeng 학생 (lit: student).

Koreans frequently refer to each other in the third person. Rather than using nŏ 너 or dan·gshin 당신 (the informal and polite forms of 'you'), it's considered more polite to refer to a person's position or to use their name. See also **grammar** (p27).

LANGUAGE TIP: WESTERN TITLES

Koreans have adopted the Western titles Mr and Miss, adapting them into mi·sŭ·t'ŏ 미스터 and mi·sŭ 미스. The latter is used even for married women, although mi·shi·jŭ 미시즈 is also becoming common. These titles precede the surname of the addressee (note that Korean women don't take their husband's surname). When addressing Westerners, though, many Koreans will use mi·sŭ·t'ŏ or mi·sŭ before the person's given name (eg 'Mr David' or 'Miss Amanda').

MAKING CONVERSATION

Nice weather, isn't it?	날씨가 좋지요? nal·shi·ga jo·chi·yo
Awful weather, isn't it?	날씨가 안 좋지요? nal·shi·ga an·jo·chi·yo
Do you live here?	여기서 사시나요? yŏ·gi·sŏ sa·shi·na·yo
Where are you going?	어디 가세요? ŏ·di ga·se·yo
What are you doing?	뭐 하세요? mwŏ ha·se·yo
Q **Do you like it here?**	여기 마음에 드시나요? yŏ·gi ma·ŭ·mé dŭ·shi·na·yo
A **I love it here.**	여기 정말 좋아요. yŏ·gi jŏng·mal jo·a·yo
What's this called?	이걸 뭐라고 하나요? i·gŏl mwŏ·ra·go ha·na·yo
That's beautiful, isn't it?	아름답지요? a·rŭm·dap·ji·yo
Can I take a photo (of you)?	(당신) 사진 찍어도 될까요? (dang·shin) sa·jin jji·gŏ·do doélk·ka·yo

☑ CULTURE TIP: ADDRESSING SERVICE PERSONNEL

In modern Korean culture, there's some uncertainty as to how to refer to a young person (eg a waiter or a shop assistant) unknown to the speaker. Calling a young man a·jŏ·shi 아저씨 (lit: uncle) seems odd, but there's no other appropriate 'relative' expression. On the other hand, calling a young woman a·ga·shi 아가씨 (lit: young lady) is now out of favour. In restaurants, young people tend to call someone over by simply saying yŏ·gi·yo 여기요 ('over here' with a polite ending).

I'll send you the photo.	사진 보내 드릴게요. sa·jin bo·nae dŭ·rilk·ke·yo
Ⓠ **How long are you here for?**	여기에 얼마 동안 계시나요? yŏ·gi·é ŏl·ma·dong·an gye·shi·na·yo
Ⓐ **I'm here for (10) days.**	(십) 일 동안 있을 거예요. (shib)·il dong·an iss·ŭl·gŏ·ye·yo
Ⓐ **I'm here for (three) weeks.**	(삼) 주 동안 있을 거예요. (sam)·ju dong·an iss·ŭl·gŏ·ye·yo
Ⓐ **I'm here for (two) months.**	(두) 달 동안 있을 거예요. (du)·dal dong·an iss·ŭl·gŏ·ye·yo
Ⓠ **Are you here on holiday?**	여행하러 오셨나요? yŏ·haeng·ha·rŏ o·shŏn·na·yo
Ⓐ **I'm here for a holiday.**	여행하러 왔어요. yŏ·haeng ha·rŏ wass·ŏ·yo
Ⓐ **I'm here on business.**	사업 때문에 왔어요. sa·ŏp·ddae·mu·né wass·ŏ·yo
Ⓐ **I'm here to study.**	공부하러 왔어요. gong·bu ha·rŏ wass·ŏ·yo

We're here with our family.	저희는 가족들과 왔어요. jŏ·hi·nŭn ga·jok·dŭl·gwa wass·ŏ·yo
I'm here with my friend.	저는 친구랑 왔어요. jŏ·nŭn ch'in·gu·rang wass·ŏ·yo

NATIONALITIES

Koreans have two different ways of naming countries: a Hangulisation of the original name (for example sing·ga·p'o·rŭ 싱가포르 for Singapore), and the Korean pronunciation of the Chinese version of that name – eg il·bon 일본 (lit: sun's origin) for Japan.

Making words for nationalities out of country names is easy – simply add sa·ram 사람 or in 인 (the pure Korean and Sino-Korean words for 'person'). Keep in mind, though, that the pronunciation may change. Thus, a person from mi·guk 미국 (America, lit: beautiful country) becomes a mi·gu·gin 미국인 (lit: America-person).

Q **Where are you from?**	어디서 오셨어요? ŏdi·sŏ o·shŏss·ŏ·yo
A **I'm from ...**	...에서 왔어요. ...·e·sŏ wass·ŏ·yo

Australia	호주/ 오스트레일리아	ho·ju/ o·sŭ·tŭ·re·il·li·a
Britain	영국	yŏng·guk
Canada	캐나다	k'ae·na·da
New Zealand	뉴질랜드	nyu·jil·laen·dŭ
the USA	미국	mi·guk

AGE

Q **How old are you? (to a child)**	몇 살이니? myŏs·sa·ri·ni

Q How old are you? (to an adult around your age or younger)	나이가 어떻게 되세요? na·i·ga ŏt·tŏ·k'é doé·se·yo
Q How old are you? (to an adult older than you)	연세가 어떻게 되세요? yŏn·se·ga ŏt·tŏ·k'é doé·se·yo
A I'm ... years old.	저는 ... 살이에요. jŏ·nŭn ... sa·ri·e·yo
Q How old is your daughter/son?	딸/아들 나이가 어떻게 되나요? ddal/a·dŭl na·i·ga ŏt·tŏ·k'é doé·na·yo
A He/She is ... years old. (while pointing to them)	... 살이에요. ... sa·ri·e·yo
Too old!	너무 늙었어요! nŏ·mu nŭl·gŏss·ŏ·yo
I'm younger than I look.	전 보기보다 젊어요. jŏn bo·gi·bo·da jŏl·mŏ·yo

For your age, see **numbers & amounts** (p38).

OCCUPATIONS & STUDIES

Q What's your occupation?	무슨 일 하세요? mu·sŭ·nil ha·se·yo
A I work in administration.	행정 일을 해요. haeng·jŏng i·rŭl hae·yo
A I'm retired.	퇴직했어요. t'oé·jik·haess·ŏ·yo
A I'm self-employed.	자영업을 해요. ja·yŏng·ŏ·bŭl hae·yo
A I'm unemployed.	현재 직업이 없어요. hyŏn·jae ji·gŏ·bi ŏp·sŏ·yo
Q What are you studying?	뭘 공부하시나요? mwŏl gong·bu·ha·shi·na·yo

Ⓐ **I'm studying ...**	저는 ...을/를 공부 해요. chŏ·nŭn ...·ŭl/·rŭl gong·bu hae·yo	

English	영어	yŏng·ŏ
humanities	인문학	in·mun·hak
Korean	한국어	han·gu·gŏ
science	과학	gwa·hak

FAMILY

Ⓠ **Do you have a ...?**	... 있으세요? ... iss·ŭ·se·yo
Ⓐ **I have a ...**	...이/가 있어요. ...·i/·ga iss·ŏ·yo
Ⓐ **I don't have a ...**	...이/가 없어요. ...·i/·ga ŏp·sŏ·yo

brother	형제	hyŏng·je
daughter	딸	ddal
granddaughter	손녀	son·nyŏ
grandson	손자	son·ja
husband	남편	nam·p'yŏn
sister	자매	ja·mae
son	아들	a·dŭl
wife	아내	a·nae

Ⓠ **Are you married?**	결혼 하셨나요? gyŏl·hon ha·shŏn·na·yo
Ⓐ **I'm married.**	전 결혼했어요. jŏn gyol·hon haess·ŏ·yo
Ⓐ **I'm single.**	전 미혼이에요. jŏn mi·hon·i·e·yo

I live with someone.	어떤 사람과 같이 살아요. ŏt·ton sa·ram·gwa ga·ch'i sa·ra·yo
We don't have any children.	아이가 없어요. a·i·ga ŏp·sŏ·yo

TALKING WITH CHILDREN

The phrases used in this section are only appropriate for talking to children – using them with adults may cause offence. For more information, see **personal pronouns** (p27).

What's your name?	이름이 뭐야? i·rŭ·mi mwŏ·ya
When's your birthday?	생일이 언제야? saeng·ir·i ŏn·je·ya
What grade are you in?	몇 학년이야? myŏ·t'ang·nyŏ·ni·ya
Do you learn (English)?	(영어) 배우니? (yŏng·ŏ) bae·u·ni
What do you do after school?	학교 끝나고 뭐 해? hak·kyo kkŭn·na·go mwŏ·hae
Do you like school?	학교 좋아하니? hak·kyo jo·a·ha·ni
Do you like sport?	운동 좋아하니? un·dong jo·a·ha·ni
Do you like your teacher?	선생님 좋아하니? sŏn·saeng·nim jo·a·ha·ni
I come from very far away.	난 먼 나라에서 왔어. nan mŏn na·ra·e·sŏ wass·ŏ
Do you go to school or kindergarten?	학교 다녀, 유치원 다녀? hak·kyo da·nyŏ yu·ch'i·wŏn da·nyŏ

LISTEN FOR

Koreans consider themselves one big family, and there are several ways of referring to a person that reflect this:

할아버지	ha·ra·bŏ·ji	elderly man (lit: grandfather)
할머니	hal·mŏ·ni	elderly woman (lit: grandmother)
아저씨	a·jŏ·shi	older man (lit: uncle)
아주머니/ 아줌마	a·ju·mŏ·ni/ a·jum·ma	older woman (lit: aunt)

Younger and middle-aged Koreans refer to 'close' people of similar age as 'older brother', 'older sister' or 'younger sibling'. Which word to use depends on the gender of the speaker. These words are sometimes attached to the person's name.

오빠	op·pa	older brother (if speaker is female)
형	hyŏng	older brother (if speaker is male)
언니	ŏn·ni	older sister (if speaker is female)
누나	nu·na	older sister (if speaker is male)
남동생	nam·dong·saeng	younger brother (regardless of speaker's gender)
여동생	yŏ·dong·saeng	younger sister (regardless of speaker's gender)

TALKING ABOUT CHILDREN

When's the baby due?	출산 예정일이 언제예요? ch'ul·san ye·jŏng·i·ri ŏn·je·ye·yo
What are you going to call the baby?	아기 이름은 뭘로 하실 거예요? a·gi i·rŭ·mŭn mwŏl·lo ha·shilk·kŏ·ye·yo
Is this your first child?	첫째인가요? chŏt·tchae·in·ga·yo
How many children do you have?	자녀가 몇 명이에요? ja·nyŏ·ga myŏn·myŏng·i·e·yo
What's his/her name?	이름이 뭐예요? i·rŭ·mi mwŏ·ye·yo
Does he/she go to school?	학교 다니나요? hak·kyo da·ni·na·yo
He/She looks like you.	닮았어요. dal·mass·ŏ·yo

FAREWELLS

Koreans greet each other with a bow, or a bow and a simultaneous handshake. The same is done when saying goodbye. They rarely hug in public, except for emotional goodbyes.

Tomorrow is my last day here.	내일이 마지막 날이에요. nae·i·ri ma·ji·mang·na·ri·e·yo
It's been great meeting you.	만나서 반가웠어요. man·na·sŏ ban·ga·wŏss·ŏ·yo
Keep in touch!	우리 서로 연락해요! u·ri sŏ·ro yŏl·la·k'ae·yo
If you come to (Scotland), you can visit my place.	(스코틀랜드)에 오시면, 저희 집에 오세요. (sŭ·k'o·t'ŭl·laen·dŭ)·é o·shi·myŏn jŏ·hi ji·bé o·se·yo

I plan to come back to Korea (next year).	(내년에) 한국에 돌아 올 거예요. (nae·nyŏ·né) han·gu·gé do·ra·olk·kŏ·ye·yo
Q **What's your (email) address?**	(이메일) 주소가 뭐예요? (i·me·il) ju·so·ga mwŏ·ye·yo
A **Here's my (email) address.**	제 (이메일) 주소예요. jé (i·me·il) ju·so·ye·yo
Q **What's your phone number?**	전화번호가 뭐예요? jŏn·hwa bŏn·ho·ga mwŏ·ye·yo
A **Here's my phone number.**	제 전화번호예요. jé jŏn·hwa bŏn·ho·ye·yo
Q **What's your Instagram?**	인스타 뭐예요? in·sŭ·ta mwŏ·ye·yo
A **Here's my Instagram.**	제 인스타예요. jé in·sŭ·ta·ye·yo

WELL-WISHING

A distinctively Korean phrase is the call of encouragement p'a·i·t'ing 파이팅 (from the English word 'fighting'), used especially when the listener is feeling down or has just suffered a setback, as if saying 'Cheer up, things will get better'. Here are some other well-wishing phrases:

Congratulations!	축하해요! ch'u·k'a hae·yo
Good luck!	행운을 빌어요! haeng·u·nŭl bi·rŏ·yo
Happy birthday!	생일 축하해요! saeng·il ch'u·k'a hae·yo
Happy New Year!	새해 복 많이 받으세요! sae·hae·bok ma·ni ba·dŭ·se·yo
Merry Christmas!	즐거운 성탄절 보내세요! jŭl·gŏ·un sŏng·t'an·jŏl bo·nae·se·yo

Interests

KEY PHRASES

What do you do in your spare time?	시간 있을 때 뭐 하세요?	shi·gan iss·ŭlt·tae mwŏ ha·se·yo
Do you like ...?	... 좋아하세요?	... jo·a·ha·se·yo
I like/ don't like ...	... 좋아해요/ 싫어해요.	... jo·a·hae·yo/ shi·rŏ·hae·yo

COMMON INTERESTS

What do you do in your spare time?	시간 있을 때 뭐 하세요? shi·gan iss·ŭlt·tae mwŏ ha·se·yo
(Q) **Do you like ...?**	... 좋아하세요? ... jo·a·ha·se·yo
(A) **I like ...**	... 좋아해요. ... jo·a·hae·yo
(A) **I don't like ...**	... 싫어해요. ... shi·rŏ·hae·yo

cooking	요리	yo·ri
gardening	정원 가꾸기	jŏng·won gak·ku·gi
hiking	등산	dŭng·san
reading	독서	dok·sŏ
sport	운동	un·dong
travelling	여행	yŏ·haeng

For types of sports, see **sports** (p158), and the **dictionary** (p221).

MUSIC

Do you dance?	춤 추시나요? ch'um ch'u·shi·na·yo
Do you go to concerts?	공연 가시나요? gong·yŏn ga·shi·na·yo
Do you listen to music?	음악 들으시나요? ŭ·mak dŭ·rŭ·shi·na·yo
Do you play an instrument?	악기 다루시나요? ak·ki da·ru·shi·na·yo
Do you sing?	노래 부르시나요? no·rae bu·rŭ·shi·na·yo
What ... do you like?	어떤 ...을/를 좋아하시나요? ŏt·tŏn ...·ŭl/·rŭl jo·a·ha·shi·na·yo

bands	밴드	baen·dŭ
music	음악	ŭ·mak
performers	공연가	gong·yŏn·ga
singers	가수	ga·su

contemporary music	현대 음악 hyŏn·dae ŭ·mak
electronic music	전자 음악 jŏn·ja ŭ·mak
Korean traditional music	국악 gu·gak
traditional opera	판소리 p'an·so·ri

Planning to go to a concert? See **buying tickets** (p54), and **going out** (p144).

☑ CULTURE TIP: KOREAN NAMES

In Korea, a person may have a Korean given name and also a se·rye·myŏng 세례명 (Christian name) if they're Catholic or belong to some Protestant churches. This name might be used in church or as an English name when interacting with foreigners, but it isn't usually used in everyday life.

Nevertheless, many Koreans try to make their Korean names easier for foreigners to read or pronounce. When a syllable in someone's name sounds like a word in English, they may use that word's spelling in their name. So a person named sŏng·dŏk 성덕 might spell his name Sung-Duck, and yu-mi 유미 might write her name as You-Me. People with surnames like wŏn 원, yu 유 and bak 박 sometimes write them as One, You and Park.

CINEMA & THEATRE

I feel like going to a/an ...	... 보러 가고 싶어요. ... bo·rŏ ga·go shi·p'ŏ·yo
How was the ...?	... 어땠나요? ... ŏt·taen·na·yo

ballet	발레	bal·lé
film	영화	yŏng·hwa
musical	뮤지컬	myu·ji·k'ŏl
opera	오페라	o·p'e·ra
performance	공연	gong·yŏn
play	연극	yŏn·gŭk

I thought it was ...

boring	지루했어요	ji·ru·hae·ssŏ·yo
entertaining	재미있었어요	jae·mi·iss·ŏss·ŏ·yo
excellent	좋았어요	jo·a·ssŏ·yo
long	길었어요	gi·rŏ·ssŏ·yo
OK	괜찮았어요	gwaen·cha·na·ssŏ·yo

What's showing at the cinema/theatre tonight?	오늘 밤 영화관에서/ 극장에서 뭐 하나요? o·nŭl·bam yŏng·hwa·gwa·ne·sŏ/ gŭk·jang·e·sŏ mwŏ ha·na·yo
Is it in (English)?	(영어)로 나오나요? (yŏng·ŏ)·ro na·o·na·yo
Does it have (English) subtitles?	(영어) 자막 나오나요? (yŏng·ŏ) ja·mang·na·o·na·yo
Is it dubbed?	더빙 되었나요? dŏ·bing doé·ŏn·na·yo
Is this seat available?	여기 자리 있나요? yŏ·gi ja·ri in·na·yo
Do you have tickets for ...?	... 표 있나요? ... p'yo in·na·yo
Are there any extra tickets?	남는 표 있나요? nam·nŭn p'yo in·na·yo
I'd like cheap tickets.	싼 표 주세요. ssan·p'yo ju·se·yo

LISTEN FOR

죄송합니다, 매진입니다.
joé·song ham·ni·da mae·jin im·ni·da
I'm sorry, it's sold out.

I'd like the best tickets.	제일 좋은 표 주세요. je·il jo·ŭn p'yo ju·se·yo
Is there a matinée show?	낮 공연 있나요? nat gong·yŏn in·na·yo
Is there a late-night showing for this film?	이 영화 심야 상영 있나요? i·yŏng·hwa shi·mya sang·yŏng in·na·yo
Have you seen ...?	... 보셨나요? ... bo·shŏn·na·yo
Q **Who's in it?**	누가 나오나요? nu·ga na·o·na·yo
A **It stars ...**	...이/가 나와요. ...·i/·ga na·wa·yo
I like ...	... 좋아해요. ... jo·a·hae·yo
I don't like ...	... 싫어해요. ... shi·rŏ·hae·yo

action movies	액션 영화	aek·shŏn yŏng·hwa
comedies	코메디	k'o·me·di
documentaries	다큐멘터리	da·k'yu·men·t'ŏ·ri
drama	드라마	dŭ·ra·ma
horror movies	공포 영화	gong·p'o yŏng·hwa
Korean cinema	한국 영화	han·guk yŏng·hwa
martial arts films	무술 영화	mu·sul yŏng·hwa
period dramas	사극	sa·gŭk
sci-fi films	공상 과학 영화	gong·sang gwa·hak yŏng·hwa
thrillers	스릴러 영화	sŭ·ril·lŏ yŏng·hwa
war movies	전쟁 영화	jŏn·jaeng yŏng·hwa

Feelings & Opinions

KEY PHRASES

How do you feel today?	오늘 기분이 어떠세요?	o·nŭl gi·bu·ni ŏt·tŏ·se·yo
I'm ...	저는 ...	jŏ·nŭn ...
What do you think of ...?	...에 대해 어떻게 생각하시나요?	...·é dae·hae ŏt·tŏ·k'é saeng·gak ha·shi·na·yo
I think it's interesting.	재미있는 것 같아요.	jae·mi·in·nŭn·gŏt ga·t'a·yo
Did you hear about ...?	... 이야기 들으셨나요?	... i·ya·gi dŭ·rŭ·shŏn·na·yo

FEELINGS

When describing oneself or another person, the subject – eg jŏ·nŭn 저는 ('I') – is omitted if it's clear from the context who is meant.

Q **How do you feel today?** 오늘 기분이 어떠세요? o·nŭl gi·bu·ni ŏt·tŏ·se·yo

Q **Are you ...?**

cold	추우세요?	ch'u·u·se·yo
happy	행복하세요?	haeng·bo·k'a·se·yo
hot	더우세요?	dŏ·u·se·yo
hungry	시장하세요?	shi·jang·ha·se·yo
sad	슬프세요?	sŭl·p'ŭ·se·yo
thirsty	목 마르세요?	mong·ma·rŭ·se·yo
tired	피곤하세요?	p'i·gon·ha·se·yo
well	건강하세요?	gŏn·gang·ha·se·yo

(A) **I'm ...** 저는 ...
jŏ·nŭn ...

cold	추워요	ch'u·wŏ·yo
happy	행복해요	haeng·bo·k'ae·yo
hot	더워요	dŏ·wŏ·yo
hungry	배고파요	bae·go·p'a·yo
sad	슬퍼요	sŭl·p'ŏ·yo
thirsty	목 말라요	mong·mal·la·yo
tired	피곤해요	p'i·gon·hae·yo
well	건강해요	gŏn·gang·hae·yo

If you're not feeling well, see **health** (p178).

OPINIONS

(Q) **Did you like it?** 좋았나요?
jo·an·na·yo

(Q) **What do you think of ...?** ...에 대해 어떻게 생각하시나요?
...·é dae·hae ŏt·tŏ·k'é saeng·gak ha·shi·na·yo

(A) **I think it's ...** 제 생각에는 ... 같아요.
jé saeng·ga·ge·nŭn ... ga·t'a·yo

awful	형편 없는 것	hyŏng·p'yŏn ŏm·nŭn·gŏt
beautiful	아름다운 것	a·rŭm·da·un·gŏt
boring	지루한 것	ji·ru·han·gŏt
great	좋은 것	jo·ŭn·gŏt
interesting	재미있는 것	jae·mi·in·nŭn·gŏt
strange	이상한 것	i·sang·han·gŏt

아름다워요.
a·rŭm·da·wŏ·yo
It's beautiful.

POLITICS & SOCIAL ISSUES

Q Who will you vote for?	누구 찍으실 거예요? nu·gu jji·gŭ·shil·gŏ·ye·yo
A I support the ... party.	전 ...을/를 지지해요. jŏn ...·ŭl/·rŭl ji·ji·hae·yo

conservative	보수당	bo·su·dang
democratic	민주당	min·ju·dang
green	녹색당	nok·saek·dang
liberal	자유당	ja·yu·dang
social-democratic	사회 민주당	sa·hoé min·ju·dang
socialist	사회당	sa·hoé·dang

I'm (American), but I didn't vote for ...	전 (미국인)인데, ... 찍지 않았어요. jŏn (mi·gu·gin) in·dé ... jjik·ji a·nass·ŏ·yo
Q How do people feel about ...?	...에 대해 사람들이 어떻게 생각하나요? ...·é dae·hae sa·ram·dŭ·ri ŏt·tŏ·k'é saeng·ga·k'a·na·yo

Ⓐ **I agree/disagree with the policy on ...**	...에 대한 정책에 찬성해요/반대해요. ...·é dae·han jŏng·ch'ae·gé ch'an·sŏng·hae·yo/ban·dae·hae·yo
Did you hear about ...?	... 이야기 들으셨나요? ... i·ya·gi dŭ·rŭ·shŏn·na·yo

the economy	경제	gyŏng·jé
immigration	이민	i·min
the war (in ...)	(...의) 전쟁	(...·é) jŏn·jaeng

Is there help for (the) ...?	...에게 도움을 주나요? ...·é·gé do·u·mŭl ju·na·yo

aged	노인	no·in
disabled	장애인	jang·ae·in
homeless	노숙자	no·suk·ja
unemployed	실업자	shi·rŏp·ja

THE ENVIRONMENT

Is there a ... problem here?	여기 ... 문제 있나요? yŏ·gi ... mun·jé in·na·yo
What should be done about ...?	...을/를 어떻게 해야 할까요? ...·ŭl/·rŭl ŏt·tŏ·k'é hae·ya halk·ka·yo
Is this a protected area?	여기 자연 보호 구역인가요? yŏ·gi ja·yŏn·bo·ho gu·yŏ·gin·ga·yo
Is this a protected species?	천연기념물인가요? ch'ŏ·nyŏn·gi·nyŏm·mu·rin·ga·yo

LOOK FOR

In Korea, recycling (jae·hwa·ryong 재활용) is the law in many places. In public, separate bins are marked 'for plastic only', 'for cans only' etc. At home, nonrecyclables can only be disposed of using special garbage bags (ssŭ·re·gi jong·nyang·jé bong·t'u 쓰레기 종량제 봉투). Food waste is also disposed of separately.

병/유리	byŏng/yu·ri	bottles only
알루미늄/캔	al·lu·mi·nyum/k'aen	cans only
종이	jong·i	paper products only
플라스틱	p'ŭl·la·sŭ·t'ik	plastic only
일반 쓰레기	il·ban ssŭ·re·gi	regular garbage
음식물 쓰레기	ŭm·shing·mul ssŭ·re·gi	food waste

Does (Gwangju) have a recycling programme?	(광주)에서는 재활용을 하나요? (gwang·ju)·e·sŏ·nŭn jae·hwa·ryong·ŭl ha·na·yo
Is this recyclable?	이것 재활용 되나요? i·gŏt jae·hwa·ryong doé·na·yo
Do we separate our rubbish?	분리수거 해야 되나요? bul·li·su·gŏ hae·ya doé·na·yo
climate change	기후 변화 gi·hu·byŏn·hwa
pollution	오염 o·yŏm

Going Out

KEY PHRASES

Is there anything interesting on tonight?	오늘 밤에 뭐 재미있는 것 없나요?	o·nŭl ba·mé mwŏ jae·mi in·nŭn·gŏt ŏm·na·yo
Where can I find clubs?	클럽 어디에 있나요?	k'ŭl·lŏb ŏ·di·é in·na·yo
Would you like to go for a coffee?	커피 마시러 가시겠어요?	k'ŏ·p'i ma·shi·rŏ ga·shi·gess·ŏ·yo
What time will we meet?	몇 시에 만날까요?	myŏs·shi·é man·nalk·ka·yo
Where shall we meet?	어디서 만날까요?	ŏ·di·sŏ man·nalk·ka·yo

WHERE TO GO

What's there to do in the evenings?	저녁에 뭐 재미있게 할 것 없나요? jŏ·nyŏ·gé mwŏ jae·mi ik·ké hal·gŏt ŏm·na·yo
Where can I find out what's on?	재미있는 할 거리 있는지 어디서 알아보나요? jae·mi in·nŭn hal·gŏ·ri in·nŭn·ji ŏ·di·sŏ a·ra·bo·na·yo
Which website are the (concerts) listed in?	(공연) 목록이 있는 웹사이트가 뭔가요? (gong·yŏn) mong·no·gi in·nŭn web·sa·i·tŭ·ga mwŏn·ga·yo

Is there anything interesting on tonight?	오늘 밤에 뭐 재미있는 것 없나요? o·nŭl ba·mé mwŏ jae·mi in·nŭn·gŏt ŏm·na·yo
Is there anything interesting on this weekend?	이번 주말에 뭐 재미있는 것 없나요? i·bŏn ju·ma·ré mwŏ jae·mi in·nŭn·gŏt ŏm·na·yo
Where can I find ...?	... 어디에 있나요? ... ŏ·di·é in·na·yo

bars	술집	sul·jip
clubs	클럽	k'ŭl·lŏb
gay/lesbian bars	게이바	ge·i·ba
music venues	음악 공연장	ŭ·mak gong·yŏn·jang
restaurants	음식점	ŭm·shik·jŏm

I feel like going to a ...	...에 가고 싶어요. ...·é ga·go shi·p'ŏ·yo

bar	술집	sul·jip
cafe	카페	k'a·p'é
concert	콘서트	k'on·sŏ·t'ŭ
cinema	영화관	yŏng·hwa·gwan
karaoke room	노래방	no·rae·bang
nightclub	나이트클럽	na·i·t'ŭ k'ŭl·lŏb
play	연극 공연	yŏn·gŭk gong·yŏn
restaurant	식당	shik·dang
teashop	찻집	ch'at·chip
traditional music performance	국악 공연	gu·gak gong·yŏn

For more on bars, drinks and partying, see **romance** (p150), **alcoholic drinks** (p201), **in the bar** (p202) and **drinking up** (p203).

INVITATIONS

What are you doing tonight?	오늘 밤에 뭐 하세요? o·nŭl ba·mé mwŏ ha·se·yo
What are you doing this weekend?	이번 주말에 뭐 하세요? i·bŏn ju·ma·ré mwŏ ha·se·yo
Would you like to go (for a) ...?	... 가시겠어요? ... ga·shi·gess·ŏ·yo
I feel like going (for a) ...	... 가고 싶어요. ... ga·go shi·p'ŏ·yo

coffee	커피 마시러	k'ŏ·p'i ma·shi·rŏ
dancing	춤추러	ch'um·ch'u·rŏ
drink	술 마시러	sul ma·shi·rŏ
meal	밥 먹으러	bam·mŏg·ŭ·rŏ
walk	산책하러	san·ch'ae·k'a·rŏ

Do you want to come to the (BTS) concert with me?	(비티에스) 공연에 같이 가시겠어요? (bi·ti·e·sŭ) gong·yŏ·né ga·ch'i ga·shi·gess·ŏ·yo
We're having a party.	우리 파티 할 거예요. u·ri p'a·t'i halk·kŏ·ye·yo
You should come along.	같이 가요. ga·ch'i ga·yo

RESPONDING TO INVITATIONS

Sure!	물론이죠! mul·lo·ni·jyo
Yes, I'd love to.	네, 가고 싶어요. né ga·go shi·p'ŏ·yo
Where shall we go?	어디 갈까요? ŏ·di galk·ka·yo

☑ CULTURE TIP: ENTERTAINMENT VENUES

In Korea, going out often means visiting various bang 방 (lit: room), venues which offer affordable entertainment options. Here are some of them:

노래방	no·rae·bang	song-room

small rooms with karaoke machines, perfect for up to a dozen people to sing along to their favourite songs

디브이디 방	di·bŭ·i·di·bang	DVD-room

a place where you can watch movies on DVD in a small room with a sofa – popular with groups of friends and couples, especially when the weather's bad

찜질방	jjim·jil·bang	steam room

public baths and saunas, with separate facilities for men and women and coed spaces to watch TV, read or relax – often open 24 hours, allowing guests to sleep overnight

피시방	p'i·shi·bang	PC-room

the Korean equivalent of an internet cafe – a big room, often dark and crowded, which attracts more computer-game addicts than internet users

I'm afraid I can't.	죄송하지만 못 갈 것 같아요. joé·song·ha·ji·man mok·kal·gŏt ga·t'a·yo
What about tomorrow?	내일은 어떠세요? nae·i·rŭn ŏt·tŏ·se·yo

ARRANGING TO MEET

Most Koreans don't meet up at a friend's home when they go out. Instead, they'll suggest meeting near a subway station, in front of a department store, or at the restaurant where they plan to go.

Ⓠ **What time will we meet?**	몇 시에 만날까요? myŏs·shi·é man·nalk·ka·yo
Ⓐ **Let's meet at (eight) o'clock.**	(여덟) 시에 만나요. (yŏ·dŏl)·shi·é man·na·yo
Ⓠ **Where shall we meet?**	어디서 만날까요? ŏ·di·sŏ man·nalk·ka·yo
Ⓐ **Let's meet at the entrance.**	입구에서 만나요. ip·gu·é·sŏ man·na·yo
Ⓐ **I'll pick you up at (six).**	(여섯) 시에 태워 드리러 올게요. (yŏ·sŏs) shi·é t'ae·wŏ dŭ·ri·rŏ olk·ke·yo
Ⓠ **Are you ready?**	준비 되셨나요? jun·bi doé·shŏn·na·yo
Ⓐ **I'm ready.**	전 준비 됐어요. jŏn jun·bi dwaess·ŏ·yo
Ⓐ **I'll be (15 minutes) late.**	(십오 분) 늦을 것 같아요. (shi·bo·bun) nŭ·jŭl·gŏt ga·t'a·yo
I'll try to make it.	노력해 볼게요. no·ryŏ·k'ae bol·ke·yo
If I'm not there by (nine), don't wait for me.	제가 (아홉) 시까지 안 오면, 기다리지 마세요. je·ga (a·hop) shik·ka·ji a·no·myŏn gi·da·ri·ji ma·se·yo
OK, I'll see you then.	네, 그때 뵐게요. né gŭt·tae boélk·ke·yo
I'm looking forward to it.	기대돼요. gi·dae dwae·yo
Sorry, I'm late.	늦어서 죄송합니다. nŭ·jŏ·sŏ joé·song·ham·ni·da
Never mind.	괜찮아요. gwaen·ch'a·na·yo

어디 갈까요?
ŏ·di galk·ka·yo
Where shall we go?

DRUGS

I don't take drugs.	전 마약 안 해요. jŏn ma·yak an·hae·yo
I'm addicted to (coffee).	전 (커피) 중독이에요. jŏn (k'ŏ·p'i) jung·do·gi·e·yo
I'm trying to quit.	끊으려고 노력 중이에요. ggŭ·nŭ·ryŏ·go no·ryŏk· jung i·e·yo
Do you want to have a smoke?	담배 피우시겠어요? dam·bae p'i·u·shi·gess·ŏ·yo
Do you have a light?	불 있으세요? bu·riss·ŭ·se·yo

If the police are talking to you about drugs, see **police** (p177), for useful phrases.

I smoke (cigarettes).	전 담배 피워요. jŏn dam·bae p'i·wŏ·yo

Romance

KEY PHRASES

Would you like to do something with me?	같이 뭐 할까요?	ga·ch'i mwŏ halk·ka·yo
I love you.	사랑해요.	sa·rang·hae·yo
Excuse me, I have to go now.	죄송하지만 지금 어디 가야 돼요.	joé·song·ha·ji·man ji·gŭm ŏ·di ga·ya dwae·yo

ASKING SOMEONE OUT

Where would you like to go (tonight)?	(오늘 밤) 어디 가고 싶으신가요? (o·nŭl·bam) ŏ·di ga·go shi·p'ŭ·shin·ga·yo
Q **Would you like to do something with me (tomorrow)?**	(내일) 같이 뭐 할까요? (nae·il) ga·ch'i mwŏ halk·ka·yo
A **Yes, I'd love to.**	네, 좋아요. né jo·a·yo
A **Sorry, I can't.**	죄송하지만 안 돼요. choé·song·ha·ji·man an·dwae·yo

PICK-UP LINES

Would you like a drink?	뭐 같이 마실까요? mwŏ ga·ch'i ma·shilk·ka·yo
Do you have a light?	라이터 있으신가요? ra·i·t'ŏ iss·ŭ·shin·ga·yo

Shall we get some fresh air?	산책 할까요? san·ch'aek halk·ka·yo
Can I dance with you?	같이 춤춰도 될까요? ga·ch'i ch'um·ch'wŏ·do doélk·ka·yo
Can I take you home?	집에 데려다 드려도 될까요? ji·bé de·ryŏ·da dŭ·ryŏ·do doélk·ka·yo

REJECTIONS

I'm here with my girlfriend/boyfriend.	여자친구랑/ 남자친구랑 같이 왔어요. yŏ·ja·ch'in·gu·rang/ nam·ja·ch'in·gu·rang ga·ch'i wass·ŏ·yo
I'm sorry, but I'd rather not.	죄송하지만 안 돼요. joé·song·ha·ji·man an·dwae·yo
Excuse me, I have to go now.	죄송하지만 지금 어디 가야 돼요. joé·song·ha·ji·man ji·gŭm ŏ·di ga·ya dwae·yo

GETTING CLOSER

I really like you.	당신이 정말 좋아요. dang·shi·ni jŏng·mal jo·a·yo
Can I kiss you?	키스해도 돼요? k'i·sŭ·hae·do dwae·yo
Do you want to come inside for a while?	안에 잠시 들어오시겠어요? a·né jam·shi dŭ·rŏ o·shi·gess·ŏ·yo

Would you like to stay over?	자고 가시겠어요? ja·go ga·shi·gess·ŏ·yo

SEX

Kiss me.	키스해 주세요. k'i·sŭ·hae·ju·se·yo
I want you.	당신을 원해요. dang·shi·nŭl wŏn·hae·yo
Let's go to bed.	잠자리에 들어요. jam·ja·ri·é dŭ·rŏ·yo
Q **Do you like this?**	좋아요? jo·a·yo
A **I like that.**	좋아요. jo·a·yo
A **I don't like that.**	싫어요. shi·rŏ·yo
That's great.	좋아요. jo·a·yo
I think we should stop now.	그만해야 될 것 같아요. gŭ·man·hae·ya doél·gŏt ga·t'a·yo
Do you have a (condom)?	(콘돔) 있나요? (k'on·dom) in·na·yo
We need to use a (condom).	(콘돔) 써야 해요. (k'on·dom) ssŏ·ya hae·yo
I won't do it without protection.	피임 없이 안 할 거예요. p'i·im ŏp·shi an·halk·kŏ·ye·yo

LOVE

I think we're good together.	우리 잘 어울리는 것 같아요. u·ri jal ŏ·ul·li·nŭn·gŏt ga·t'a·yo

I'm really happy with you.	당신과 있으면 행복해요. dang·shin·gwa iss·ŭ·myŏn haeng·bo·k'ae·yo
I love you.	사랑해요. sa·rang·hae·yo
Will you marry me?	결혼해 주시겠어요? gyŏl·hon hae·ju·shi·gess·ŏ·yo
I'd like you to meet my parents.	부모님께 인사드리러 가요. bu·mo·nimk·ké in·sa·dŭ·ri·rŏ ga·yo

PROBLEMS

I don't think it's working out.	안 될 것 같네요. an·doél·gŏt ga·t'a·yo
Q **Are you seeing someone else?**	다른 사람 만나나요? da·rŭn sa·ram man·na·na·yo
A **He/She is just a friend.**	그냥 친구예요. gŭ·nyang ch'in·gu·ye·yo
We'll work it out.	잘 해결할 수 있을 거예요. jal hae·gyŏl hal·su iss·ŭlk·kŏ·ye·yo
I want to stay friends.	친구로 남았으면 좋겠어요. ch'in·gu·ro na·mass·ŭ·myŏn jo·k'ess·ŏ·yo

LEAVING

I have to leave (tomorrow).	저 (내일) 떠나야 돼요. jŏ (nae·il) ddŏ·na·ya dwae·yo
I'll keep in touch.	연락할게요. yŏl·la·k'alk·ke·yo
I'll miss you.	보고 싶을 거예요. bo·go shi·p'ŭlk·kŏ·ye·yo

Beliefs & Culture

KEY PHRASES

What's your religion?	종교가 뭐예요?	jong·gyo·ga mwŏ·ye·yo
I'm ...	전 ...	jŏn ...
I'm sorry, it's against my beliefs.	죄송하지만, 그것은 저의 믿음에 위배돼요.	joé·song·ha·ji·man gŭ·gŏ·sŭn jŏ·é mi·dŭm·é wi·bae dwae·yo

RELIGION

Q **What's your religion?**	종교가 뭐예요? jong·gyo·ga mwŏ·ye·yo
A **I'm agnostic.**	전 불가지론자예요. jŏn bul·ga·ji·ron·ja·ye·yo
A **I'm an atheist.**	전 무신론자예요. jŏn mu·shin·non·ja·ye·yo
A **I'm (a/an) ...**	전 ... jŏn ...

Buddhist	불교예요	bul·gyo·ye·yo
Catholic	천주교예요	ch'ŏn·ju·gyo·ye·yo
Christian	기독교예요	gi·dok·kyo·ye·yo
Confucianist	유교예요	yu·gyo·ye·yo
Hindu	힌두교예요	hin·du·gyo·ye·yo
Jewish	유태교예요	yu·t'ae·gyo·ye·yo
Muslim	이슬람교예요	i·sŭl·lam·gyo·ye·yo

Ⓐ **I believe in religious freedom.**	전 종교의 자유를 믿어요. jŏn jong·gyo·é ja·yu·rŭl mi·dŏ·yo
Ⓐ **I don't have any religion.**	전 종교가 없어요. jŏn jong·gyo·ga ŏp·sŏ·yo
I (don't) believe in ...	전 ...을/를 (안) 믿어요. jŏn ...·ŭl/·rŭl (an) mi·dŏ·yo

a god	신	shin
astrology	점성학	jŏm·sŏng·hak
fate	운명	un·myŏng
God (Judeo-Christian)	하나님	ha·na·nim

Can I attend a service/mass here?	여기서 예배/미사 드려도 되나요? yŏ·gi·sŏ ye·bae/mi·sa dŭ·ryŏ·do doé·na·yo
Can I pray here?	여기서 기도해도 되나요? yŏ·gi·sŏ gi·do·hae·do doé·na·yo
Can I worship here?	여기서 찬양 예배 드려도 되나요? yŏ·gi·sŏ ch'a·nyang ye·bae dŭ·ryŏ·do doé·na·yo
Where can I attend a service/mass?	어디 서예배/미사 드릴 수 있나요? ŏ·di·sŏ ye·bae/mi·sa dŭ·ril·su in·na·yo
Where can I pray?	어디서 기도할 수 있나요? ŏ·di·sŏ gi·do·hal·su in·na·yo
Where can I worship?	어디서 찬양 예배 드릴 수 있나요? ŏ·di·sŏ ch'a·nyang ye·bae dŭ·ril·su in·na·yo

CULTURAL DIFFERENCES

How do you do this in (Korea)?	(한국)에서는 이걸 어떻게 하나요? (han·gug)·e·sŏ·nŭn i·gŏl ŏt·to·k'é ha·na·yo
I didn't mean to do/say anything wrong.	일부러 그런 게 아니예요. il·bu·rŏ gŭ·rŏn·gé a·ni·ye·yo
Is this a local or national custom?	이 지방의 관습인가요, 한국 전체의 관습인가요? i·ji·bang·é gwan·sŭ·bin·ga·yo han·guk jŏn·ch'e·é gwan·sŭ·bin·ga·yo
I don't want to offend you.	기분 나쁘게 하려던 게 아니예요. gi·bun nap·pŭ·gé ha·ryŏ·dŏn·gé a·ni·ye·yo
I respect your beliefs.	당신의 믿음을 존중해요. dang·shi·né mi·dŭm·ŭl jon·jung·hae·yo
I'm not used to this.	이것에 익숙하지 않아요. i·gŏ·sé ik·su·k'a·ji a·na·yo

☑ CULTURE TIP: SHAMANISM

An important part of Korean spirituality is mu·sok·shi·nang 무속신앙 (shamanism). It's not a religion, but it does involve communication with spirits through intermediaries known as mu·dang 무당 (shamans). Shamanist ceremonies are held for a variety of reasons: to cure illness, to ward off financial problems or to guide a deceased family member safely into the spirit world. A gut 굿 (ceremony) might be held by a village on a regular basis to ensure the safety of its citizens and a good harvest of rice or fish.

☑ CULTURE TIP: SUPERSTITIONS

In Korean the number four, sa 사, sounds like one of the Chinese characters for 'death' – the Korean word for 'death', sa·mang 사망, is based on this. The resulting superstition is the reason the 4th floor in lifts and office listings is often named with the letter 'F' instead of the number four.

When writing a person's name, it's preferable to use any colour except bbal·gang 빨강 (red). Though the source of this superstition is uncertain, many older people associate writing someone's name in red ink with death.

Finally, a dwae·ji 돼지 (pig) appearing in a dream is considered a sign of good luck – if it happens to you, Korean friends might advise you to buy a lottery ticket!

I'd rather not join in.	하지 않는 게 낫겠어요. ha·ji an·nŭn·gé nak·kess·ŏ·yo
I'll try it.	한번 해 볼게요. han·bŏn hae·bolk·ke·yo
I'm sorry, it's against my beliefs.	죄송하지만, 그것은 저의 믿음에 위배돼요. joé·song·ha·ji·man gŭ·gŏ·sŭn jŏ·é mi·dŭm·é wi·bae dwae·yo
I'm sorry, it's against my culture.	죄송하지만, 그것은 저의 문화에 위배돼요. joé·song·ha·ji·man gŭ·gŏ·sŭn jŏ·é mun·hwa·é wi·bae dwae·yo
I'm sorry, it's against my religion.	죄송하지만, 그것은 저의 종교에 위배돼요. joé·song·ha·ji·man gŭ·gŏ·sŭn jŏ·é jong·gyo·é wi·bae dwae·yo
This is different.	이건 색달라요. i·gŏn saek·tal·la·yo
This is interesting.	이건 흥미로워요. i·gŏn hŭng·mi·ro·wŏ·yo

Sports

KEY PHRASES

Which sport do you play?	어떤 운동 하세요?	**ŏt·tŏn un·dong ha·se·yo**
What's your favourite team?	제일 좋아하는 팀이 뭐예요?	**je·il jo·a·ha·nŭn t'i·mi mwŏ·ye·yo**
What's the score?	점수가 어떻게 되나요?	**jŏm·su·ga ŏt·tŏ·k'é doé·na·yo**

SPORTING INTERESTS

Q **Which sport do you follow?**	어떤 운동 관심 있으세요? **ŏt·tŏn un·dong gwan·shim iss·ŭ·se·yo**
Q **Which sport do you play?**	어떤 운동 하세요? **ŏt·tŏn un·dong ha·se·yo**
A **I follow ...**	...에 관심 있어요. **...·é gwan·shim iss·ŏ·yo**
A **I play/do ...**	저는 ...을/를 해요. **jŏ·nŭn ...·ŭl/·rŭl hae·yo**

aerobics	에어로빅	**e·ŏ·ro·bik**
archery	양궁	**yang·gung**
baseball	야구	**ya·gu**
basketball	농구	**nong·gu**
football/soccer	축구	**ch'uk·ku**
golf	골프	**gol·pŭ**
karate	가라테	**ga·ra·t'e**
martial arts	무술	**mu·sul**

mixed martial arts	종합격투기	jong·hap·gyŏk·tu·gi
scuba diving	스쿠버 다이빙	sŭ·k'u·bŏ da·i·bing
table tennis	탁구	tak-ku
taekwondo	태권도	tae·gwŏn·do
tennis	테니스	t'e·ni·sŭ
volleyball	배구	bae·gu
weightlifting	역도	yŏk·to

Ⓐ **I cycle.**	전 자전거를 타요. jŏn ja·jŏn·gŏ·rŭl t'a·yo
Ⓐ **I run.**	전 달리기를 해요. jŏn dal·li·gi·rŭl hae·yo
Ⓐ **I walk.**	전 걷기를 해요. jŏn gŏk·ki·rŭl hae·yo
Ⓐ **I swim.**	전 수영을 해요. jŏn su·yŏng·ŭl hae·yo
Ⓠ **Do you like (baseball)?**	(야구) 좋아하시나요? (ya·gu) jo·a·ha·shi·na·yo
Ⓐ **Yes, very much.**	많이 좋아해요. ma·ni jo·a·hae·yo
Ⓐ **Not really.**	별로요. byŏl·lo·yo
Ⓐ **I like watching it.**	보는 것은 좋아해요. bo·nŭn·gŏ·sŭn jo·a·hae·yo

어떤 운동 하세요?

ŏt·tŏn un·dong ha·se·yo

Which sport do you play?

Who's your favourite sportsperson?	특히 좋아하는 운동 선수가 누구예요? t'ŭ·k'i jo·a·ha·nŭn un·dong sŏn·su·ga nu·gu·ye·yo
What's your favourite team?	제일 좋아하는 팀이 뭐예요? je·il jo·a·ha·nŭn t'i·mi mwŏ·ye·yo

For more sports, see the **dictionary** (p221).

GOING TO A GAME

Would you like to go to a game?	경기 보러 가시겠어요? gyŏng·gi bo·rŏ ga·shi·gess·ŏ·yo
Who are you supporting?	어느 팀을 응원하세요? ŏ·nŭ t'i·mŭl ŭng·wŏn·ha·se·yo
What's the score?	점수가 어떻게 되나요? jŏm·su·ga ŏt·tŏ·k'é doé·na·yo
Who's playing?	누가 경기해요? nu·ga gyŏng·gi·hae·yo
Who's winning?	누가 이기고 있나요? nu·ga i·gi·go in·na·yo

LISTEN FOR

무승부	mu·sŭng·bu	draw/even
무득점	mu·dŭk·jŏm	love (zero)
매치포인트	mae·ch'i·p'o·in·t'ŭ	match point
영점	yŏng·jŏm	nil (zero)

That was a boring game!	지루한 경기였어요! ji·ru·han gyŏng·gi·yŏss·ŏ·yo
That was a great game!	굉장한 경기였어요! goéng·jang·han gyŏng·gi·yŏss·ŏ·yo

PLAYING SPORT

Q **Do you want to play a game?**	저랑 운동경기 하시겠어요? jŏ·rang un·dong·gyŏng·gi ha·shi·gess·ŏ·yo
A **I'm sorry, I can't.**	죄송하지만, 안 돼요. joé·song·ha·ji·man an·dwae·yo
Can I join in?	같이 해도 되나요? ga·ch'i hae·do doé·na·yo
Your/My point.	제/당신 점수예요. jé/dang·shin jŏm·su·ye·yo
Kick/Pass it to me!	저한테 차/패스해 주세요! jŏ·han·t'e ch'a/p'ae·sŭ·hae ju·se·yo
Where's a good place to ...?	...하기 좋은 곳이 어디예요? ... ha·gi jo·ŭn go·shi ŏ·di·ye·yo

fish	낚시	nakk·shi
go hiking	등산	dŭng·san
go horse riding	승마	sŭng·ma
go scuba diving	스쿠버 다이빙	sŭ·k'u·bŏ da·i·bing
go windsurfing	윈드서핑	win·dŭ·sŏ·p'ing
run	육상	yuk·sang
ski	스키	sŭ·k'i

Where's the nearest ...?	제일 가까운 ... 어디예요? je·il gak·ka·un ... ŏ·di·ye·yo

basketball court	농구장	nong·gu·jang
golf course	골프장	gol·p'ŭ·jang
gym	헬스장	hel·sŭ·jang
ice rink	빙상경기장	bing·sang·gyŏng·gi·jang
swimming pool	수영장	su·yŏng·jang
tennis court	테니스장	t'e·ni·sŭ·jang

Can I hire a ...?	... 빌릴 수 있나요? ... bil·lil·su in·na·yo

ball	공	gong
bicycle	자전거	ja·jŏn·gŏ
court	경기장	gyŏng·gi·jang
racquet	라켓	ra·k'et

What's the charge per day?	하루당 얼마예요? ha·ru·dang ŏl·ma·ye·yo
What's the charge per game?	게임당 얼마예요? ge·im·dang ŏl·ma·ye·yo
What's the charge per hour?	시간당 얼마예요? shi·gan·dang ŏl·ma·ye·yo
Is there a women-only session/pool?	여성 전용 강습/수영장 있나요? yŏ·sŏng·jŏ·nyong gang·sŭp/su·yŏng·jang in·na·yo
Where are the changing rooms?	탈의실이 어디예요? t'a·ri·shi·ri ŏ·di·ye·yo

FOOTBALL/SOCCER

Who plays for (the Korean National Football Team)?	(한국 국가대표팀)에 어떤 선수가 뛰나요? (han·guk guk·ka·dae·p'yo·t'im)·é ŏt·tŏn sŏn·su·ga ddwi·na·yo
He's/She's a great player.	그는/그녀는 실력있는 선수예요. gŭ·nŭn/gŭ·nyŏ·nŭn shil·lyŏ·gin·nŭn sŏn·su·ye·yo
What a great/terrible team!	굉장한/ 형편없는 팀이네요! goéng·jang·han/ hyŏng·p'yŏn·ŏm·nŭn t'i·mi·ne·yo
Down with ...!	... 져라! ... jyŏ·ra
What a goal!	골 멋져요! gol mŏt·jyŏ·yo
What a pass!	패스 멋져요! p'ae·sŭ mŏt·jyŏ·yo
What a kick!	킥 멋져요! k'ik mŏt·jyŏ·yo

Off to see a match? Check out **going to a game** (p160) and **buying tickets** (p54).

LISTEN FOR

공	gong	ball
퇴장	t'oé·jang	expulsion
골대	gol·dae	goal posts
선수	sŏn·su	player
심판	shim·p'an	referee
공격수	gong·gyŏk·su	striker

Outdoors

KEY PHRASES

Where can we buy hiking supplies?	등산 용품 어디서 살 수 있나요?	dŭng·san yong·p'um ŏ·di·sŏ sal·su in·na·yo
Is there a trail I can follow?	등산로가 있나요?	deung·san·no·ga in·na·yo
I'm lost.	길을 잃었어요.	gi·rŭl i·rŏss·ŏ·yo
Is it safe to dive/ swim here?	여기서 다이빙해도/ 수영해도 안전한가요?	yŏ·gi·sŏ da·i·bing·hae·do/ su·yŏng·hae·do an·jŏn han·ga·yo
What's the weather like?	날씨 어떤가요?	nal·shi ŏt·tŏn·ga·yo

HIKING

Is there a trail I can follow?	등산로가 있나요? deung·san·no·ga in·na·yo
How long is the trail?	등산로가 얼마나 긴가요? dŭng·san·no·ga ŏl·ma·na gin·ga·yo
Is it possible to go rock climbing here?	여기서 암벽 등반해도 되나요? yŏ·gi·sŏ am·byŏk dŭng·ban hae·do doé·na·yo
Is it safe to climb this mountain?	이 산 올라가기에 안전한가요? i·san ol·la·ga·gi·é an·jŏn·han·ga·yo

How high is the climb?	얼마나 높나요? ŏl·ma·na nom·na·yo
Is it very scenic?	경치가 아주 좋은가요? gyŏng·ch'i·ga a·ju jo·ŭn·ga·yo
When does it get dark?	언제 어두워 지나요? ŏn·jé ŏ·du·wŏ ji·na·yo
Where's the nearest village?	가장 가까운 마을이 어디 있나요? ga·jang gak·ka·un ma·ŭ·ri ŏ·di in·na·yo
Where's the nearest temple?	가장 가까운 절이 어디 있나요? ga·jang gak·ka·un jŏ·ri ŏ·di in·na·yo
Is there a mountain hut up there?	저 위에 산장이 있나요? jŏ wi·é san·jang·i in·na·yo
Where can we buy hiking supplies?	등산 용품 어디서 살 수 있나요? dŭng·san yong·p'um ŏ·di·sŏ sal·su in·na·yo
Do you employ local guides?	현지 가이드가 있나요? hyŏn·ji ga·i·dŭ·ga in·na·yo
Where can we spend the night?	어디서 잘 수 있나요? ŏ·di·sŏ jal·su in·na·yo
Can I leave some things here for a while?	여기 잠깐 물건 놔둬도 되나요? yŏ·gi jamk·kan mul·gŏn nwa·dwŏ·do doé·na·yo
Do we have to pay?	돈 내야 하나요? don nae·ya ha·na·yo
Can I cook here?	여기서 취사해도 되나요? yŏ·gi·sŏ ch'wi·sa·hae·do doé·na·yo

Where can I ...?	어디서 ... 있나요? ŏ·di·sŏ ... in·na·yo

buy things	물건 살 수	mul·gŏn sal·su
find someone who knows this area	여기 잘 아는 사람을 찾을 수	yŏ·gi jal a·nŭn sa·ra·mŭl ch'a·jŭl·su
get a map	지도 구할 수	ji·do gu·hal·su
hire hiking gear	등산 장비 빌릴 수	dŭng·san jang·bi bil·lil·su

Where can I find the ...?	... 어디 있나요? ... ŏ·di in·na·yo

campsite	야영 장소	ya·yŏng jang·so
nearest village	제일 가까운 마을	je·il gak·ka·un ma·ŭl
showers	샤워 시설	sha·wŏ shi·sŏl
toilets	화장실	hwa·jang·shil

Do we need to take food?	음식 가져 가야 되나요? ŭm·shik ga·jŏ·ga·ya doé·na·yo
Do we need to take water?	물 가져 가야 되나요? mul ga·jŏ·ga·ya doé·na·yo
Which is the easiest route?	제일 쉬운 경로가 뭐예요? je·il shi·un gyŏng·no·ga mwŏ·ye·yo
Which is the most interesting route?	제일 재미있는 경로가 뭐예요? je·il jae·mi·in·nŭn gyŏng·no·ga mwŏ·ye·yo

Which is the shortest route?	제일 짧은 경로가 뭐예요? je·il jjal·bŭn gyŏng·no·ga mwŏ·ye·yo
Is the track open?	이 길 개방되어 있나요? i·gil gae·bang·doé·ŏ in·na·yo
Is the track scenic?	이 길 경치가 좋은가요? i·gil gyŏng·ch'i·ga jo·ŭn·ga·yo
Is the track well-marked?	이 길 보기 쉽게 표시되어 있나요? i·gil bo·gi ship·ké p'yo·shi·doé·ŏ in·na·yo
Where have you come from?	어디서 오시는 길이에요? ŏ·di·sŏ o·shi·nŭn gi·ri·e·yo
How long did it take?	얼마나 걸리셨나요? ŏl·ma·na gŏl·li·shŏn·na·yo
Does this path go to (Dobongsan)?	이 길이 (도봉산) 가는 길인가요? i·gi·ri (do·bong·san) ga·nŭn gi·rin·ga·yo
Can I go through here?	여기 지나가도 되나요? yŏ·gi ji·na·ga·do doé·na·yo
I'm lost.	길을 잃었어요. gi·rŭl i·rŏss·ŏ·yo
Is the water OK to drink?	마셔도 괜찮은 물인가요? ma·shŏ·do gwaen·ch'a·nŭn mu·rin·ga·yo

LISTEN FOR

물살 조심하세요!	mul·sal jo·shim ha·se·yo	Be careful of the undertow!
위험해요!	wi·hŏm·hae·yo	It's dangerous!

AT THE BEACH

Is there a beach near here?	주위에 해수욕장 있나요? ju·wi·é hae·su·yok·jang in·na·yo
Is it safe to dive/swim here?	여기서 다이빙해도/수영해도 안전한가요? yŏ·gi·sŏ da·i·bing·hae·do/su·yŏng·hae·do an·jŏn han·ga·yo
What time is high/low tide?	밀물이/썰물이 언제예요? mil·mu·ri/ssŏl·mu·ri ŏn·je·ye·yo
How much to rent a chair?	의자 빌리는 데 얼마예요? ŭi·ja bil·li·nŭn·dé ŏl·ma·ye·yo
How much to rent a parasol?	파라솔 빌리는 데 얼마예요? p'a·ra·sol bil·li·nŭn·dé ŏl·ma·ye·yo

WEATHER

Q **What will the weather be like tomorrow?**	내일 날씨가 어떨까요? nae·il nal·shi·ga ŏt·tŏlk·ka·yo
Q **What's the weather like?**	날씨 어떤가요? nal·shi ŏt·tŏn·ga·yo

LOOK FOR

낚시 금지	nak·shi gŭm·ji	No fishing
다이빙 금지	da·i·bing gŭm·ji	No diving
수영 금지	su·yŏng gŭm·ji	No swimming

It's ...

cloudy	구름이 많아요.	gu·rŭ·mi ma·na·yo
cold	추워요.	ch'u·wŏ·yo
fine	맑아요.	mal·ga·yo
freezing	정말 추워요.	jŏng·mal ch'u·wŏ·yo
hot	더워요.	dŏ·wŏ·yo
humid	습도가 높아요.	sŭp·do·ga no·p'a·yo
muggy	푹푹 쪄요.	p'uk·p'uk jjyŏ·yo
raining	비가 와요.	bi·ga wa·yo
snowing	눈이 와요.	nu·ni wa·yo
sunny	햇빛이 밝아요.	haep·pi·ch'i bal·ga·yo
warm	따뜻해요.	ddat·tŭ·t'ae·yo
windy	바람이 많이 불어요.	ba·ra·mi ma·ni bu·rŏ·yo

Where can I buy a rain jacket?	우비 어디서 사나요? u·bi ŏ·di·sŏ sa·na·yo
Where can I buy an umbrella?	우산 어디서 살 수 있어요? u·san ŏ·di·sŏ sal·su iss·ŏ·yo

FLORA & FAUNA

What ... is that?	이게 무슨 ...이에요/예요? i·gé mu·sŭn ...·i·e·yo/·ye·yo

animal	동물	dong·mul
flower	꽃	ggot
plant	식물	shing·mul
tree	나무	na·mu

LISTEN FOR

진달래	jin·dal·lae	azalea
벚꽃	bŏk·kot	cherry blossom
개나리	gae·na·ri	forsythia
은행나무	ŭn·haeng na·mu	gingko tree
고라니	go·ra·ni	Korean water deer
단풍나무	dan·p'ung na·mu	maple tree
무궁화	mu·gung·hwa	Korean rose (national flower of South Korea)

Is it ...?

common	흔한가요?	hŭn·han·ga·yo
dangerous	위험한가요?	wi·hŏm·han·ga·yo
endangered	멸종 위기에 있나요?	myŏl·jong wi·gi·é in·na·yo
poisonous	독이 있나요?	do·gi in·na·yo
protected	보호를 받고 있나요?	bo·ho·rŭl bak·ko in·na·yo

What's it used for?	뭐에 쓰나요? mwŏ·é ssŭ·na·yo
Can you eat the fruit?	열매 먹을 수 있나요? yŏl·mae mŏ·gŭl·su in·na·yo

For geographical and agricultural terms, and more names of animals and plants, see the **dictionary** (p221).

SAFE TRAVEL

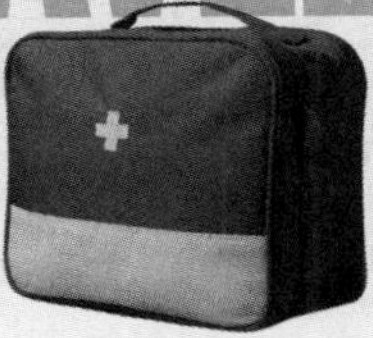

Emergencies

KEY PHRASES

Help!	도와주세요!	do·wa·ju·se·yo
There's been an accident.	사고가 났어요.	sa·go·ga nass·ŏ·yo
It's an emergency!	응급 상황이에요!	ŭng·gŭp sang·hwang·i·e·yo

Help!	도와주세요! do·wa·ju·se·yo
Stop!	그만 하세요! gŭ·man ha·se·yo
Go away!	저리 가세요! jŏ·ri ka·se·yo
Thief!	도둑이야! do·du·gi·ya
Fire!	불이야! bu·ri·ya
Watch out!	조심하세요! jo·shim·ha·se·yo
Call an ambulance!	구급차 불러주세요! gu·gŭp·ch'a bul·lŏ·ju·se·yo
Call a doctor!	의사 불러주세요! ŭi·sa bul·lŏ·ju·se·yo
Call the police!	경찰 불러주세요! gyŏng·ch'al bul·lŏ·ju·se·yo
It's an emergency!	응급 상황이에요! ŭng·gŭp sang·hwang·i·e·yo

LOOK FOR

경찰서	gyŏng·ch'al·sŏ	Police station
병원	byŏng·won	Hospital
응급실	ŭng·gŭp·shil	Emergency department
파출소	p'a·ch'ul·so	Police substation

There's been an accident.
사고가 났어요.
sa·go·ga nass·ŏ·yo

Can I use your phone?
전화 좀 써도 되나요?
jŏn·hwa jom ssŏ·do doé·na·yo

Could you help me, please?
좀 도와주시겠어요?
jom do·wa·ju·shi·gess·ŏ·yo

Where are the toilets?
화장실이 어디예요?
hwa·jang·shi·ri ŏ·di·ye·yo

I'm lost.
길을 잃었어요.
gi·rŭl i·rŏss·ŏ·yo

She's having a baby.
아기가 곧 나올 것 같아요.
a·gi·ga got na·ol·gŏt ga·t'a·yo

He/She is having a/an ...

allergic reaction	알레르기 반응을 보여요.	al·le·rŭ·gi ba·nŭng·ŭl bo·yŏ·yo
asthma attack	천식 발작해요.	ch'ŏn·shik bal·ja·k'ae·yo
epileptic fit	간질 발작해요.	gan·jil bal·ja·k'ae·yo
heart attack	심장 마비예요.	shim·jang ma·bi·ye·yo

☑ LANGUAGE TIP: TONGUE TWISTERS

Try rolling these two beauties off your tongue:

경찰청 쇠창살 외철창살,
검찰청 쇠창살 쌍철창살.
gyŏng·ch'al·chŏng soé·ch'ang·sal oé·ch'ŏl·ch'ang·sal
gŏm·ch'al·ch'ŏng soé·ch'ang·sal ssang·ch'ŏl·ch'ang·sal
An iron bar in the National Police Agency window is a single iron bar, and an iron bar in the Public Prosecutor's Office window is a double iron bar.

간장 공장 공장장은 강 공장장이고,
된장 공장 공장장은 공 공장장이다.
gan·jang gong·jang gong·jang·jang·ŭn gang gong·jang·jang·i·go
doén·jang gong·jang gong·jang·jang·ŭn gong gong·jang·jang·i·da
The manager of the soy sauce factory is manager Gang, and the manager of the soy bean paste factory is manager Gong.

Is it safe ...?	... 안전한가요?	... an·jŏn han·ga·yo

at night	밤에	ba·mé
for gay people	동성 커플에게	dong·sŏng k'ŏ·p'ŭ·re·gé
for travellers	여행자에게	yŏ·haeng·ja·e·gé
for women	여자에게	yŏ·ja·e·gé
on your own	혼자서도	hon·ja·sŏ·do

Police

KEY PHRASES

Where's the police station?	경찰서가 어디예요?	gyŏng·chal·sŏ·ga ŏ·di·ye·yo
I want to contact my embassy/ consulate.	대사관에/ 영사관에 연락하고 싶습니다.	dae·sa·gwa·né/ yŏng·sa·gwa·né yŏl·la·k'a·go ship·sŭm·ni·da
My bags were stolen.	가방 도둑 맞았어요.	ga·bang do·dung·ma·jass·ŏ·yo

Korean police in general are willing to give extra leeway to foreigners, but not if they give attitude. Apologising and/or admitting fault can be a quick way to end a sticky situation, as the disadvantaged party is often only looking for a face-saving admission that they were wronged. Most police speak only rudimentary English. In a bind, you can call the 1330 Korea Travel Helpline for help.

Where's the police station?	경찰서가 어디예요? gyŏng·chal·sŏ·ga ŏ·di·ye·yo
I want to report an offence.	신고하려고 해요. shin·go ha·ryŏ·go hae·yo
I've been assaulted.	저는 폭행 당했어요. jŏ·nŭn p'o·k'aeng·dang haess·ŏ·yo
I've been raped.	저는 강간 당했어요. jŏ·nŭn gang·gan·dang haess·ŏ·yo
I've been robbed.	저는 도둑 맞았어요. jŏ·nŭn do·dung ma·jass·ŏ·yo
I have insurance.	전 보험에 들었어요. jŏn bo·hŏ·mé dŭ·rŏss·ŏ·yo

I've lost my ...	... 잃어버렸어요. ... i·rŏ·bŏ·ryŏss·ŏ·yo
My ... was/were stolen.	... 도둑 맞았어요. ... do·dung·ma·jass·ŏ·yo

backpack	배낭	bae·nang
bags	가방	ga·bang
car keys	차 열쇠	ch'a yŏl·soé
credit card	신용 카드	shi·nyong k'a·dŭ
handbag	핸드백	haen·dŭ·baek
jewellery	보석	bo·sŏk
money	돈	don
papers	서류	sŏ·ryu
passport	여권	yŏ·gwŏn
wallet	지갑	ji·gap

I need an (English) interpreter.	(영어) 통역사가 필요해요. (yŏng·ŏ) t'ong·yŏk·sa·ga p'i·ryo·hae·yo
What am I accused of?	제가 무슨 혐의가 있나요? je·ga mu·sŭn hyŏ·mi·ga in·na·yo
I didn't do it.	전 그런 적 없습니다. jŏn gŭ·rŏn·jŏk ŏp·sŭm·ni·da
I'm sorry.	죄송합니다. joé·song·ham·ni·da
I apologise.	사과드립니다. sa·gwa dŭ·rim·ni·da

LISTEN FOR

교통 위반 벌금입니다.	gyo·t'ong wi·ban bŏl·gŭm im·ni·da It's a traffic violation fine.
속도 위반 벌금입니다.	sok·do wi·ban bŏl·gŭm im·ni·da It's a speeding fine.
주차 위반 벌금입니다.	ju·ch'a wi·ban bŏl·gŭm im·ni·da It's a parking fine.

I didn't realise I was doing anything illegal.	전 그게 불법인지 몰랐습니다. jŏn gŭ·gé bul·bŏ·bin·ji mol·lass·sŭm·ni·da
Is there a fine we can pay to clear this?	벌금을 내면 됩니까? bŏl·gŭ·mŭl nae·myŏn doém·nik·ka
I want to contact my embassy/consulate.	대사관에/영사관에 연락하고 싶습니다. dae·sa·gwa·né/yŏng·sa·gwa·né yŏl·la·k'a·go ship·sŭm·ni·da
Can I make a phone call?	전화 좀 써도 되겠습니까? jŏn·hwa jom ssŏ·do doé·gess·sŭm·nik·ka
Can I have a lawyer (who speaks English)?	(영어하는) 변호사 쓸 수 있습니까? (yŏng·ŏ·ha·nŭn) byŏn·ho·sa ssŭl·su iss·sŭm·nik·ka
This medicine is for personal use.	이 약은 제가 쓸 겁니다. i·ya·gŭn je·ga ssŭl gŏm·ni·da
I have a prescription for this drug.	이 약 처방전이 있습니다. i·yak chŏ·bang·jŏ·ni iss·sŭm·ni·da

Health

KEY PHRASES

Where's the nearest hospital?	제일 가까운 병원 어디 있나요?	je·il gak·ka·un byŏng·wŏn ŏ·di in·na·yo
I'm sick.	전 아파요.	jŏn a·p'a·yo
I need a doctor.	의사가 필요해요.	ŭi·sa·ga p'i·ryo hae·yo
I'm on medication for ...	전 ... 약을 먹어요.	jŏn ... ya·gŭl mŏ·gŏ·yo
I'm allergic to ...	전 ...에 알레르기가 있어요.	jŏn ...·é al·le·rŭ·gi·ga iss·ŏ·yo

DOCTOR

Where's the nearest ...?
제일 가까운 ... 어디 있나요?
je·il gak·ka·un ... ŏ·di in·na·yo

dental clinic	치과	ch'i·gwa
emergency department	응급실	ŭng·gŭp·shil
hospital	병원	byŏng·wŏn
optometrist	안경점	an·gyŏng·jŏm
pharmacy	약국	yak·kuk

I need a doctor (who speaks English).
(영어 하는) 의사가 필요해요.
(yŏng·ŏ ha·nŭn) ŭi·sa·ga p'i·ryo hae·yo

Could I see a female doctor?	여자 의사 있나요? yŏ·ja ŭi·sa in·na·yo
Could the doctor come here?	왕진 올 수 있나요? wang·jin ol·su in·na·yo
I've run out of my medication.	약이 다 떨어졌어요. ya·gi da ddŏ·rŏ·jŏss·ŏ·yo
This is my usual medicine.	제가 늘 먹는 약이에요. je·ga nŭl mŏng·nŭn ya·gi·e·yo
My child weighs (20) kilos.	제 아이는 (이십) 킬로그램이에요. jé a·i·nŭn (i·ship) k'il·lo·gŭ·rae·mi·e·yo
What's the correct dosage?	정확한 복용량이 뭐예요? jŏng·hwa·k'an bo·gyong·nyang·i mwŏ·ye·yo
I don't want a blood transfusion.	수혈은 싫어요. su·hyŏ·rŭn shi·rŏ·yo
I've been vaccinated against ...	전 ... 예방주사 맞았어요. jŏn ... ye·bang·ju·sa ma·jass·ŏ·yo

diptheria and tetanus	디프테리아, 파상풍	di·p'ŭ·t'e·ri·a p'a·sang·p'ung
hepatitis A/B	A형/B형 간염	e·i·hyŏng/bi·hyŏng ga·nyŏm
Japanese B encephalitis	일본 뇌염	il·bon noé·yŏm
measles, mumps and rubella	MMR	e·me·mal
rabies	광견병	gwang·gyŏn·byŏng
tuberculosis	결핵	gyŏl·haek
typhoid	장티푸스	jang·t'i·p'u·sŭ
varicella/ chickenpox	수두	su·du

LANGUAGE TIP: ADDRESSING DOCTORS

Doctors and other medical professionals can be referred to as sŏn·saeng·nim 선생님 (a term for someone to whom you wish to show respect). Using English and calling your doctor or dentist 'Dr Kim', for example, is also perfectly acceptable.

I need new contact lenses.	새 콘택트렌즈가 필요해요. sae k'on·t'aek·t'ŭ·ren·jŭ ga p'i·ryo·hae·yo
I need new glasses.	새 안경이 필요해요. sae an·gyŏng·i p'i·ryo·hae·yo
I have foreign medical insurance.	외국 의료보험이 있어요. oé·guk ŭi·ryo·bo·hŏ·mi iss·ŏ·yo
I have Korean national medical insurance.	한국 의료보험이 있어요. han·guk ŭi·ryo·bo·hŏ·mi iss·ŏ·yo
Can I have a receipt for my insurance?	보험용 영수증 좀 주시겠어요? bo·hŏm·nyong yŏng·su·jŭng jom ju·shi·gess·ŏ·yo

SYMPTOMS & CONDITIONS

I'm sick.	전 아파요. jŏn a·p'a·yo
My friend/child is (very) sick.	제 친구가/아이가 (많이) 아파요. jé ch'in·gu·ga/a·i·ga (ma·ni) a·p'a·yo

It hurts here.	여기가 아파요. yŏ·gi·ga a·p'a·yo
I'm dehydrated.	전 탈수 상태예요. jŏn t'al·su sang·t'ae·ye·yo
I can't sleep.	잠이 안 와요. ja·mi an·wa·yo
I'm on medication for ...	전 ... 약을 먹어요. jŏn ... ya·gŭl mŏ·gŏ·yo
I have (a/an) ...	저는 ...에 걸렸어요. jŏ·nŭn ...·é gŏl·lyŏss·ŏ·yo
I've recently had (a/an) ...	저는 최근에 ...에 걸렸었어요. jŏ·nŭn ch'oé·gŭ·né ...·é gŏl·lyŏss·ŏss·ŏ·yo

LISTEN FOR

아프세요?	a·p'ŭ·se·yo Do you feel any pain?
어디가 아프세요?	ŏ·di·ga a·p'ŭ·se·yo Where does it hurt?
이렇게 하면 아파요?	i·rŏ·k'é ha·myŏn a·p'a·yo Does it hurt if I do this?
열이 있나요?	yŏ·ri in·na·yo Do you have a temperature?
언제부터 이랬나요?	ŏn·je·bu·t'ŏ i·raen·na·yo How long have you been like this?
전에도 이런 적 있나요?	jŏ·ne·do i·rŏn·jŏ·gin·na·yo Have you had this before?
약 복용 중인가요?	yak bo·gyong·jung in·ga·yo Are you on medication?
알레르기 있나요?	al·le·rŭ·gi in·na·yo Are you allergic to anything?

I've been injured.	전 다쳤어요	jŏn da·ch'ŏss·ŏ·yo
I've been vomiting.	전 계속 토했어요	jŏn gye·sok t'o·haess·ŏ·yo
I have (a) ...	저는 ...	jŏ·nŭn ...

asthma	천식이 있어요	ch'ŏn·shi·gi iss·ŏ·yo
cold	감기에 걸렸어요	gam·gi·é gŏl·lyŏss·ŏ·yo
constipation	변비가 있어요	byŏn·bi·ga iss·ŏ·yo
cough	기침을 해요	gi·ch'i·mŭl hae·yo
diabetes	당뇨병이 있어요	dang·nyo·byŏng·i iss·ŏ·yo
diarrhoea	설사를 해요	sŏl·sa·rŭl hae·yo
fever	열이 나요	yŏ·ri na·yo
headache	두통이 있어요	du·t'ong·i iss·ŏ·yo
nausea	메슥거려요	me·sŭk·kŏ·ryŏ·yo
pain	통증이 있어요	t'ong·jŭng·i iss·ŏ·yo
sore throat	목이 아파요	mo·gi a·p'a·yo

I feel ...

dizzy	어지러워요.	ŏ·ji·rŏ·wŏ·yo
hot and cold	더운데 춥기도 해요.	dŏ·un·dé ch'up·ki·do hae·yo
nauseous	메슥거려요.	me·sŭk·kŏ·ryŏ·yo
shivery	덜덜 떨려요.	dŏl·dŏl ddŏl·lyŏ·yo
weak	힘이 없어요.	hi·mi ŏp·sŏ·yo

WOMEN'S HEALTH

Could I see a female doctor?	여자 의사 있나요? yŏ·ja ŭi·sa in·na·yo
I'm pregnant.	전 임신 중이에요. jŏn im·shin·jung i·e·yo
I think I'm pregnant.	임신한 것 같아요. im·shin han·gŏt ka·t'a·yo
I'm on the pill.	피임약을 먹고 있어요. p'i·im·nya·gŭl mŏk·ko iss·ŏ·yo
I haven't had my period for (eight) weeks.	(팔) 주 동안 생리가 없어요. (p'al) ju·dong·an saeng·ni·ga ŏp·sŏ·yo
Do you have something for (period pain)?	(생리통) 약 있나요? (saeng·ni·t'ong) yak in·na·yo

LISTEN FOR

섹스 하시나요?	sek·sŭ ha·shi·na·yo Are you sexually active?
피임 하시나요?	p'i·im ha·shi·na·yo Are you using contraception?
생리 중인가요?	saeng·ni·jung in·ga·yo Are you menstruating?
마지막 생리가 언제였나요?	ma·ji·mak saeng·ni·ga ŏn·jé yŏn·na·yo When did you last have your period?
임신 중인가요?	im·shin·jung in·ga·yo Are you pregnant?
임신하셨습니다.	im·shin ha·shŏss·sŭm·ni·da You're pregnant.

I've noticed a lump here.	여기 혹이 있어요.	yŏ·gi ho·gi iss·ŏ·yo
I have a urinary tract infection.	요도염에 걸렸어요.	yo·do·yŏ·mé gŏl·lyŏss·ŏ·yo
I have a yeast infection.	진균감염에 걸렸어요.	jin·gyun·ga·myŏ·mé gŏl·lyŏss·ŏ·yo
I need contraception.	피임을 하고 싶어요.	p'i·i·mŭl ha·go shi·p'ŏ·yo
I need the morning-after pill.	사후피임약이 필요해요.	sa·hu·p'i·im·nya·gi p'i·ryo·hae·yo
I need a pregnancy test.	임신 검사 하고 싶어요.	im·shin gŏm·sa ha·go shi·p'ŏ·yo

ALLERGIES

I have a skin allergy.	전 피부 알레르기가 있어요.	jŏn p'i·bu al·le·rŭ·gi·ga iss·ŏ·yo
I'm allergic to ...	전 ...에 알레르기가 있어요.	jŏn ...·é al·le·rŭ·gi·ga iss·ŏ·yo

antibiotics	항생제	hang·saeng·jé
anti-inflammatories	소염제	so·yŏm·jé
aspirin	아스피린	a·sŭ·p'i·rin
bees	벌	bŏl
codeine	코데인	k'o·de·in
dairy products	유제품	yu·je·p'um
penicillin	페니실린	p'e·ni·shil·lin
pollen	꽃가루	ggok·ka·ru
sulphur-based drugs	황화물이 들어간 약	hwang·hwa·mu·ri dŭ·rŏ·gan·nyak

For food-related allergies, see **vegetarian & special meals** (p209).

LISTEN FOR

오늘 뭘 드셨나요?	o·nŭl mwŏl dŭ·shŏn·na·yo What did you eat today?
담배 피우시나요?	dam·bae p'i·u·shi·na·yo Do you smoke?
술 드시나요?	sul dŭ·shi·na·yo Do you drink?
어제 술 드셨나요?	ŏ·jé sul dŭ·shŏn·na·yo Did you drink yesterday?
마약 하시나요?	ma·yak ha·shi·na·yo Do you take drugs?

ALTERNATIVE TREATMENTS

I don't use (Western medicine).	전 (양약)을 안 써요. jŏn (yang·yag)·ŭl an·ssŏ·yo
Where can I find an Eastern medical clinic?	한의원 어디에 있나요? ha·ni·wŏn ŏ·di·é in·na·yo
Can I see someone who practises ...?	... 찾을 수 있나요? ... ch'a·jŭl·su in·na·yo

acupuncture	침 놓는 분	ch'im non·nŭn·bun
aromatherapy	아로마테라피 하시는 분	a·ro·ma t'e·ra·p'i ha·shi·nŭn·bun
massage	안마사	an·ma·sa
moxibustion	뜸 놓는 분	ddŭm non·nŭn·bun
yoga	요가 가르치시는 분	yo·ga ga·rŭ·ch'i·shi·nŭn·bun

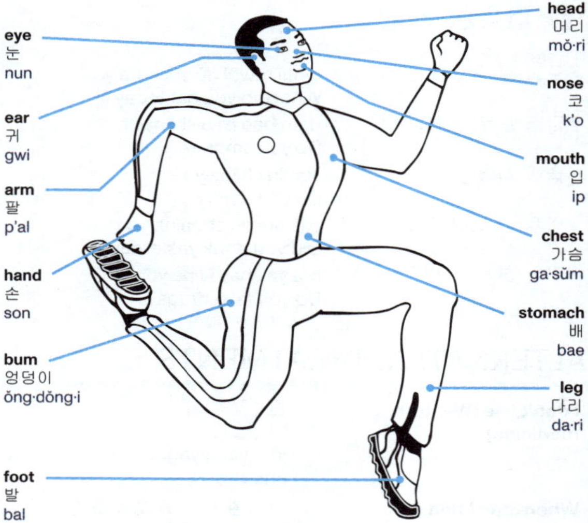

PARTS OF THE BODY

My ... hurts.	...이/가 아파요. ...i/·ga a·p'a·yo
I have a pain in my ...	...에 통증이 있어요. ...·é t'ong·jŭng·i iss·ŏ·yo
I can't move my ...	...을/를 움직일 수가 없어요. ...·ŭl/·rŭl um·ji·gil·su·ga ŏp·sŏ·yo
I have a cramp in my ...	...에 경련이 났어요. ...·é gyŏng·nyŏ·ni nass·ŏ·yo
My ... is swollen.	...이/가 부었어요. ...·i/·ga bu·ŏss·ŏ·yo

PHARMACIST

I need something for (a headache).	(두통) 약 주세요. (du·t'ong) yak ju·se·yo
Do I need a prescription for (antihistamines)?	(항히스타민제) 사려면 처방전 필요한가요? (hang·hi·sŭ·t'a·min·jé) sa·ryŏ·myŏn ch'ŏ·bang·jŏn p'i·ryo han·ga·yo
I have a prescription.	처방전 있어요. ch'ŏ·bang·jŏn iss·ŏ·yo
How many times a day?	하루에 몇 번인가요? ha·ru·é myŏp·pŏn in·ga·yo
Will it make me drowsy?	먹으면 졸릴까요? mŏ·gŭ·myŏn jol·liik·ka·yo

For more pharmaceutical items, see the **dictionary** (p221).

DENTIST

I have a broken tooth.	이가 깨졌어요. i·ga ggae·jyŏss·ŏ·yo
I have a cavity.	충치가 있어요. ch'ung·ch'i·ga iss·ŏ·yo

LISTEN FOR

하루에 (세) 번	ha·ru·é (se)·bŏn	(three) times a day
(네) 시간마다	(ne) shi·gan·ma·da	every (four) hours
식전 (삼십 분)	shik·jŏn (sam·ship·pun)	(half an hour) before eating
식후 (삼십 분)	shi·k'u (sam·ship·pun)	(half an hour) after eating
식간	shik·kan	while eating

LISTEN FOR

아 하세요.	a ha·se·yo	Open wide.
꽉 물어 보세요.	ggwak mu·rŏ·bo·se·yo	Bite down on this.
움직이지 마세요.	um·ji·gi·ji ma·se·yo	Don't move.
입 헹구세요.	ip heng·gu·se·yo	Rinse.

I have a toothache.	이가 아파요. i·ga a·p'a·yo
One of my teeth is loose.	이가 흔들려요. i·ga hŭn·dŭl·lyŏ·yo
It keeps bleeding.	피가 안 멈춰요. p'i·ga an·mŏm·ch'wŏ·yo
I need an anaesthetic.	마취 해 주세요. ma·ch'wi hae ju·se·yo
I need a filling.	때워 주세요. ddae·wŏ ju·se·yo
I've lost a filling.	때운 데가 떨어졌어요. ddae·un·de·ga ddŏ·rŏ·jyŏss·ŏ·yo
My braces fell off.	교정기가 떨어졌어요. gyo·jŏng·gi·ga ddŏ·rŏ·jyŏss·ŏ·yo
My dentures are broken.	틀니가 깨졌어요. t'ul·li·ga ggae·jyŏss·ŏ·yo
My gums hurt.	잇몸이 아파요. in·mo·mi a·p'a·yo
I don't want it extracted.	뽑지 마세요. bbop·ji ma·se·yo

FOOD

Eating Out

KEY PHRASES

Can you recommend a restaurant?	음식점 추천해 주시겠어요?	ŭm·shik·jŏm ch'u·ch'ŏn hae· ju·shi·gess·ŏ·yo
A table for (two), please.	(두) 명 자리 주세요.	(du)·myŏng ja·ri ju·se·yo
May we see the menu?	메뉴 볼 수 있나요?	me·nyu bol·su in·na·yo
I'd like a beer, please.	맥주 주세요.	maek·ju ju·se·yo
Please bring the bill.	계산서 가져다 주세요.	gye·san·sŏ ga·jŏ·da ju·se·yo

BASICS

breakfast	아침 a·ch'im
lunch	점심 jŏm·shim
dinner	저녁 jŏ·nyŏk
snack	간식 gan·shik
to eat	먹어요 (먹~) mŏ·gŏ·yo (mŏk~)
to drink	마셔요 (마시~) ma·shŏ·yo (ma·shi~)
I'd like ...	... 주세요. ... ju·se·yo

I'm hungry!	배고파요! bae·go·p'a·yo

FINDING A PLACE TO EAT

Where would you go for a celebration?	축하할 일이 있으면 어디가 좋아요? ch'u·k'a·hal i·ri iss·ŭ·myŏn ŏ·di·ga jo·a·yo
Where would you go for a cheap meal?	저렴한 식사는 어디서 하나요? jŏ·ryŏm·han shik·sa·nŭn ŏ·di·sŏ ha·na·yo
Where would you go for local specialities?	이 지방의 특별한 음식을 어디가 잘 하나요? i·ji·bang·é t'ŭk·byŏl·han ŭm·shi·gŭl ŏ·di·ga jal ha·na·yo
Can you recommend a bar/restaurant?	술집/음식점 추천해 주시겠어요? sul·jip/ŭm·shik·jŏm ch'u·ch'ŏn hae·ju·shi·gess·ŏ·yo
I'd like to reserve a table for (two) people.	(두) 명 테이블 예약해 주세요. (du)·myŏng t'e·i·bŭl ye·ya·k'ae ju·se·yo

☑ CULTURE TIP: MEAL OPTIONS

You can eat out well in Korea on any budget. Street stalls selling freshly made cheap gan·shik 간식 (snacks) can be found all over any city. Many offer light meals as well, with enclosed seating that's heated in winter. Small family-run restaurants offer full meals including side dishes, called ban·ch'an 반찬, at budget prices. Formal dining in foreign restaurants has become very popular, and many such establishments offer se·t'ŭ me·nyu 세트 메뉴 (set menus), which include a full meal from starter to coffee and dessert.

LISTEN FOR

끝났어요.	ggŭn·nass·ŏ·yo	We're closed.
자리가 없어요.	ja·ri·ga ŏp·sŏ·yo	We're full.
잠시만요.	jam·shi·man·nyo	One moment.

I'd like to reserve a table for (eight) o'clock.	(여덟) 시 테이블 예약해 주세요. (yŏ·dŏl)·shi t'e·i·bŭl ye·ya·k'ae ju·se·yo
Are you still serving food?	아직 음식 되나요? a·jik ŭm·shik doé·na·yo
How long is the wait?	얼마나 기다려야 되나요? ŏl·ma·na gi·da·ryŏ·ya doé·na·yo

AT THE RESTAURANT

A table for (two), please.	(두) 명 자리 주세요. (du)·myŏng ja·ri ju·se·yo

For two, please.	두 명이요.	du·myŏng·i·yo

We'd like a table by the window, please.	창가 자리로 주세요. chang·ga ja·ri·ro ju·se·yo
What would you recommend?	추천 해 주시겠어요? ch'u·ch'ŏn hae·ju·shi·gess·ŏ·yo
Do you have an English menu?	영어로 된 메뉴 있나요? yŏng·ŏ·ro·doén me·nyu in·na·yo
Can we see the menu?	메뉴 볼 수 있나요? me·nyu bol·su in·na·yo

Menu, please.	메뉴 주세요.	me·nyu ju·se·yo

Eating Out

CAN I SEE THE MENU, PLEASE?
메뉴 볼 수 있나요?
me·nyu bol·su in·na·yo

WHAT WOULD YOU RECOMMEND FOR ...?
...로 뭘 추천하시겠어요?
...ro mwŏl ch'u·ch'ŏn ha·shi·gess·ŏ·yo

THE MAIN COURSE
주요리
ju·yo·ri

DESSERT
디저트
di·jŏ·t'ŭ

DRINKS
술
sul

CAN YOU BRING ME SOME ..., PLEASE?
... 가져다 주세요.
... ga·jŏ·da ju·se·yo

I'D LIKE THE BILL, PLEASE.
계산서 가져다 주세요.
gye·san·sŏ ga·jŏ·da ju·se·yo

What comes with the set menu?	세트 시키면 뭐가 나오나요? se·t'ŭ shi·k'i·myŏn mwŏ·ga na·o·na·yo
I'll have what they're having.	저 분 들이랑 같은 걸로 주세요. jŏ·bun·dŭ·ri·rang ga·t'ŭn·gŏl·lo ju·se·yo
What's that called?	저거 이름이 뭔가요? jŏ·gŏ i·rŭ·mi mwŏn·ga·yo
What's in that dish?	저 음식에 뭐가 들어있나요? jŏ·ŭm·shi·gé mwŏ·ga dŭ·rŏ·in·na·yo
Does it take long to prepare?	나오는 데 오래 걸리나요? na·o·nŭn·dé o·rae gŏl·li·na·yo
Is this dish spicy?	이 음식 맵나요? i·ŭm·shing·maem·na·yo
I'd like some more of this side dish.	이 반찬 좀 더 주세요. i·ban·ch'an jom dŏ ju·se·yo
Is this drink refillable?	이 음료 리필 되나요? i·ŭm·nyo ri·p'il doé·na·yo
I'd like a refill.	리필 해 주세요. ri·p'il hae·ju·se·yo

☑ CULTURE TIP: ORDERING FOOD

Foreign chains usually offer English-language menus and at least one staff member will speak English. Menus often come with pictures, or very realistic models of the food served are displayed in the window. Many restaurants now have tablets for ordering at each table, and these often have pictures or English translations. Koreans don't mind if you ask a lot of questions or even point to someone else's meal. At most restaurants, simply head to the front counter to pay your bill after your meal.

Are these complimentary?	이거 공짜인가요? i·gŏ gong·jja in·ga·yo
Could I please see the wine list?	와인 리스트 볼 수 있나요? wa·in ri·sŭ·t'ŭ bol·su in·na·yo
Can you recommend a good wine?	좋은 와인 추천해 주시겠어요? jo·ŭn wa·in ch'u·ch'ŏn hae·ju·shi·gess·ŏ·yo
I'd like (a/the) ..., please.	... 주세요. ... ju·se·yo

one serving	일인분	i·rin·bun
two servings	이인분	i·in·bun
three servings	삼인분	sa·min·bun
children's menu	어린이 메뉴	ŏ·ri·ni me·nyu
drink menu	음료수 메뉴	ŭm·nyo·su me·nyu
half portion	반만	ban·man
huge portion	양 많은 것	yang ma·nŭn·gŏt
local speciality	이 지역의 유명한 음식	i·ji·yŏ·gé yu·myŏng·han ŭm·shik

REQUESTS

Please bring (a/the) ...	... 가져다 주세요. ... ga·jŏ·da ju·se·yo

chopsticks	젓가락	jŏk·ka·rak
fork	포크	p'o·k'ŭ
(wine)glass	(와인) 잔	(wa·in)·jan
plates	개인 접시	gae·in jŏp·shi
knife	나이프	na·i·p'ŭ
napkin	냅킨	naep·k'in
spoon	숟가락	suk·ka·rak

LISTEN FOR

뭐 드릴까요?	mwŏ dŭ·rilk·ka·yo What can I get you?
... 좋아하세요?	... jo·a·ha·se·yo Do you like ...?
... 맛있어요.	... ma·shiss·ŏ·yo I suggest the ...
여기 있습니다!	yŏ·gi iss·sŭm·ni·da Here you go!
맛있게 드세요.	ma·shik·ké dŭ·se·yo Enjoy your meal.

I'd like it with ...	... 넣어 주세요. ... nŏ·ŏ ju·se·yo
I'd like it without ...	... 넣지 마세요. ... nŏ·ch'i ma·se·yo

cheese	치즈	ch'i·jŭ
gochujang (chilli sauce)	고추장	go·ch'u·jang
garlic	마늘	ma·nŭl
ginger	생강	saeng·gang
ground pepper	후춧가루	hu·ch'uk·ka·ru
mayonnaise	마요네즈	ma·yo·ne·jŭ
mustard (Asian)	겨자	gyŏ·ja
nuts	견과류	gyŏn·gwa·ryu
oil	기름	gi·rŭm
chillies	고추	go·ch'u
red pepper powder	고춧가루	go·ch'uk·ka·ru
salt	소금	so·gŭm
soy sauce	간장	gan·jang
vinegar	식초	shik·ch'o

LOOK FOR

애피타이저	ae·p'i·t'a·i·jŏ	Appetisers
앙트레	ang·t'ŭ·ré	Starters
수프	su·p'ŭ	Soups
샐러드	sael·lŏ·dŭ	Salads
메인 코스	me·in k'o·sŭ	Main courses
반찬	ban·ch'an	Side dishes
후식	hu·shik	Desserts
음료수	ŭm·nyo·su	Drinks
탄산음료	t'an·san ŭm·nyo	Soft drinks
맥주	maek·ju	Beers
샴페인	sham·p'e·in	Sparkling wines
화이트와인	hwa·i·t'ŭ wa·in	White wines
레드 와인	re·dŭ wa·in	Red wines

For additional items, see the **menu decoder** (p212).

Can you make it less spicy?	덜 맵게 해 주시겠어요? dŏl maep·ké hae·ju·shi·gess·ŏ·yo
I don't want it ...	... 마세요. ... ma·se·yo

boiled	끓이지	ggŭ·ri·ji
grilled/broiled	굽지	gup·chi
deep-fried	튀기지	t'wi·gi·ji
fried	볶지	bok·chi
mashed	으깨지	ŭk·kae·ji

I want it ...	... 주세요. ... ju·se·yo

boiled	끓여	ggŭ·ryŏ
grilled/broiled	구워	gu·wŏ
deep-fried	튀겨	t'wi·gyŏ
fried	볶아	bok·ka
mashed	으깨	ŭk·kae
medium	미디엄으로	mi·di·ŏ·mŭ·ro
rare	레어로	re·ŏ·ro
reheated	다시 데워	da·shi de·wŏ
well done	웰던으로	wel·dŏ·nŭ·ro
without ...	... 없이	... ŏp·shi
with the dressing on the side	드레싱 따로	dŭ·re·shing dda·ro

For other specific meal requests, see **vegetarian & special meals** (p209).

COMPLIMENTS & COMPLAINTS

I love this dish.	이거 맛있어요. i·gŏ ma·shiss·ŏ·yo
I love the local cuisine.	이 지역 음식이 맛있어요. i·ji·yŏk ŭm·shi·gi ma·shiss·ŏ·yo
That was delicious!	맛있었어요! ma·shiss·ŏss·ŏ·yo
I'm full.	배불러요. bae·bul·lŏ·yo
I didn't order this.	이거 주문 안 했는데요. i·gŏ ju·mun an·haen·nŭn·de·yo

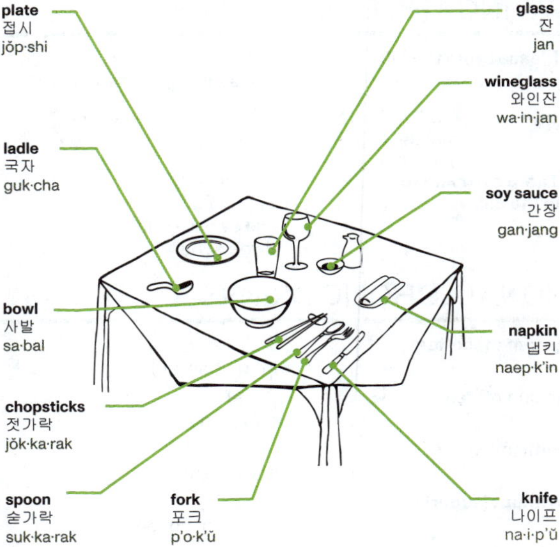

This is ...

burnt	탔어요.	t'ass·ŏ·yo
cold	차가워요.	ch'a·ga·wŏ·yo
(too) spicy	(너무) 매워요.	(nŏ·mu) mae·wŏ·yo
stale	싱싱하지 않아요.	shing·shing·ha·ji a·na·yo
superb	최고예요.	ch'oé·go·ye·yo

PAYING THE BILL

Please bring the bill.	계산서 가져다 주세요. gye·san·sŏ ga·jŏ·da ju·se·yo
Bill, please.	계산서 주세요. gye·san·sŏ ju·se·yo
There's a mistake in the bill.	계산서가 잘못 되었네요. gye·san·sŏ·ga jal·mot dwoé·ŏt·ne·yo

NONALCOHOLIC DRINKS

(a cup of) coffee	커피 (한 잔) k'ŏ·p'i (han·jan)
(a cup of) tea	차 (한 잔) ch'a (han·jan)
with (milk)	(우유) 넣은 (u·yu) nŏ·ŭn
without (sugar)	(설탕) 뺀 (sŏl·t'ang) bbaen
mineral water	생수 saeng·su
orange juice	오렌지 주스 o·ren·ji jus·sŭ

LOOK FOR

홍차	hong·ch'a	black tea
유자차	yu·ja·ch'a	citron tea
대추차	dae·ch'u·ch'a	jujube tea
생강차	saeng·gang·ch'a	ginger tea
녹차	nok·ch'a	green tea

LOOK FOR

블랙	bŭl·laek	black
무카페인	mu·k'a·p'e·in	decaffeinated
아이스	a·i·sŭ	iced
진한	jin·han	strong
약한	ya·k'an	weak
크림 넣은	k'ŭ·rim nŏ·ŭn	with cream
크림과 설탕 넣은	k'ŭ·rim·gwa sŏl·t'ang nŏ·ŭn	with cream and sugar

persimmon punch	수정과 su·jŏng·gwa
soft drink	탄산 음료 t'an·san ŭm·nyo
(boiled) water	(끓인) 물 (ggŭ·rin) mul

ALCOHOLIC DRINKS

beer	맥주 maek·ju
brandy	브랜디 bŭ·raen·di
champagne	샴페인 sham·p'e·in
cocktail	칵테일 k'ak·t'e·il
glass of red wine	레드 와인 한 잔 re·dŭ wa·in han·jan
glass of sparkling wine	샴페인 한 잔 sham·p'e·in han·jan
glass of white wine	화이트와인 한 잔 hwa·i·t'ŭ wa·in han·jan

☑ LANGUAGE TIP: 'ALCOHOL' SUFFIX

A helpful hint when poring over a Korean menu: lots of names for Korean alcoholic drinks end in ·ju 주 (based on the Chinese character for 'alcohol') – what precedes that is usually the other main ingredient.

a shot of ...		... 한 잔 ... han·jan
gin	진	jin
rum	럼	rŏm
tequila	테킬라	t'e·k'il·la
vodka	보드카	bo·dŭ·k'a
whisky	위스키	wi·sŭ·k'i

For additional items, see the **menu decoder** (p212) and the **dictionary** (p221).

IN THE BAR

I'll buy you a drink.	제가 살게요. je·ga salk·ke·yo
Q **What would you like to drink?**	뭐 마시고 싶으세요? mwŏ ma·shi·go shi·p'ŭ·se·yo
A **I'll have ...**	... 주세요. ... ju·se·yo
What side dish would you like to have?	안주 뭐 드시겠어요? an·ju mwŏ dŭ·shi·gess·ŏ·yo
What kind of side dishes do you have?	안주 뭐가 있나요? an·ju mwŏ·ga in·na·yo

Do you serve meals here?	여기 식사도 되나요? yŏ·gi shik·sa·do doé·na·yo
Is food served here?	여기 식사 나오나요? yŏ·gi shik·sa na·o·na·yo
No ice, please.	얼음 빼고 주세요. ŏ·rŭm bbae·go ju·se·yo
It's my round.	제 차례예요. jé ch'a·rye·ye·yo
I'm next.	다음에 제가 살 차례예요. da·ŭ·mé je·ga sal ch'a·rye·ye·yo
You can get the next one.	다음 번에 사세요. da·ŭm·bŏ·né sa·se·yo
Same again, please.	똑같은 걸로 주세요. ddok·ka·t'ŭn·gŏl·lo ju·se·yo

DRINKING UP

Cheers!	건배!/짠! gŏn·bae/jjan

CULTURE TIP: ORDERING BEER

Beer is typically ordered by the bottle, mug or pitcher, which are ordered according to size. Rather than referring to the number of pints, litres or quarts, beer is ordered by shi·shi 시시 (millilitre, literally 'cc' for 'cubic centimetre').

... of beer	맥주 ...	maek·ju ...
half a litre (500mL)	오백 시시	o·baek·shi·shi
a litre (1000mL)	천 시시	ch'ŏn·shi·shi
one bottle	한 병	han·byŏng
two bottles	두 병	du·byŏng
a pitcher	피처 한 개	p'i·chŏ han·gae

Thanks, but I don't feel like it.	고맙지만 오늘은 별로 내키지가 않네요. go·map·ji·man o·nŭ·rŭn byŏl·lo nae·k'i·ji·ga an·ne·yo
I don't usually drink much.	보통 많이 안 마셔요. bo·t'ong ma·ni an·ma·shŏ·yo
I don't drink alcohol.	전 술 안 마셔요. jŏn sul an·ma·shŏ·yo
I'm tired, so I'd better get home.	피곤해서 집에 가야겠어요. p'i·gon·hae·sŏ ji·bé ga·ya·gess·ŏ·yo
This is hitting the spot.	정말 딱인데요. jŏng·mal dda·gin·de·yo
I'm feeling drunk.	저 취한 것 같아요. jŏ ch'wi·han·gŏt ga·t'a·yo
I feel fantastic!	환상적인 기분이에요. hwan·sang·jŏ·gin gi·bu·ni·e·yo
I really, really love you.	정말 정말 사랑해요. jŏng·mal jŏng·mal sa·rang·hae·yo
I think I've had one too many.	저 약간 취한 것 같아요. jŏ yak·kan ch'wi·han·gŏt ga·t'a·yo

☑ CULTURE TIP: PAYING FOR DRINKS

Drinking in Korea is a group activity, a chance to let loose with friends or colleagues. The bill is usually settled when the party is ready to leave, but there's also a trend towards paying as you go. Many bars still require a table of patrons to order an·ju 안주 ('side dishes' of snacks, chips/fries, fruit etc) as a kind of cover charge.

LISTEN FOR

뭐 드릴까요?	mwŏ dŭ·rilk·ka·yo What are you having?
많이 드신 것 같은데요.	ma·ni dŭ·shin·gŏt ga·t'ŭn·de·yo I think you've had enough.
마지막 주문 받습니다.	ma·ji·mak ju·mun bat·sŭm·ni·da Last orders.

I'm drunk.	저 취했어요. jŏ ch'wi·haess·ŏ·yo
I feel ill.	몸이 안 좋아요. mo·mi an·jo·a·yo
I think I'm going to throw up.	토할 것 같아요. t'o·hal·gŏt ga·t'a·yo
Please help me catch a taxi.	택시 잡는 것 도와 주세요. t'aek·shi jam·nŭn·gŏt do·wa ju·se·yo
I don't think you should drive.	운전하시면 안 될 것 같아요. un·jŏn·ha·shi·myŏn an·doél·gŏt ga·t'a·yo

Self-Catering

KEY PHRASES

What's the local speciality?	지방 특산품에 뭐가 있나요?	ji·bang t'ŭk·san·p'u·mé mwŏ·ga in·na·yo
Where can I find the ... section?	... 코너 어디 있나요?	... k'o·nŏ ŏ·di in·na·yo
I'd like some ...	... 조금 주세요.	... jo·gŭm ju·se·yo

BUYING FOOD

What's that?	저게 뭐예요? jŏ·gé mwŏ·ye·yo
What's the local speciality?	지방 특산품에 뭐가 있나요? ji·bang t'ŭk·san·p'u·mé mwŏ·ga in·na·yo
How much is (a kilo of kimchi)?	(김치 일 킬로그램)에 얼마예요? (gim·ch'i il k'il·lo·gŭ·raem)·é ŏl·ma·ye·yo
Can I taste it?	맛 볼 수 있나요? map·pol·su in·na·yo
Can I have a bag, please?	봉투 주시겠어요? bong·t'u ju·shi·gess·ŏ·yo
I don't need a bag, thanks.	봉투 없어도 돼요. bong·t'u ŏp·sŏ·do dwae·yo

맛 볼 수 있나요?
map·pol·su in·na·yo
Can I taste it?

I'd like ...	... 주세요.	... ju·se·yo
(200) grams	(이백) 그램	(i·baek) gŭ·raem
half a kilo	오백 그램	o·baek gŭ·raem
a kilo	일 킬로그램	il k'il·lo·gŭ·raem
(two) kilos	(이) 킬로그램	(i) k'il·lo·gŭ·raem
a bottle	한 병	han·byŏng
a piece	한 개	han·gae
(three) pieces	(세) 개	(se)·gae
a slice	한 쪽	han·jjok
(six) slices	(여섯) 쪽	(yŏ·sŏt)·jjok
a can/tin	한 캔	han·k'aen
some ...	... 조금	... cho·gŭm

I'd like that/this one.	저거/이거 주세요. jŏ·gŏ/i·gŏ ju·se·yo
Do you have anything cheaper?	더 싼 것 있나요? dŏ·ssan·gŏt in·na·yo
Do you have other kinds?	다른 것 있나요? da·rŭn·gŏt in·na·yo

Where can I find the ... section? ... 코너 어디 있나요? ... k'o·nŏ ŏ·di in·na·yo

dairy	유제품	yu·je·p'um
fish	생선	saeng·sŏn
frozen goods	냉동식품	naeng·dong·shik·p'um
fruit and vegetable	과일 야채	gwa·il ya·ch'ae
health-food	건강식품	gŏn·gang shik·p'um
meat	고기	go·gi
poultry	닭	dak

For more food items, see the **menu decoder** (p212) and the **dictionary** (p221).

COOKING

I need a ... ...이/가 필요해요. ...:i/·ga p'i·ryo·hae·yo

chopping board	도마	do·ma
frying pan	프라이팬	p'ŭ·ra·i·p'aen
knife	나이프	na·i·p'ŭ
saucepan	냄비	naem·bi

For more cooking implements, see the **dictionary** (p221).

Vegetarian & Special Meals

KEY PHRASES

Do you have vegetarian food?	채식주의 음식 있나요?	ch'ae·shik·ju·i ŭm·shik in·na·yo
Could you prepare a meal without ...?	... 빼고 해 주시겠어요?	... bbae·go hae·ju·shi·gess·ŏ·yo
I'm allergic to ...	전 ... 알레르기가 있어요.	jŏn ... al·le·rŭ·gi·ga iss·ŏ·yo

SPECIAL DIETS & ALLERGIES

I'm allergic to ...
전 ... 알레르기가 있어요.
jŏn ... al·le·rŭ·gi·ga iss·ŏ·yo

dairy produce	유제품	yu·je·p'um
eggs	계란	gye·ran
gelatine	젤라틴	jel·la·t'in
gluten	글루텐	gŭl·lu·t'en
honey	꿀	ggul
MSG	화학조미료	hwa·hak·jo·mi·ryo
nuts	견과류	gyŏn·gwa·ryu
peanuts	땅콩	ddang·k'ong
shellfish	조개	jo·gae

To explain your dietary restrictions with reference to religious beliefs, see **beliefs & culture** (p154).

LOOK FOR

입구	ip·gu	Entrance
출구	ch'ul·gu	Exit
관계자 외 출입금지	gwan·gye·ja·oé ch'u·rip·gŭm·ji	Authorised personnel only
연중무휴	yŏn·jung·mu·hyu	Open all year

Is there a vegetarian restaurant near here?	주위에 채식주의 음식점 있나요? ju·wi·é ch'ae·shik·ju·i ŭm·shik·jŏm in·na·yo
I'm a vegan.	전 철저한 채식주의자예요. jŏn ch'ŏl·jŏ·han ch'ae·shik·ju·i·ja·ye·yo
I'm a vegetarian.	전 채식주의자예요. jŏn ch'ae·shik·ju·i·ja·ye·yo
I don't eat ...	전 ... 안 먹어요. jŏn ... an·mŏ·gŏ·yo

ORDERING FOOD

Do you have any vegetarian dishes?	채식주의 음식 있나요? ch'ae·shik·ju·i ŭm·shik in·na·yo
Do you have halal food?	할랄 음식 있나요? hal·lal ŭm·shik in·na·yo
Do you have kosher food?	유대인 음식 있나요? yu·dae·in ŭm·shik in·na·yo
Is it cooked in/with ...?	... 들어 가나요? ... dŭ·rŏ ga·na·yo

Could you prepare a meal without ...? ... 빼고 해 주시겠어요? ... bbae·go hae·ju·shi·gess·ŏ·yo

butter	버터	bŏ·t'ŏ
chicken	닭고기	dak·ko·gi
fish (stock)	생선 (국물)	saeng·sŏn (gung·mul)
ham	햄	haem
meat	고기	go·gi
meat stock	육수	yuk·su
oil	기름	gi·rŭm
pork	돼지고기	dwae·ji·go·gi
beef	쇠고기	soé·go·gi
seafood	해물	hae·mul

Is this ...? 이거 ...? i·gŏ ...

decaffeinated	무카페인인가요	mu·k'a·p'e·in in·ga·yo
free of animal produce	고기 안 들었나요	go·gi an·dŭ·rŏn·na·yo
free-range	방목했나요	bang·mo·k'aen·na·yo
genetically modified	유전자 변형 식품인가요	yu·jŏn·ja byŏn·hyŏng shik·p'u·min·ga·yo
low-fat	저지방인가요	jŏ·ji·bang in·ga·yo
low in sugar	설탕 조금 들었나요	sŏl·t'ang jo·gŭm dŭ·rŏn·na·yo
low in salt	저염도인가요	jŏ·yŏm·do·in·ga·yo
salt-free	무염인가요	mu·yŏ·min·ga·yo
organic	유기농인가요	yu·gi·nong in·ga·yo

MENU Decoder

음식 사전

These Korean dishes and ingredients are listed in alphabetical order according to their pronunciation, so you can easily understand what's on offer and ask for what takes your fancy when you're eating out.

A

a·bo·k'a·do 아보카도 avocado
a·ch'im 아침 breakfast
ae·ho·bak 애호박 courgette • squash • zucchini
aek·sang k'ŭ·rim 액상 크림 cream
ae·p'i·t'a·i·jŏ 애피타이저 appetiser
a·gwi·jjim 아귀찜 steamed spicy angler fish
a·i·sŭ k'ŏ·p'i 아이스 커피 iced coffee
a·i·sŭ·k'ŭ·rim 아이스크림 ice cream
a·mon·dŭ 아몬드 almonds
ang·t'ŭ·ré 앙트레 starter
an·shim·(sal) 안심(살) tenderloin
a·sŭ·p'a·ra·gŏ·sŭ 아스파라거스 asparagus

B

ba·bi·k'yu 바비큐 barbecue
ba·da·ga·jae 바다가재 lobster
bae 배 pear
bae·ch'u 배추 cabbage (Chinese)
bae·ch'u gim·ch'i 배추김치 pickled cabbage seasoned with garlic & red chilli
baek·gim·ch'i 백김치 pickled white cabbage – non-spicy & with a sour taste
ba·k'a 박하 mint
bam 밤 chestnuts
ba·na·na 바나나 banana
ban·ch'an 반찬 side dishes
ban·su·k'an 반숙한 soft-boiled
bap 밥 steamed rice
bbang 빵 bread
be·i·k'ŏn 베이컨 bacon
bi·bim·bap 비빔밥 rice, vegetables & meat topped with an egg
bi·bim·naeng·myŏn 비빔냉면 cold buckwheat noodles with vegetables & meat in hot sauce
bi·sŭ·k'it 비스킷 biscuit
bi·t'ŭp·pu·ri 비트 뿌리 beetroot
bo·dŭ·k'a 보드카 vodka
bo·gŏ 복어 blowfish • puffer fish
bok·kŭm·bap 볶음밥 fried rice
bok·kŭm·na·myŏn 볶음 라면 fried ramen noodles
bok·kŭn 볶은 sautéed
bok·kŭn·ddang·k'ong 볶은 땅콩 roasted peanuts
bog·sung·a 복숭아 peach
bŏn·de·gi 번데기 silkworm larvae snack
bo·ri·bap 보리밥 boiled/steamed rice with steamed barley
bo·ri·ch'a 보리차 barley tea

bo·shin·t'ang 보신탕 dog-meat soup
bŏ·sŏp·pap 버섯밥 rice with mushrooms
bŏ·sŏt 버섯 mushrooms
bŏ·sŏt·jŏn·gol 버섯전골 mushroom hotpot
bo·ssam 보쌈 steamed pork & cabbage
bŏ·t'ŏ 버터 butter
bu·dae·jji·gae 부대찌개 ham-and-everything stew
bul·go·gi 불고기 marinated beef or pork grilled at the table & eaten with lettuce & other vegetables
bŭl·laek k'ŏ·p'i 블랙커피 black coffee
bul·dak 불닭 very spicy chicken
bung·ŏp·pang 붕어빵 fish-shaped cake with red bean filling
bŭ·raen·di 브랜디 brandy
bŭ·ro·k'ol·li 브로콜리 broccoli
bwi·p'é 뷔페 buffet

C

ch'a 차 tea
ch'ae·shik bwi·p'é 채식 뷔페 vegetarian buffet
ch'ae·shik·ju·i·ja 채식주의자 vegetarian
ch'am·ch'i 참치 tuna
ch'am·ch'i ch'o·bap 참치 초밥 tuna sushi
ch'am·gi·rŭm 참기름 sesame oil
cha·moé 참외 honeydew melon
ch'e·ri 체리 cherries
ch'i·jŭ 치즈 cheese
ch'i·jŭ gim·bap 치즈 김밥 rice-and-seaweed roll with cheese
chi·kin 치킨 fried chicken
ch'il·myŏn·jo 칠면조 turkey
ch'o·k'ol·lik·k'e·i·k'ŭ 초콜릿 케이크 chocolate cake
ch'o·k'ol·lit 초콜릿 chocolate
ch'ŏn·do bok·sung·a 천도복숭아 nectarine
ch'ong·gak·kim·ch'i 총각김치 pickled radish seasoned with garlic & red chilli
ch'ŏng·ŏ 청어 herring
ch'ŏng·p'o·do 청포도 white/green grapes
ch'u·ŏ·t'ang 추어탕 mudfish soup

D

dae·ch'u 대추 jujube (red date)
dae·ch'u·ch'a 대추차 jujube tea
dae·ch'u·sul 대추술 red date liquor
dae·gu 대구 cod
dae·ha 대하 prawn
dae·hap·jo·gae 대합조개 clams
da·jin·go·gi 다진 고기 mincemeat
dak·ba·bi·k'yu 닭 바비큐 barbecued chicken
dak bok·kŭm·t'ang 닭 볶음탕 a spicy stew of chicken pieces, transparent noodles, potatoes & vegetables
dak·kal·bi 닭갈비 spicy chicken pieces, cabbage, vegetables & finger-sized pressed rice cakes that are grilled at your table
dak·ko·ch'i 닭꼬치 grilled chicken on skewers
dak·ko·gi 닭고기 chicken
dak·ku·i 닭구이 roasted chicken
dak·kuk 닭국 chicken stew
dan 단 sweet
dang·gŭn 당근 carrot
dan·mu·ji 단무지 pickled daikon radish
ddal·gi 딸기 strawberries
ddang·k'ong 땅콩 peanuts
ddŏk 떡 rice cakes
ddŏk·bok·ki 떡볶이 rice cakes cooked in red pepper sauce
ddŭ·gŏ·un ŭm·nyo 뜨거운 음료 hot drinks
de·ch'in 데친 poached
dŏ·dŏk·ku·i 더덕구이 grilled deodeok (a mountain herb) root seasoned with a red pepper sauce, sesame oil & sugar
doén·jang 된장 soybean paste

doén·jang·jji·gae 된장찌개 soybean paste stew with tofu, vegetables, some meat & tiny shellfish
do·ga·ni·t'ang 도가니탕 cow knee cartilage soup
dol·sop·pap 돌솥밥 hotpot rice
dol·sop·pi·bim·bap 돌솥비빔밥 rice, vegetables & meat topped with an egg & cooked in a stone hotpot
dong·dong·ju 동동주 clear rice wine
dong·gŭ·rang·ddaeng 동그랑땡 large mincemeat patty
donk·ka·sŭ 돈가스 pork cutlet with rice & salad
do·nŏt 도넛 doughnuts
do·ra·ji mu·ch'im 도라지 무침 a red-coloured salad of raw bellflower roots dressed with salt, vinegar, red pepper powder, sesame seeds & oil
do·t'o·ri·muk 도토리묵 acorn jelly
du·bu 두부 tofu
du·bu·jji·gae 두부찌개 spicy tofu stew with soybean paste & kimchi
du·bu·jo·rim 두부조림 sliced tofu marinated in soy sauce, red pepper powder, garlic, green onions & hot green pepper, then fried or steamed
dŭng·shim(·sal) 등심(살) sirloin
du·yu 두유 soy milk
dwae·ji ba·bi·k'yu 돼지 바비큐 barbecued pork
dwae·ji·bul·go·gi 돼지불고기 marinated pork grilled at the table & eaten with lettuce & other vegetables
dwae·ji·gal·bi ba·bi·k'yu 돼지갈비 바비큐 barbecued pork ribs
dwae·ji·go·gi 돼지고기 pork

G

ga·jae 가재 crayfish
ga·ji 가지 aubergine · eggplant
gal·bi 갈비 ribs
gal·bi·gu·i 갈비구이 grilled ribs
gal·bi·jjim 갈비찜 steamed short ribs
gal·bi·t'ang 갈비탕 short rib stew – ribs are cooked with pyogo mushrooms, carrots, gingko nuts & jujubes in a sauce featuring soy sauce, green onions, garlic, pepper, sesame seeds, pear juice & ginger juice
gam 감 persimmon
gam·ja 감자 potatoes
gam·ja·bok·kŭm 감자볶음 fried potatoes
gam·ja·jŏn 감자전 potato pancake
gam·ja·t'ang 감자탕 spicy soup with meat & potatoes
gam·ja·t'wi·gim 감자튀김 chips · French fries
gan 간 liver
gang·nang·k'ong 강낭콩 kidney beans
ga·ni·doen 간이 된 salted
gan·jang 간장 soy sauce
gan·shik 간식 snack
gé 게 crab
ge·jang 게장 pickled raw crab served with rice
ge·jjim 게찜 steamed crab
ggak·du·gi 깍두기 pickled cubed radish seasoned with garlic & red chilli
ggo·ch'i 꼬치 Korean-style shish kebabs
ggo·ri·gom·t'ang 꼬리곰탕 oxtail soup
ggul 꿀 honey
ggŭ·rin 끓인 boiled
ggwŏng·baek·suk 꿩백숙 pheasant stew
gim 김 laver, often dried and salted
gim·bap 김밥 rice rolled in seaweed
gim·ch'i 김치 kimchi – Korean national dish of pickled vegetables; Napa cabbage pickled with ground red pepper is most common but there are hundreds of varieties, both mild and spicy.
gim·ch'i·bok·kŭm·bap 김치볶음밥 fried rice with kimchi
gim·ch'i·jji·gae 김치찌개 kimchi stew

gim·ch'i·man·du 김치만두 kimchi dumplings
go·ch'u 고추 chilli pepper
go·ch'u·jang 고추장 chilli sauce • red pepper paste
go·ch'uk·ka·ru 고춧가루 chilli pepper • red pepper powder
go·dŭng·ŏ·gu·i 고등어구이 grilled mackerel
go·gi 고기 meat
go·gu·ma 고구마 sweet potato
gol·baeng·i mu·ch'im 골뱅이무침 seasoned river snails with mixed vegetables
gŏ·mŭn·k'ong 검은콩 black beans
go·myŏng 고명 garnish
gŏn·jo 건조 dried
gŏn·p'o·do 건포도 raisins
gop·ch'ang·gu·i 곱창구이 grilled intestines (typically pork) cooked on a metal plate over charcoal & served with a light bean paste sauce & chopped green onions
gop·ch'ang jŏn·gol 곱창전골 tripe hotpot
guk·su 국수 noodles
gul 굴 oyster
gul·so·sŭ 굴소스 oyster sauce
gu·un 구운 baked • broiled • grilled • roasted
gu·un·gam·ja 구운 감자 plain roasted potatoes
gwa·il 과일 fruit
gwa·il jus·sŭ 과일 주스 fruit juice
gwang·ŏ·hoé 광어회 raw halibut
gwi·ri 귀리 oats
gye·ran 계란 egg
gye·ran·jjim 계란찜 steamed egg
gye·ranp·pang 계란빵 small cake with egg inside
gye·ran sael·lŏ·dŭ 계란 샐러드 egg salad
gyŏ·ja 겨자 mustard (Korean-style)
gyŏn·gwa·ryu 견과류 nuts
gyul 귤 mandarin • tangerine

H

hae·ba·ra·gi 해바라기 sunflower
hae·jang·guk 해장국 'sunrise soup' – a hangover remedy consisting of boiled bones, chopped radish, radish leaves, cabbage, green onions & blood
haem 햄 ham
haem·bŏ·gŏ 햄버거 hamburger
hae·mul 해물 seafood
hae·mul bok·kŭm·bap 해물볶음밥 fried rice with seafood
hae·mul·t'ang 해물탕 spicy assorted seafood soup
hae·san·mul ya·ch'ae t'wi·gim 해산물 야채 튀김 seafood & vegetables fried in batter
ham·hŭng·naeng·myŏn 함흥냉면 North Korean cold noodles
han·gwa 한과 traditional whole-grain cookies
han·jŏng·shik 한정식 banquet of traditional meats, seafood & vegetables
hat·to·gŭ 핫도그 corn dog • hot dog
he·i·jŭl·lŏt 헤이즐넛 hazelnuts
hin·k'ong 흰콩 white soybeans
ho·bak·jŏn 호박전 fried squash slices
hŏ·bŭ 허브 herbs
hŏ·bŭ·t'i 허브티 herbal tea
ho·du 호두 walnuts
ho·du·gwa·ja 호두과자 pastry filled with walnut pieces and red bean paste
hoé 회 sashimi without the rice
hoé·dŏp·bap 회덮밥 raw fish on rice
hoé·naeng·myŏn 회냉면 cold buckwheat noodles with raw fish in hot sauce
hong·ch'a 홍차 black tea
hong·hap 홍합 mussels
hong·hap·pap 홍합밥 rice with mussels (& side dishes)
hop·pang 호빵 large steamed buns stuffed with sweet red beans, mincemeat or minced vegetables

hot·tŏk 호떡 fried dough filled with brown sugar, nuts, and cinnamon
hu·ch'u 후추 black pepper
hu·ch'uk·ka·ru 후춧가루 ground pepper
hŭ·gyŏm·so jung·t'ang 흑염소 중탕 goat soup
hun·jé 훈제 smoked
hu·shik 후식 dessert
hwa·i·t'ŭ wa·in 화이트와인 white wine

I

in·sam 인삼 ginseng
in·sam·ch'a 인삼차 ginseng tea
in·sam·ju 인삼주 ginseng liquor
in·sŭ·t'ŏn·t'ŭ k'ŏ·p'i 인스턴트 커피 instant coffee

J

ja·du 자두 plums
jaem 잼 jam
jan·ch'i·guk·su 잔치국수 thin noodles, usually in a broth made from anchovies & courgette/zucchini
jang·ŏ·gu·i 장어구이 grilled eel
jap·ch'ae 잡채 transparent noodles stir-fried in sesame oil with strips of egg, meat & vegetables
jin 진 gin
jja·jang·myŏn 짜장면 noodles in black-bean sauce
jjamp·pong 짬뽕 spicy seafood noodle soup of Chinese origin
jjan 짠 salty
jji·gae 찌개 stew
jjim·dak 찜닭 braised chicken pieces with noodles & vegetables
jjin 찐 steamed
jjin·man·du 찐만두 steamed dumplings
jji·nok·su·su 찐 옥수수 corn on the cob
jjinp·pang 찐빵 giant steamed bun with sweet bean paste
jo·gae 조개 shellfish • clam
jo·gak 조각 slice
jok·bal 족발 steamed pork hocks
jŏk·p'o·do 적포도 red grapes
jŏm·shim 점심 lunch
jŏn·bok·juk 전복죽 rice porridge with abalone
jŏng·ŏ·ri 정어리 sardine
jŏng·su·gi·mul 정수기 물 filtered water
jŏ·nyŏk 저녁 dinner
jo·ri·doén 조리 된 cooked
jo·rin 졸인 braised
jŏ·rin 절인 pickled
jŏ·rin ya·ch'ae 절인 야채 pickled vegetables
juk 죽 rice poridge
jŭng·nyu·su 증류수 distilled water
jus·sŭ 주스 juice
ju·yo·ri 주요리 main course

K

k'ak·t'e·il 칵테일 cocktail
k'al·guk·su 칼국수 thick handmade white noodles in broth
k'a·p'u·ch'i·no 카푸치노 cappuccino
k'a·ré 카레 curry
k'e·ch'ŏp 케첩 ketchup
k'e·i·k'ŭ 케이크 cake
k'i·wi 키위 kiwi fruit
k'o·k'o·a 코코아 cocoa
k'o·k'o·nŏt 코코넛 coconut
k'ol·li·p'ŭl·la·wŏ 콜리플라워 cauliflower
k'ong 콩 beans
k'ong·guk·su 콩국수 noodles in cold soy milk broth
k'ong·na·mul 콩나물 bean sprouts
k'ong·na·mul·guk 콩나물국 bean sprout soup
k'ong·nyu 콩류 legumes
k'ŏ·p'i 커피 coffee
k'ŏ·sŭ·t'ŏ·dŭ 커스터드 custard
k'ŭ·rae·k'ŏ 크래커 cracker
k'ŭ·rim·gwa sŏl·t'ang nŏ·ŭn k'ŏ·p'i 크림과 설탕 넣은 커피 coffee with cream & sugar

k'ŭ·rim nŏ·ŭn k'ŏ·p'i 크림 넣은 커피 coffee with cream
k'ŭ·ru·a·sang 크루아상 croissant
gu·un 구운 baked • broiled • grilled • roasted
gu·un·gam·ja 구운 감자 plain roasted potatoes
gwa·il 과일 fruit
gwa·il jus·sŭ 과일 주스 fruit juice
gwang·ŏ·hoé 광어회 raw halibut
gwi·ri 귀리 oats
gye·ran 계란 egg
gye·ranp·pang 계란빵 small cake with egg inside
gye·ran sael·lŏ·dŭ 계란 샐러드 egg salad
gye·ran·jjim 계란찜 steamed egg
gyŏ·ja 겨자 mustard (Korean-style)
gyŏn·gwa·ryu 견과류 nuts
gyul 귤 mandarin • tangerine

M

maek·ju 맥주 beer
mae·shil·ju 매실주 green plum wine
mae·un 매운 hot (spicy)
mae·un·t'ang 매운탕 spicy fish soup
ma·ga·rin 마가린 margarine
mak·kŏl·li 막걸리 fermented/unstrained rice wine • a milky liquor with a low alcohol content
mak·kuk·su 막국수 buckwheat noodles with vegetables, meat & chicken broth
mal·lin gwa·il 말린 과일 dried fruit
ma·mŏl·le·i·dŭ 마멀레이드 marmalade
man·du 만두 small dumplings filled with mincemeat, seafood, vegetables & herbs
man·du·guk·su 만두 국수 dumpling & noodle soup
man·duk·kuk 만둣국 soup with meat-filled dumplings
man·du·t'wi·gim 만두 튀김 fried dumplings
mang·go 망고 mango
man·ju 만쥬 freshly baked minicakes filled with custard
ma·nŭl 마늘 garlic
ma·rŭn o·jing·ŏ 마른 오징어 dried squid – at street stalls, this is roasted over a bed of pebbles
mat·t'ang 맛탕 honey-coated & roasted sweet potatoes
ma·yo·ne·jŭ 마요네즈 mayonnaise
me·ch'u·ri·al 메추리알 quail eggs
me·in k'o·sŭ 메인 코스 main course
mel·lon 멜론 melon
me·mil·ju 메밀주 liquor flavoured with buckwheat flowers
met·tu·gi·bok·kŭm 메뚜기볶음 fried grasshoppers
met·twae·ji 멧돼지 wild pig
mi·di·ŏm 미디엄 medium (of meat)
mil 밀 wheat
mil·ga·ru 밀가루 flour
mi·so 미소 see **doén·jang**
mi·t'ŭ·bol 미트볼 meatballs
mi·yŏk 미역 sea mustard (seaweed)
mi·yŏk·kuk 미역국 brown seaweed soup
mo·dum·hoé 모둠회 mixed raw fish platter
mo·dum saeng·sŏn ch'o·bap 모둠 생선초밥 assorted sushi
mo·gwa 모과 Chinese quince
mŏ·sŭ·t'ŏ·dŭ 머스터드 mustard (Western-style)
mu 무 radish
mu·hwa·gwa 무화과 fig
muk 묵 jellied food
mu·k'a·pe·in k'ŏ·p'i 무카페인 커피 decaffeinated coffee
mul 물 water
mul·gim·ch'i 물김치 cold nonspicy kimchi floating in cool water
mul·laeng·myŏn 물냉면 cold buckwheat noodles in an icy, sweetish broth, garnished with shredded vegetables & half a hard-boiled egg

myŏl·ch'i 멸치 anchovies
myŏl·ch'i·bok·kŭm 멸치볶음 anchovies stir-fried with garlic, ginger, soy sauce, corn syrup & cooking wine, then deep-fried

N

nae·jang 내장 giblets (meat)
nak·ji 낙지 octopus
nak·ji·bok·kŭm 낙지볶음 octopus or baby octopus chopped up in a mixture of red pepper paste & soy sauce, then stir-fried with onions, chilli & green onions
nak·ji·jŏn·gol 낙지전골 octopus hotpot
noé 뇌 brains
nok·ch'a 녹차 green tea
nok·du bin·daet·tŏk 녹두빈대떡 mung bean pancake
nŭl·gŭn ho·bak 늙은 호박 pumpkin
nu·rung·ji 누룽지 crunchy scorched rice snack

O

o·gok·bap 오곡밥 five-grain rice, usually consisting of glutinous & regular rice, glutinous sorghum, glutinous millet, dried black beans & dried sweet beans
o·gol·gyé 오골계 black chicken
o·i 오이 cucumber
o·i·so·ba·gi 오이소박이 pickled stuffed cucumber seasoned with garlic & red chilli
o·jing·ŏ 오징어 cuttlefish • squid
o·jing·ŏ·dŏp·bap 오징어 덮밥 rice topped with cuttlefish roasted in hot pepper paste
o·jing·ŏ sun·dae 오징어순대 stuffed squid
ok·su·su 옥수수 corn
ok·su·su·ch'a 옥수수차 roasted corn tea
ol·li·bŭ 올리브 olive
ol·li·bŭ o·il 올리브오일 olive oil
ŏ·muk 어묵 pressed fish & seafood cakes in broth
o·mŭl·let 오믈렛 omelette
o·mŭ·ra·i·sŭ 오므라이스 omelette with rice
o·ren·ji 오렌지 orange
o·ren·ji jus·sŭ 오렌지주스 orange juice
o·ri 오리 duck
o·ri·gu·i 오리구이 roast duck
o·ri·t'ang 오리탕 duck soup
ŏ·rŭm 얼음 ice

P

p'a 파 leek
p'aen·k'e·i·k'ŭ 팬케이크 pancakes
p'a·i 파이 pie
p'a·i·nae·p'ŭl 파인애플 pineapple
p'a·jŏn 파전 green onion pancake
p'ap·ping·su 팥빙수 red bean shaved ice
p'a·sŭl·li 파슬리 parsley
p'a·sŭ·t'a 파스타 pasta
p'at 팥 red bean paste
p'e·i·sŭ·t'ŭ·ri 페이스트리 pastry
p'i·ja 피자 pizza
p'i·k'ŭl 피클 pickles
p'i·mang 피망 bell pepper • paprika
p'i·sŭ·t'a·ch'i·o 피스타치오 pistachio
p'o·do 포도 grapes
p'o·do·jus·sŭ 포도 주스 grape juice
p'o·do·na·mu 포도나무 grapevine
p'uk·ko·ch'u 풋고추 green chilli pepper
p'ŭ·ri·ma 프리마 creamer (for coffee)

R

ra·im 라임 lime
ra·jŭ·be·ri 라즈베리 raspberries
ra·myŏn 라면 instant ramen noodles
re·dŭ wa·in 레드 와인 red wine
re·mon 레몬 lemon
re·mo·ne·i·dŭ 레모네이드 lemonade
ren·jŭ·k'ong 렌즈콩 lentils

re·ŏ 레어 rare (of meat)
rolp·pang 롤빵 bread roll
rŏm 럼 rum

S

sael·lŏ·dŭ 샐러드 salad
saen·dŭ·wi·ch'i 샌드위치 sandwich
saeng 생 raw
saeng·gang 생강 ginger
saeng·gang·ch'a 생강차 ginger tea
saeng·gwa·il jus·sŭ 생과일주스 freshly squeezed fruit juice
saeng·maek·ju 생맥주 draught beer
saeng·sŏn 생선 fish
saeng·sŏn ch'o·bap 생선초밥 sushi
saeng·sŏn·gu·i 생선구이 broiled & salted fish • grilled fish
saeng·sŏn·hoé 생선회 raw fish
saeng·sŏn t'wi·gim 생선 튀김 seasoned fish dipped in batter & fried
saeng·su 생수 mineral spring water
sae·u 새우 shrimp
sae·u·gu·i 새우구이 grilled prawns
sae·u·t'wi·gim 새우튀김 prawn pieces dipped in batter & deep-fried
sa·gwa 사과 apple
sal·gu 살구 apricot
sal·la·mi so·shi·ji 살라미 소시지 salami
sal·mŭn 삶은 boiled
sal·sa 살사 salsa
sam·gak·kim·bap 삼각 김밥 triangular rice and fillings wrapped in dried seaweed
sam·gye·t'ang 삼계탕 a small whole chicken stuffed with glutinous rice, red dates, garlic & ginseng boiled in broth
sam·gyŏp·sal 삼겹살 barbecued pork belly
san·ch'ae·bi·bim·bap 산채비빔밥 rice, mountain vegetables & meat topped with an egg
san·ch'ae·jŏng·shik 산채 정식 banquet of mountain vegetables
sang·ŏ 상어 shark
san·nak·ji 산낙지 live baby octopus
sa·wŏ·k'ŭ·rim 사워크림 sour cream
sel·lŏ·ri 셀러리 celery
sha·bŭ·sha·bŭ 샤브샤브 beef & vegetable hot pot
sham·p'e·in 샴페인 champagne • sparkling wine
sha·rŭ·do·né 샤르도네 chardonnay
shi·gol·bap·sang 시골 밥상 countryside-style meal
shi·gŭm·ch'i 시금치 spinach
shi·gŭm·ch'i mu·ch'im 시금치무침 whole spinach cut into pieces & seasoned with soy sauce, sesame oil & a touch of sugar
shik·ch'o 식초 vinegar
shi·k'yé 식혜 dessert of sweet rice punch with grains of rice
shin·sŏl·lo 신선로 a special-occasion dish of specially arranged meatballs, fried egg slivers, fried fish fillets, mushrooms, fried liver, pre-cooked carrots, gingko nuts, walnuts & pine nuts
shin·sŏn·han 신선한 fresh
shi·ri·ŏl 시리얼 cereal
so·bul·go·gi 소불고기 marinated beef grilled at the table & eaten with lettuce & other vegetables
soé·gal·bi 쇠갈비 barbecued beef ribs
soé·go·gi 쇠고기 beef
soé·go·gi gim·bap 쇠고기 김밥 rice-and-seaweed roll with beef
soé·go·gi ssam 쇠고기 쌈 barbecued beef slices & lettuce wrap (with side dishes)
soé·go·gi·guk 쇠고기 국 beef soup
soé·go·gi·guk·bap 쇠고기 국밥 beef & rice soup
so·gal·bi·jjim 소갈비찜 braised beef rib stew
so·gal·bi·t'ang 소갈비탕 beef ribs soup
so·gŭl ch'ae·un 속을 채운 stuffed
so·gŭm 소금 salt
so·ju 소주 traditional Korean liquor generally made from rice or sweet potatoes (similar to vodka, but less potent)

sŏl·t'ang 설탕 sugar
song·a·ji·go·gi 송아지 고기 veal
sŏng·nyu 석류 pomegranate
song·p'yŏn 송편 crescent-shaped rice-flour cakes stuffed with beans, chestnuts or sesame seeds & steamed on a layer of pine needles – associated with Chusok (Harvest Moon Festival)
sŏn·jik·kuk 선짓국 rice with ox-blood soup
so·shi·ji 소시지 sausage
so·sŭ 소스 sauce
ssal·gwa·ja 쌀과자 rice crackers
ssam·bap 쌈밥 rice with side dishes & leaf wraps
su·bak 수박 watermelon
su·je·bi 수제비 dough flakes in shellfish broth
su·jŏng·gwa 수정과 persimmon punch with cinnamon flavouring
sŭ·k'ŭ·raem·bŭl·dŭ e·gŭ 스크램블드에그 scrambled eggs
sul 술 alcoholic drink
sun·dae 순대 noodle & vegetable sausage
sun·du·bu·jji·gae 순두부찌개 spicy soft tofu stew
sung·nyung 숭늉 burnt-rice tea
su·p'ŭ 수프 soup
sŭ·t'e·i·k'ŭ 스테이크 steak

T

t'a·ba·sŭ·k'o so·sŭ 타바스코 소스 Tabasco sauce
t'al·ji u·yu 탈지 우유 skim milk
t'ang·su·yuk 탕수육 sweet & sour pork
t'an·san ŭm·nyo 탄산음료 soft drink
de·ch'in 데친 poached
t'e·k'il·la 테킬라 tequila
t'o·ma·t'o 토마토 tomatoes
t'o·ma·t'o so·sŭ 토마토소스 tomato sauce
t'ong·milp·pang 통밀빵 wholemeal bread
t'o·sŭ·t'ŭ 토스트 fried sandwich on toasted bread
t'wi·gin 튀긴 deep-fried

U

ŭk·kaen 으깬 mashed
ŭm·nyo·su 음료수 drink
ŭn·haeng 은행 gingko nuts
u·yu 우유 milk

W

wa·in 와인 wine
wan·du·k'ong 완두콩 peas
wan·su·gé 완숙의 hard-boiled
wa·p'ŭl 와플 waffles
wel·dŏn 웰던 well-done (of meat)
wi·sŭ·k'i 위스키 whisky

Y

ya·ch'ae 야채 vegetables
ya·ch'ae't'wi·gim 야채튀김 deep-fried vegetables in tempura
yak·shik 약식 flavoured glutinous rice mixed with honey, dates & chestnuts
yang·bae·ch'u 양배추 cabbage (Western)
yang·go·gi 양고기 lamb • mutton
yang·p'a 양파 onion
yang·sang·ch'u 양상추 lettuce
yo·gu·rŭ·t'ŭ 요구르트 yoghurt
yŏl·mu·naeng·myŏn 열무 냉면 cold noodles with radish kimchi soup
yŏn·hoé 연회 banquet
yŏ·nŏ 연어 salmon
yŏt 엿 hard taffy
yu·ja·ch'a 유자차 citron tea
yuk·kae·jang 육개장 spicy beef soup with noodles and vegetables
yu·k'oé 육회 seasoned raw beef
yul·mu·ch'a 율무차 'Job's tears' tea – a hot drink that has a nutty flavour, made from the powdered seeds of the 'Job's tears' tropical grass

DICTIONARY

English to Korean

영어 – 한국어

Words in this dictionary are marked as nouns n, adjectives a, adverbs adv, verbs v, pronouns pron or prepositions prep for clarity where required. The abbreviations sg (singular), pl (plural), inf (informal) and pol (polite) are also used where applicable. Korean verbs are given in their polite form (ending in ~yo ~요). The verb stem is repeated between brackets after the verb. For more information, see **grammar** (p18).

A

aboard 탑승한 tap·sŭng·han
abortion 낙태 nak·t'ae
about ... prep ...에 대하여 ...·é dae·ha·yŏ
above ... prep ... 위에 ... wi·é
abroad 외국에 oé·gu·gé
accept 받아들여요 (받아들이~) ba·da·dŭ·ryŏ·yo (pa·da·dŭ·ri~)
accident 사고 sa·go
accommodation 숙박 suk·bak
account (bill) n 계산서 gye·san·sŏ
across ... prep ... 맞은 편에 ... ma·jŭn·p'yŏ·né
actor 배우 bae·u
acupuncture 침 ch'im
adaptor 어댑터 ŏ·daep·t'ŏ
addiction 중독 jung·dok
address n 주소 ju·so
administration 관리 gwal·li
administrator 관리자 gwal·li·ja
admission (price) 입장료 ip·jang·nyo
admit (let in) 허락해요 (허락하~) hŏ·ra·k'ae·yo (hŏ·ra·k'a~)
adult n 성인 sŏng·in
advertisement 광고 gwang·go
advice 조언 jo·ŏn
aeroplane 비행기 bi·haeng·gi
after ... prep ... 후에 ... hu·é
afternoon 오후 o·hu
again 다시 da·shi
against ... prep ...에 반대하여 ...·é ban·dae·ha·yŏ
age n inf/pol 나이/연세 na·i/yŏn·sé
ago 전에 jŏ·né
agree 동의해요 (동의하~) dong·i·hae·yo (dong·i·ha~)
agriculture 농사 nong·sa
ahead 앞 쪽에 ap·jjo·gé
AIDS 에이즈 é·i·jŭ
air n 공기 gong·gi
air-conditioned 냉방 중 naeng·bang·jung
air conditioning 냉방 naeng·bang
airline 항공사 hang·gong·sa
airmail 항공 우편 hang·gong u·p'yŏn
airplane 비행기 bi·haeng·gi
airport 공항 gong·hang
airport tax 공항세 gong·hang·sé

aisle (on plane) 통로 t'ong·no
alarm clock 알람 시계 al·lam shi·gyé
alcohol 술 sul
all 모든 mo·dŭn
allergic to ... ...에 알레르기가 있는 ...é al·le·rŭ·gi·ga in·nŭn
allergy 알레르기 al·le·rŭ·gi
almond 아몬드 a·mon·dŭ
almost 거의 gŏ·i
alone 홀로 hol·lo
already 벌써 bŏl·ssŏ
also 또한 ddo·han
altitude 고도 go·do
always 언제나 ŏn·je·na
ambassador 대사 dae·sa
ambulance 구급차 gu·gŭp·ch'a
amusement park 유원지 yu·wŏn·ji
anaemia 빈혈 bin·hyŏl
anchovy 멸치 myŏl·ch'i
ancient a 고대의 go·dae·ŭi
and 그리고 gŭ·ri·go
angry 화난 hwa·nan
animal 동물 dong·mul
ankle 발목 bal·mok
another 또 하나의 ddo ha·na·é
answer n 대답 dae·dap
answer v 대답해요 (대답하~) dae·da·p'ae·yo (dae·da·p'a-)
ant 개미 gae·mi
antibiotics 항생제 hang·saeng·jé
antihistamines 항히스타민제 hang·hi·sŭ·t'a·min·jé
antinuclear movement 반핵 운동 ban·haek un·dong
antique n 골동품 gol·dong·p'um
antiseptic n 소독약 so·dong·nyak
any 무엇이든 mu·ŏ·shi·dŭn
apartment 아파트 a·p'a·t'ŭ
appendicitis 맹장염 maeng·jang·nyŏm
appendix (body) 맹장 maeng·jang
apple 사과 sa·gwa
appointment 약속 yak·sok
apricot 살구 sal·gu
aquarium 수족관 su·jok·kwan
archaeology 고고학 go·go·hak
architect 건축가 gŏn·ch'uk·ka
architecture 건축 gŏn·ch'uk
argue 논쟁해요 (논쟁하~) non·jaeng·hae·yo (non·jaeng·ha-)
arm (body) 팔 p'al
arrest 체포해요 (체포하~) ch'e·p'o·hae·yo (ch'e·p'o·ha-)
arrivals 도착 do·ch'ak
arrive 도착해요 (도착하~) do·ch'a·k'ae·yo (do·ch'a·k'a-)
art 미술 mi·sul
art gallery 미술관 mi·sul·gwan
artist (painter) 화가 hwa·ga
ashtray 재떨이 jaet·tŏ·ri
ask (a question) 물어봐요 (물어보~) mu·rŏ·bwa·yo (mu·rŏ·bo-)
ask (for something) 부탁해요 (부탁하~) bu·t'a·k'ae·yo (bu·t'a·k'a-)
asparagus 아스파라거스 a·sŭ·p'a·ra·gŏ·sŭ
aspirin 아스피린 a·sŭ·p'i·rin
asthma 천식 ch'ŏn·shik
at ... prep ...에서 ...e·sŏ
athletics 운동 un·dong
atmosphere 분위기 bu·nwi·gi
aubergine 가지 ga·ji
aunt (maternal) 이모 i·mo
aunt (paternal) 고모 go·mo
Australia 호주/오스트레일리아 ho·ju/o·sŭ·t'ŭ·re·il·li·a
ATM 현금인출기 hyŏn·gŭ·min·ch'ul·gi
autumn 가을 ga·ŭl
avenue 대로 dae·ro
avocado 아보카도 a·bo·k'a·do
awful 형편없는 hyŏng·p'yŏn·ŏm·nŭn

B

baby 아기 a·gi
baby food 유아식 yu·a·shik
babysitter 육아 도우미 yu·ga do·u·mi
back (body) 허리 hŏ·ri
back (position) 뒤쪽 dwi·jjok
backpack 배낭 bae·nang
bacon 베이컨 be·i·k'ŏn
bad 나쁜 nap·pŭn
bag 가방 ga·bang

baggage 짐/수하물 jim/su·ha·mul
baggage allowance 수하물 허용량 su·ha·mul hŏ·yong·nyang
baggage claim 수하물 수취대 su·ha·mul su·ch'wi·dae
bakery 빵집 bbang·jip
balance (account) 잔액 ja·naek
balcony 발코니 bal·k'o·ni
ball (sport) 공 gong
ballet 발레 bal·lé
banana 바나나 ba·na·na
band (music) 밴드 baen·dŭ
bandage 붕대 bung·dae
Band-Aid 반창고 ban·ch'ang·go
bank n 은행 ŭn·haeng
bank account 은행 계좌 ŭn·haeng gye·jwa
banknote 지폐 ji·p'yé
banquet 연회 yŏn·hoé
bar n 술집 sul·jip
barbecue 바비큐 ba·bi·k'yu
barber shop 이발소 i·bal·so
baseball 야구 ya·gu
basket 바구니 ba·gu·ni
basketball 농구 nong·gu
bath n 목욕 mo·gyok
bathing suit 수영복 su·yŏng·bok
bathroom 욕실/화장실 yok·shil/hwa·jang·shil
battery 배터리 bae·t'ŏ·ri
bay 만 man
be ... ...이에요/예요 ...i·e·yo/·ye·yo
beach (for swimming) 해수욕장 hae·su·yok·jang
beach (geographic) 해변 hae·byŏn
bean 콩 k'ong
bean sprouts 콩나물 k'ong·na·mul
beautician 미용사 mi·yong·sa
beautiful 아름다운 a·rŭm·da·un
beauty salon 미용실 mi·yong·shil
because 왜냐하면 wae·nya·ha·myŏn
bed 침대 ch'im·dae
bedding 이부자리 i·bu·ja·ri
bedroom 침실 ch'im·shil
bed sheet 침대 시트 ch'im·dae shi·t'ŭ
bee 벌 bŏl
beef 쇠고기 soé·go·gi
beer 맥주 maek·ju
beetroot 비트 뿌리 bi·t'ŭp·pu·ri
begin 시작해요 (시작하~) shi·ja·k'ae·yo (shi·ja·k'a~)
before ... prep ... 전에 ... jŏ·né
beggar 거지 gŏ·ji
behind ... prep ... 뒤에 ... dwi·é
below ... prep ... 아래 ... a·rae
beside ... prep ... 옆에 ... yŏ·p'é
best 최고의 ch'oé·go·é
bet n 내기 nae·gi
bet v 내기해요 (내기하~) nae·gi·hae·yo (nae·gi·ha~)
better 더 나은 dŏ·na·ŭn
between ... prep ... 사이의 ... sa·i·é
bicycle 자전거 ja·jŏn·gŏ
big 큰 k'ŭn
bigger 더 큰 dŏ·k'ŭn
biggest 제일 큰 je·il·k'ŭn
bike chain 자전거 체인 ja·jŏn·gŏ ch'e·in
bike lock 자전거 자물쇠 ja·jŏn·gŏ ja·mul·soé
bike path 자전거 도로 ja·jŏn·gŏ do·ro
bike shop 자전거 매장 ja·jŏn·gŏ mae·jang
bill (restaurant) n 계산서 gye·san·sŏ
billiards 당구 dang·gu
billion 십억 shi·bŏk
binoculars 쌍안경 ssang·an·gyŏng
bird 새 sae
birth certificate 출생증명서 ch'ul·saeng·jŭng·myŏng·sŏ
birthday 생일 saeng·il
biscuit 비스킷 bi·sŭ·k'it
bite (insect/mammal) n 물림 mul·lim
bitter 쓴 ssŭn
black 검은 gŏ·mŭn
bladder 방광 bang·gwang
blanket 담요 dam·nyo
blind a 시각 장애의 shi·gak jang·ae·ŭi
blister n 물집 mul·jip
blocked 막힌 ma·k'in
blood 혈액 hyŏ·raek
blood group 혈액형 hyŏ·rae·k'yŏng

blood pressure 혈압 hyŏ·rap
blood test 혈액 검사 hyŏ·raek·gŏm·sa
blue 파란 p'a·ran
board (plane, ship) v 타요 (타~) t'a·yo (t'a-)
boarding house 하숙집 ha·suk·jip
boarding pass 탑승권 t'ap·sŭng·gwŏn
boat 배 bae
body 몸 mom
boiled 끓인 ggŭ·rin
bone 뼈 bbyŏ
book n 책 ch'aek
book (make a booking) v 예약해요 (예약하~) ye·ya·k'ae·yo (ye·ya·k'a-)
booked out 매진 mae·jin
bookshop 서점 sŏ·jŏm
boot (footwear) 부츠 bu·ch'ŭ
border (national) n 국경 guk·kyŏng
bored 심심한 shim·shim·han
boring 재미없는 jae·mi·ŏm·nŭn
borrow 빌려요 (빌리~) bil·lyŏ·yo (bil·li-)
botanic garden 수목원 su·mo·gwŏn
both 둘 다 dul·da
bottle 병 byŏng
bottle opener 병따개 byŏngt·ta·gae
bottom (body) 엉덩이 ŏng·dŏng·i
bottom (position) 바닥 ba·dak
boutique (fashion) 의류 매장 ŭi·ryu mae·jang
bowl (plate) n 사발 sa·bal
box n 상자 sang·ja
boxing 권투 gwŏn·t'u
boy 남자 아이 nam·ja·a·i
boyfriend 남자 친구 nam·ja ch'in·gu
bra 브래지어 bŭ·rae·ji·ŏ
brakes 브레이크 bŭ·re·i·k'ŭ
brassware 놋쇠 제품 nos·soé je·p'um
brave 용감한 yong·gam·han
bread 빵 bbang
break v 깨뜨려요 (깨뜨리~) ggaet·tŭ·ryŏ·yo (ggaet·tŭ·ri-)
break down 고장나요 (고장나~) go·jang·na·yo (go·jang·na-)
breakfast 아침 a·ch'im
breast (body) 가슴 ga·sŭm
breathe 숨 쉬어요 (숨 쉬~) sum·shi·ŏ·yo (sum·shi-)
bribe n 뇌물 noé·mul
bridge (structure) n 다리 da·ri
briefcase 서류가방 sŏ·ryu·ga·bang
bring 가지고 와요 (가지고 오~) ga·ji·go·wa·yo (ga·ji·go·o-)
brochure 소책자 so·ch'aek·ja
broken 깨진 ggae·jin
broken down 고장난 go·jang·nan
bronchitis 기관지염 gi·gwan·ji·yŏm
brother 형제 hyŏng·jé
brown 갈색 gal·saek
bruise n 멍 mŏng
brush n 솔 sol
bucket 양동이 yang·dong·i
budget n 예산 ye·san
buffet 뷔페 bwi·p'é
bug n 벌레 bŏl·lé
build 지어요 (짓~) ji·ŏ·yo (jit-)
building 빌딩 bil·ding
bumbag 여행 복대 yŏ·haeng·bok·tae
burn n 화상 hwa·sang
burnt 탄 t'an
bus 버스 bŏ·sŭ
business n 사업 sa·ŏp
business class 비즈니스석 bi·jŭ·ni·sŭ·sŏk
businessperson 사업가 sa·ŏp·ga
business trip 출장 ch'ul·jang
busker 길거리 공연가 gil·gŏ·ri gong·yŏn·ga
bus station 버스 터미널 bŏ·su t'ŏ·mi·nŏl
bus stop 버스 정류장 bŏ·su jŏng·nyu·jang
busy (person) 바쁜 bap·pŭn
busy (phone) 통화중 t'ong·hwa·jung
but 하지만 ha·ji·man
butcher's shop 정육점 jŏng·yuk·jŏm
butter n 버터 bŏ·t'ŏ
button n 단추 dan·ch'u
buy 사요 (사~) sa·yo (sa-)

C

cafe 카페 k'a·pé
cake 케이크 k'e·i·k'ŭ
calculator 계산기 gye·san·gi
calendar 달력 dal·lyŏk
call (phone) v 전화해요 (전화하~) jŏn·hwa·hae·yo (jŏn·hwa·ha~)
calligraphy 서예 sŏ·yé
camera 카메라 k'a·me·ra
camp v 야영해요 (야영하~) ya·yŏng·hae·yo (ya·yŏng·ha~)
camping store 야영용품점 ya·yŏng·yong·p'um·jŏm
campsite 야영장 ya·yŏng·jang
can n 캔 k'aen
can (be able) 할 수 있어요 (할 수 있~) hal·su iss·ŏ·yo (hal·su iss~)
can (have permission) 해도 돼요 (해도 되~) hae·do dwae·yo (hae·do doé~)
Canada 캐나다 k'ae·na·da
cancel 취소해요 (취소하~) ch'wi·so·hae·yo (ch'wi·so·ha~)
cancer 암 am
candle 초 ch'o
candy 사탕 sa·t'ang
can opener 캔따개 k'aent·ta·gae
capsicum 고추 go·ch'u
car 차 ch'a
cardiac arrest 심장마비 shim·jang·ma·bi
cards (playing) 카드 k'a·dŭ
care (for someone) 아껴요 (아끼~) ak·kyŏ·yo (ak·ki~)
car hire 렌트카 ren·t'ŭ·k'a
car park 주차장 ju·ch'a·jang
carpenter 목수 mok·su
carpet 카펫 k'a·p'et
car registration 자동차 등록증 ja·dong·ch'a dŭng·nok·jŭng
carrot 당근 dang·gŭn
carry 날라요 (나르~) nal·la·yo (na·rŭ~)
carton 팩 p'aek
cash n 현금 hyŏn·gŭm
cash (a cheque) v 현금으로 바꿔요 (현금으로 바꾸~) hyŏn·gŭ·mŭ·ro bak·kwŏ·yo (hyŏn·gŭ·mŭ·ro bak·ku~)
cash register 금전 등록기 gŭm·jŏn dŭng·nok·ki
casino 카지노 k'a·ji·no
castle 성 sŏng
cat 고양이 go·yang·i
cathedral 성당 sŏng·dang
cauliflower 콜리플라워 k'ol·li·p'ŭl·la·wŏ
cave n 동굴 dong·gul
cavity (dental) 충치 ch'ung·ch'i
CD 시디 shi·di
celebration 축하 ch'u·k'a
celery 셀러리 sel·lŏ·ri
cell phone 휴대폰 hyu·dae·p'on
cemetery 묘지 myo·ji
centimetre 센티미터 sen·t'i·mi·t'ŏ
centre n 중앙 jung·ang
ceramics 도자기 do·ja·gi
cereal (breakfast) 시리얼 shi·ri·ŏl
ceremony 의식 ŭi·shik
certificate 증명서 jŭng·myŏng·sŏ
chain n 체인 ch'e·in
chair n 의자 ŭi·ja
chairlift (skiing) 리프트 ri·p'ŭ·t'ŭ
championships 선수권 대회 sŏn·suk·gwŏn dae·hoé
chance n 기회 gi·hoé
change n 변화 byŏn·hwa
change (coins) n 잔돈 jan·don
change (money) v 환전해요 (환전하~) hwan·jŏn·hae·yo (hwan·jŏn·ha~)
changing room 탈의실 t'a·ri·shil
chapel 예배당 ye·bae·dang
charm 매력 mae·ryŏk
charming 매력적인 mae·ryŏk·jŏ·gin
chat up 말 걸어요 (말 걸~) mal gŏ·rŏ·yo (mal gŏl~)
cheap 싼 ssan
cheat n 속임수 so·gim·su
cheat v 속여요 (속이~) so·gyŏ·yo (so·gi~)
check (banking) n 수표 su·p'yo
check (bill) n 계산서 gye·san·sŏ

check v 점검해요 (점검하~) jŏm·gŏm·hae·yo (jŏm·gŏm·ha~)
check-in (desk) 체크인 ch'e·k'ŭ·in
checkpoint 검문소 gŏm·mun·so
cheese 치즈 ch'i·jŭ
chef 요리사 yo·ri·sa
chemist (pharmacist) 약사 yak·sa
chemist (pharmacy) 약국 yak·kuk
cheque (banking) 수표 su·p'yo
cherry 체리 ch'e·ri
chess 체스 ch'e·sŭ
chessboard 체스판 ch'e·sŭ·p'an
chest (body) 가슴 ga·sŭm
chestnut 밤 bam
chewing gum 껌 ggŏm
chicken (animal) 닭 dak
chicken (meat) 닭고기 dak·ko·gi
chicken pox 수두 su·du
child 어린이 ŏ·ri·ni
child-minding service 아이 돌보기 a·i·dol·bo·gi
children (general) 어린이 ŏ·ri·ni
children (offspring) 자녀 ja·nyŏ
child seat 어린이용 좌석 ŏ·ri·ni·yong jwa·sŏk
chilli 고추 go·ch'u
China 중국 jung·guk
chiropractor 척추 지압사 ch'ŏk·ch'u ji·ap·sa
chocolate 초콜릿 ch'o·k'ol·lit
choose 선택해요 (선택하~) sŏn·tae·k'ae·yo (sŏn·tae·k'a~)
chopping board 도마 do·ma
chopsticks 젓가락 jŏk·ka·rak
church 교회 gyo·hoé
cigar 시가 shi·ga
cigarette 담배 dam·bae
cigarette lighter 라이터 ra·i·t'ŏ
cinema 영화관 yŏng·hwa·gwan
circus 서커스 sŏ·k'ŏ·sŭ
citizenship 시민권 shi·min·gwŏn
city 도시 do·shi
city centre 시내 shi·nae
civil rights 시민권 shi·min·gwŏn
class (category) n 종류 jong·nyu
class (school) 수업 su·ŏp
classical 고전 go·jŏn
class system 계급 제도 gye·gŭp·je·do
clean a 깨끗한 ggaek·kŭ·t'an
clean v 청소해요 (청소하~) ch'ŏng·so·hae·yo (ch'ŏng·so·ha~)
cleaning 청소 ch'ŏng·so
client 고객 go·gaek
cliff 절벽 jŏl·byŏk
climb v 올라요 (오르~) ol·la·yo (o·rŭ~)
cloakroom 휴대품 보관소 hyu·dae·p'um bo·gwan·so
clock n 시계 shi·gyé
close a 가까운 gak·ka·un
close v 닫아요 (닫~) da·da·yo (dad~)
closed 휴무 hyu·mu
clothesline 빨랫줄 bbal·laet·chul
clothing 옷 ot
clothing store 옷가게 ok·ka·gé
cloud n 구름 gu·rŭm
cloudy 구름이 많은 gu·rŭ·mi ma·nŭn
clutch (car) 클러치 k'ŭl·lŏ·ch'i
coach (trainer) n 코치 k'o·ch'i
coach v 가르쳐요 (가르치~) ga·rŭ·ch'ŏ·yo (ga·rŭ·ch'i~)
coast n 해안 hae·an
coat n 코트 k'ŏ·t'ŭ
cockroach 바퀴벌레 ba·k'wi·bŏl·lé
cod 대구 dae·gu
coffee 커피 k'ŏ·p'i
coins 동전 dong·jŏn
cold (illness) n 감기 gam·gi
cold (to senses) a 차가운 ch'a·ga·un
cold (weather) a 추운 ch'u·un
colleague 동료 dong·nyo
collect call 수신자 부담 통화 su·shin·ja bu·dam t'ong·hwa
college 대학 dae·hak
colour n 색깔 saek·kal
comb n 빗 bit
come 와요 (오~) wa·yo (o~)
comedy 코메디 k'o·me·di
comfortable 편안한 p'yŏ·nan·han
commission 수수료 su·su·ryo
communion 영성체 yŏng·sŏng·ch'é
communism 공산주의 gong·san·ju·i

communist n 공산주의자 gong·san·ju·i·ja
company (firm) 회사 hoé·sa
compass 나침반 na·ch'im·ban
complain 불평해요 (불평하~) bul·p'yŏng·hae·yo (bul·p'yŏng·ha~)
complaint 불평 bul·p'yŏng
complimentary (free) 공짜 gong·tcha
computer 컴퓨터 k'ŏm·p'yu·t'ŏ
computer game 컴퓨터 게임 k'ŏm·p'yu·t'ŏ ge·im
concert 콘서트 k'on·sŏ·t'ŭ
concussion 진동 jin·dong
conditioner (hair) 컨디셔너 k'ŏn·di·shŏ·nŏ
condom 콘돔 k'on·dom
conference 회의 hoé·i
confession (religious) 고해성사 go·hae·sŏng·sa
confirm (a booking) 확인해요 (확인하~) hwa·gin·hae·yo (hwa·gin·ha~)
conjunctivitis 결막염 gyŏl·mang·nyŏm
connection (transport) n 환승 hwan·sŭng
conservative a 보수적인 bo·su·jŏ·gin
constipation 변비 byŏn·bi
consulate 영사관 yŏng·sa·gwan
contact lenses 콘택트 렌즈 k'on·t'aek·t'ŭ ren·jŭ
contact lens solution 콘택트 렌즈 용액 k'on·t'aek·t'ŭ ren·jŭ yong·aek
contraceptives 피임 p'i·im
contract n 계약서 gye·yak·sŏ
convenience store 편의점 p'yŏ·ni·jŏm
convent 수도원 su·do·wŏn
cook n 요리사 yo·ri·sa
cook v 요리해요 (요리하~) yo·ri·hae·yo (yo·ri·ha~)
cookie 과자 gwa·ja
cooking 요리 yo·ri
cool (groovy) 멋진 mŏt·jin
cool (temperature) 시원한 shi·wŏn·han
corkscrew 코르크 따개 k'o·rŭ·k'ŭ dda·gae
corn 옥수수 ok·su·su
corner n 모퉁이 mo·t'ung·i
corrupt a 부패한 bu·p'ae·han
corruption 부패 bu·p'ae
cost n 비용 bi·yong
cost v 들어요 (들~) dŭ·rŏ·yo (dŭl~)
cotton (fabric) n 면 myŏn
cotton balls 솜 som
cough n 기침 gi·ch'im
cough v 기침 해요 (기침 하~) gi·ch'im hae·yo (gi·ch'im ha~)
cough medicine 기침약 ki·ch'im·nyak
count v 세요 (세~) se·yo (se~)
country 나라 na·ra
countryside 시골 shi·gol
coupon 쿠폰 k'u·p'on
courgette 애호박 ae·ho·bak
court (legal) 법정 bŏp·jŏng
court (tennis) 코트 k'o·t'ŭ
cover charge 팁 t'ip
cow 소 so
crab 게 gé
cracker 크래커 k'ŭ·rae·k'ŏ
crafts 공예품 gong·ye·p'um
crash n 충돌 ch'ung·dol
crazy 미친 mi·ch'in
cream (food) 액상 크림 aek·sang k'ŭ·rim
cream (lotion) 크림 k'ŭ·rim
credit card 신용카드 shi·nyong k'a·dŭ
croissant 크루아상 k'ŭ·ru·a·sang
crop (riding) n 채찍 ch'ae·jjik
cross (religious) n 십자가 ship·ja·ga
crossing (pedestrian) 건널목 gŏn·nŏl·mok
crowded 붐비는 bum·bi·nŭn
cucumber 오이 o·i
cup 컵 k'ŏp
cupboard 찬장 ch'an·jang
currency exchange 환율 hwa·nyul
current (electricity) 전류 jŏl·lyu
current affairs 시사 shi·sa
curry 카레 k'a·ré
custom 풍습 p'ung·sŭp
customs 세관 se·gwan
cut n 삭제 sak·jé

cut v 잘라요 (자르~) jal·la·yo (ja·rŭ~)
cutlery 수저와 포크 su·jŏ·wa p'o·k'ŭ
CV 이력서 i·ryŏk·sŏ
cycle (ride) v 자전거를 타요 (자전거를 타~) ja·jŏn·gŏ·rŭl t'a·yo (ja·jŏn·gŏ·rŭl t'a~)
cycling 사이클 sa·i·k'ŭl
cyclist 사이클 선수 sa·i·k'ŭl sŏn·su
cystitis 방광염 bang·gwang·nyŏm

D

dad 아빠 ap·pa
daily adv 매일 mae·il
dairy products 유제품 yu·je·p'um
dance n 춤 ch'um
dance v 춤 춰요 (춤 추~) ch'um·ch'wŏ·yo (ch'um·ch'u~)
dangerous 위험한 wi·hŏm·han
dark 어두운 ŏ·du·un
date (appointment) 약속 yak·sok
date (day) 날짜 nal·jja
date (fruit) 대추 dae·ch'u
date (romantic) 데이트 de·i·t'ŭ
date of birth 생년월일 saeng·nyŏn·wŏ·ril
daughter 딸 ddal
dawn 새벽 sae·byŏk
day 하루 ha·ru
daytime 낮 nat
dead 죽은 ju·gŭn
deaf 귀가 먼 gwi·ga·mŏn
decide 결정해요 (결정하~) gyŏl·jŏng·hae·yo (gyŏl·jŏng·ha~)
deep 깊은 gi·p'ŭn
deer 사슴 sa·sŭm
deforestation 삼림 벌채 sam·nim bŏl·ch'ae
degrees (temperature) 도 do
delay n 지연 ji·yŏn
delicatessen 식품점 shik·p'um·jŏm
deliver 배달해요 (배달하~) bae·dal·hae·yo (bae·dal·ha~)
demilitarized zone (DMZ) 비무장지대 bi·mu·jang ji·dae
democracy 민주주의 min·ju·ju·i
Democratic People's Republic of Korea 조선인민공화국 jo·sŏn in·min gong·hwa·guk
demonstration (display) 시연 shi·yŏn
demonstration (rally) 시위 shi·wi
dental floss 치실 ch'i·shil
dentist 치과의사 ch'i·gwa ŭi·sa
deodorant 데오드란트 de·o·dŭ·ran·t'ŭ
depart 떠나요 (떠나~) ddŏ·na·yo (ddŏ·na~)
department store 백화점 bae·k'wa·jŏm
departure 출발 ch'ul·bal
departure hall 출국장 ch'ul·guk·jang
deposit n 보증금 bo·jŭng·gŭm
derailleur 변속 장치 byŏn·sok jang·ch'i
descendant 후손 hu·son
desert n 사막 sa·mak
design n 디자인 di·ja·in
dessert 후식 hu·shik
destination 목적지 mok·jŏk·ji
details 자세한 내용 ja·se·han nae·yong
diabetes 당뇨병 dang·nyo·byŏng
dial tone 발신음 bal·shi·nŭm
diaper 기저귀 gi·jŏ·gwi
diaphragm (contraceptive) 페서리 p'e·sŏ·ri
diarrhoea 설사 sŏl·sa
diary 일기 il·gi
dice 주사위 ju·sa·wi
dictionary 사전 sa·jŏn
die 죽어요 (죽~) ju·gŏ·yo (jug~)
diet (to lose weight) n 다이어트 da·i·ŏ·t'ŭ
different 다른 da·rŭn
difficult 어려운 ŏ·ryŏ·un
digital a 디지털 di·ji·t'ŏl
dinner 저녁 jŏ·nyŏk
direct a 직접적인 jik·jŏp·jŏ·gin
direction 방향 bang·hyang
director 지휘자 ji·hwi·ja
dirty 더러운 dŏ·rŏ·un
disabled person 장애인 jang·ae·in
disco 디스코 di·sŭ·k'o
discount n 할인 ha·rin

discrimination 차별 ch'a·byŏl
disease 병 byŏng
dish n 접시 jŏp·shi
diving 다이빙 da·i·bing
diving equipment 다이빙 용품 da·i·bing yong·p'um
divorced 이혼한 i·hon·han
dizzy 어지러운 ŏ·ji·rŏ·un
do 해요 (하~) hae·yo (ha~)
doctor 의사 ŭi·sa
doctor of Eastern medicine 한의사 ha·ni·sa
dog 개 gae
doll 인형 in·hyŏng
dollar 달러 dal·lŏ
door 문 mun
dope (illicit drugs) 마약 ma·yak
double a 두 배의 du·bae·é
double bed 더블베드 dŏ·bŭl·be·dŭ
double room 더블 룸 dŏ·bŭl·lum
doughnut 도넛 do·nŏt
down 아래로 a·rae·ro
downhill 내리막 nae·ri·mak
drama 드라마 dŭ·ra·ma
draught beer 생맥주 saeng·maek·chu
dream n 꿈 ggum
dress n 드레스 dŭ·re·sŭ
dried 말린 mal·lin
dried fruit 말린 과일 mal·lin gwa·il
drink n 음료수 ŭm·nyo·su
drink v 마셔요 (마시~) ma·shŏ·yo (ma·shi~)
drink (alcoholic) 술 sul
drinking fountain 급수대 gŭp·su·dae
drive v 운전해요 (운전하~) un·jŏn·hae·yo (un·jŏn·ha~)
driver's licence 운전면허증 un·jŏn myŏn·hŏ·jŭng
drug (medication) n 약 yak
drug addiction 마약 중독 ma·yak·jung·dok
drug dealer 마약상 ma·yak·sang
drugs (illicit) 마약 ma·yak
drug trafficking 마약 밀매 ma·yang·mil·mae
drug user 마약 사용자 ma·yak sa·yong·ja
drum (instrument) n 드럼 dŭ·rŏm
drunk 술 취한 sul·ch'wi·han
dry a 마른 ma·rŭn
dry v 말려요 (말리~) mal·lyŏ·yo (mal·li~)
duck n 오리 o·ri
dummy (pacifier) 노리개젖꼭지 no·ri·gae jŏk·kok·ji
dumplings 만두 man·du
duty-free n 면세 myŏn·sé
dynasty 왕조 wang·jo

E

each 각각의 gak·ka·gé
ear 귀 gwi
early adv 이른 i·rŭn
earn 벌어요 (벌~) bŏ·rŏ·yo (bŏl~)
earplugs 귀마개 gwi·ma·gae
earrings 귀고리 gwi·go·ri
earth 땅 ddang
earthquake 지진 ji·jin
east n 동쪽 dong·jjok
Eastern medical clinic 한의원 ha·ni·wŏn
Eastern medicine 한약 ha·nyak
easy 쉬운 shi·un
eat 먹어요 (먹~) mŏ·gŏ·yo (mŏg~)
economy class 이코노미석 i·k'o·no·mi·sŏk
eczema 습진 sŭp·jin
education 교육 gyo·yuk
eel 장어 jang·ŏ
egg 계란 gye·ran
eggplant 가지 ga·ji
election 선거 sŏn·gŏ
electrical store 전파사 jŏn·p'a·sa
electrician 전기 기사 jŏn·gi gi·sa
electricity 전기 jŏn·gi
electronics 전자제품 jŏn·ja·je·p'um
elevator 엘리베이터 el·li·be·i·t'ŏ
email n 이메일 i·me·il
embarrassed 창피한 ch'ang·p'i·han
embassy 대사관 dae·sa·gwan

embroidery 자수품 ja·su·p'um
emergency 응급 상황 ŭng·gŭp sang·hwang
emergency exit 비상구 bi·sang·gu
emotional 감정적인 gam·jŏng·jŏ·gin
employee 직원 ji·gwŏn
employer 고용인 go·yong·in
empty a 빈 bin
end n 끝 ggŭt
end v 끝나요 (끝나~) gŭn·na·yo (gŭn·na~)
endangered species 멸종 위기의 종 myŏl·jong wi·gi·ŭi jong
engaged (phone) 통화 중인 t'ong·hwa·jung·in
engaged (to be married) 약혼한 ya·k'on·han
engagement (to marry) 약혼 ya·k'on
engine 엔진 en·jin
engineer n 엔지니어 en·ji·n·i·ŏ
engineering 공학 gong·hak
England 영국 yŏng·guk
English (language) 영어 yŏng·ŏ
enjoy (oneself) 즐겨요 (즐기~) jŭl·gyŏ·yo (jŭl·gi~)
enough 충분한 ch'ung·bun·han
enter 들어가요 (들어가~) dŭ·rŏ·ga·yo (dŭ·rŏ·ga~)
entrance 입구 ip·gu
entry n 입장 ip·jang
envelope n 봉투 bong·t'u
environment 환경 hwan·gyŏng
epilepsy 간질 gan·jil
equality 평등 p'yŏng·dŭng
equipment 장비 jang·bi
escalator 에스컬레이터 e·sŭ·k'ŏl·le·i·t'ŏ
estate agency 부동산 bu·dong·san
euro 유로 yu·ro
Europe 유럽 yu·rŏp
euthanasia 안락사 al·lak·sa
evening 저녁 jŏ·nyŏk
every a 모든 mo·dŭn
everyone 모두 mo·du
everything 전부 jŏn·bu
exactly 정확히 jŏng·hwa·k'i
example 예 yé
excellent 뛰어난 ddwi·ŏ·nan
excess baggage 초과 수하물 ch'o·gwa su·ha·mul
exchange n 교환 gyo·hwan
exchange v 교환해요 (교환하~) gyo·hwan·hae·yo (gyo·hwan·ha~)
exchange rate 환율 hwa·nyul
excluded 제외된 je·oé·doén
exhaust (car) 매연 mae·yŏn
exhibition 전시회 jŏn·shi·hoé
exit n 출구 ch'ul·gu
expensive 비싼 biss·an
experience n 경험 gyŏng·hŏm
exploitation 이용 i·yong
express a 고속의 go·so·gé
express mail 빠른 우편 bba·rŭn u·p'yŏn
extension (visa) (비자) 연장 (bi·ja) yŏn·jang
eye 눈 nun
eye drops 안약 a·nyak

F

fabric 천 ch'ŏn
face n 얼굴 ŏl·gul
face cloth 세수 수건 se·su su·gŏn
factory 공장 gong·jang
factory worker 공장 직원 gong·jang ji·gwŏn
fall (autumn) n 가을 ga·ŭl
fall (down) v 떨어져요 (떨어지~) ddŏ·rŏ·jŏ·yo (ddŏ·rŏ·ji~)
family 가족 ga·jok
family name 성 sŏng
famous 유명한 yu·myŏng·han
fan (hand-held) 부채 bu·ch'ae
fan (machine) 선풍기 sŏn·p'ung·gi
fan (politics/sport) 팬 p'aen
fan belt 팬 벨트 p'aen·bel·t'ŭ
far adv 멀리 mŏl·li
fare n 요금 yo·gŭm
farm n 농장 nong·jang
farmer 농부 nong·bu
fashion n 패션 p'ae·shŏn
fat a 뚱뚱한 ddungt·tung·han
father 아버지 a·bŏ·ji

father-in-law (husband's father) 시아버지 shi·a·bŏ·ji
father-in-law (wife's father) 장인어른 jang·i·nŏ·rŭn
faucet (tap) 수도꼭지 su·dok·kok·ji
(someone's) fault n 잘못 jal·mot
faulty 불량인 bul·lyang·in
feed 먹여요 (먹이~) mŏ·gyŏ·yo (mŏ·gi~)
feel (touch) v 느껴요 (느끼~) nŭk·kyŏ·yo (nŭk·ki~)
feelings 감정 gam·jŏng
female a 여성의 yŏ·sŏng·é
fence n 담장 dam·jang
ferry n 페리 p'e·ri
festival 축제 ch'uk·jé
fever 열 yŏl
few 몇 개 myŏk·kae
fiancé 약혼자 ya·k'on·ja
fiancée 약혼녀 ya·k'on·nyŏ
fiction 소설 so·sŏl
fig 무화과 mu·hwa·gwa
fight v 싸워요 (싸우~) ssa·wŏ·yo (ssa·u~)
fill 채워요 (채우~) ch'ae·wŏ·yo (ch'ae·u~)
film (cinema) 영화 yŏng·hwa
filtered 걸러진 gŏl·lŏ·jin
find 찾아요 (찾~) ch'a·ja·yo (ch'aj~)
fine n 벌금 bŏl·gŭm
fine a 좋은 jo·ŭn
finger 손가락 son·ga·rak
finish n 끝 ggŭt
finish v 마쳐요 (마치~) ma·chŏ·yo (ma·ch'i~)
fire n 불 bul
firewood 장작 jang·jak
first a 첫 ch'ŏt
first adv 처음으로 ch'ŏ·ŭ·mŭ·ro
first-aid kit 구급상자 gu·gŭp·sang·ja
first class 퍼스트 클래스 p'ŏ·sŭ·t'ŭ k'ŭl·lae·sŭ
first name 이름 i·rŭm
fish (animal) 물고기 mul·go·gi
fish (food) 생선 saeng·sŏn
fishing 낚시 nakk·shi
fishmonger 생선 장수 saeng·sŏn jang·su
fish shop 생선 가게 saeng·sŏn ga·gé
flag n 깃발 gip·bal
flash (camera) 플래시 p'ŭl·lae·shi
flashlight 손전등 son·jŏn·dŭng
flat (apartment) n 아파트 a·p'a·t'ŭ
flat a 평평한 p'yŏng·p'yŏng·han
flea 벼룩 byŏ·ruk
flea market 벼룩시장 byŏ·ruk·shi·jang
flight 비행 bi·haeng
flood n 홍수 hong·su
floor n 바닥 ba·dak
floor (storey) 층 ch'ŭng
florist 꽃집 ggot·jip
flour 밀가루 mil·ga·ru
flower n 꽃 ggot
flu 독감 dok·kam
fly n 파리 p'a·ri
fly v 날아요 (날~) na·ra·yo (nal~)
foggy 안개 낀 an·gaek·kin
folk music 민속 음악 min·sok ŭ·mak
folk village 민속촌 min·sok·ch'on
follow 따라가요 (따라가~) dda·ra·ga·yo (dda·ra·ga~)
food 음식 ŭm·shik
food court 푸드 코트 p'u·dŭ k'o·t'ŭ
food poisoning 식중독 shik·jung·dok
food shop 슈퍼 shu·p'ŏ
foot (body) 발 bal
football (soccer) 축구 ch'uk·ku
footpath 보도 bo·do
foreign 외국의 oé·gu·gé
foreigner 외국인 oé·gu·gin
forest 숲 sup
forever 영원히 yŏng·wŏn·hi
forget 잊어요 (잊~) i·jŏ·yo (ij~)
forgive 용서해요 (용서하~) yong·sŏ·hae·yo (yong·sŏ·ha~)
fork 포크 p'o·k'ŭ
fortnight 이 주일 i·ju·il
fortress 요새 yo·sae
fortune-teller 점쟁이 jŏm·jaeng·i
fortune-telling 점 jŏm
foul (football/soccer) n 파울 p'a·ul
fountain 분수 bun·su

fragile 깨지기 쉬운 ggae·ji·gi shi·un
France 프랑스 p'ŭ·rang·sŭ
free (available) a 한가한 han·ga·han
free (gratis) a 공짜의 gong·jja·é
free (not bound) a 자유로운 ja·yu·ro·un
free (of charge) 서비스 sŏ·bi·sŭ
freeze 얼려요 (얼리~) ŏl·lyŏ·yo (ŏl·li~)
fresh 신선한 shin·sŏn·han
fridge 냉장고 naeng·jang·go
fried 튀긴 t'wi·gin
friend 친구 ch'in·gu
from ... prep ...에서 ...·e·sŏ
frost 서리 sŏ·ri
frozen food 냉동 식품 naeng·dong shik·p'um
fruit 과일 gwa·il
fruit juice 과일 주스 gwa·il jus·sŭ
fry 튀겨요 (튀기~) t'wi·gyŏ·yo (t'wi·gi~)
frying pan 프라이팬 p'ŭ·ra·i·p'aen
full 가득 찬 ga·dŭk·ch'an
full-time 전 시간의 jŏn·shi·ga·né
fun a 재미있는 jae·mi·in·nŭn
funeral 장례식 jang·nye·shik
funny 우스운 u·sŭ·un
furniture 가구 ga·gu
future n 미래 mi·rae

G

game (sport) 경기 gyŏng·gi
garage 차고 ch'a·go
garbage 쓰레기 ssŭ·re·gi
garbage can 쓰레기통 ssŭ·re·gi·t'ong
garden n 정원 jŏng·wŏn
gardener 정원사 jŏng·wŏn·sa
gardening 정원 가꾸기 jŏng·wŏn gak·ku·gi
garlic 마늘 ma·nŭl
gas (for cooking) 가스 ga·sŭ
gas (petrol) 휘발유 hwi·bal·yu
gas cartridge 부탄 가스통 bu·t'an·ga·sŭ·t'ong
gastroenteritis 위장염 wi·jang·nyŏm
gate (airport, etc) 문 mun
gauze 거즈 gŏ·jŭ
gay (homosexual) n 동성애자 dong·sŏng·ae·ja
gearbox 변속장치 byŏn·sok jang·ch'i
Germany 독일 do·gil
get 얻어요 (얻~) ŏ·dŏ·yo (ŏd~)
get off (bus, train) 내려요 (내리~) nae·ryŏ·yo (nae·ri~)
gift 선물 sŏn·mul
gig 공연장 gyong·yŏn·jang
ginger 생강 saeng·gang
gingko nut 은행 ŭn·haeng
ginseng 인삼 in·sam
girl 여자 아이 yŏ·ja·a·i
girlfriend 여자 친구 yŏ·ja ch'in·gu
give 줘요 (주~) jwŏ·yo (ju~)
given name 이름 i·rŭm
glandular fever 선열 sŏ·nyŏl
glass (drinking) 잔 jan
glasses (spectacles) 안경 an·gyŏng
gloves (clothing) 장갑 jang·gap
gloves (latex) 고무 장갑 go·mu jang·gap
glue n 풀 p'ul
go 가요 (가~) ga·yo (ga~)
goal (sport) 골 gol
goalkeeper 골키퍼 gol·k'i·pŏ
goat 염소 yŏm·so
god (general) 신 shin
goggles (skiing) 스키 고글 sŭ·k'i·go·gŭl
goggles (swimming) 물안경 mu·ran·gyŏng
gold n 금 gŭm
golf 골프 gol·p'ŭ
golf ball 골프공 gol·p'ŭ·gong
golf course 골프장 gol·p'ŭ·jang
good 좋은 jo·ŭn
go out 나가요 (나가~) na·ga·yo (na·ga~)
gorge 골짜기 gol·jja·gi
go shopping 쇼핑해요 (쇼핑하~) sho·p'ing·hae·yo (sho·p'ing·ha~)
government 정부 jŏng·bu
gram 그램 gŭ·raem
granddaughter 손녀 son·nyŏ
grandfather 할아버지 ha·ra·bŏ·ji

grandmother 할머니 hal·mŏ·ni
grandson 손자 son·ja
grass (lawn) 잔디 jan·di
grateful 감사해요 (감사하~) gam·sa·hae·yo (gam·sa·ha~)
grave n 무덤 mu·dŏm
great (fantastic) 좋은 jo·ŭn
green 초록색 ch'o·rok·saek
greengrocer 청과상 chŏng·gwa·sang
grey 회색의 hoé·sae·gé
grilled 구운 gu·un
grocery 슈퍼 shu·p'ŏ
grow 자라요 (자라~) ja·ra·yo (ja·ra~)
guarantee n 보증 bo·jŭng
guess v 추측해요 (추측하~) ch'u·chŭ·k'ae·yo (ch'u·chŭ·k'a~)
guesthouse 민박집 min·bak·jip
guide (audio) 음성 안내 ŭm·sŏng an·nae
guide (person) 가이드 ga·i·dŭ
guidebook 가이드 책자 ga·i·dŭ ch'aek·ja
guide dog 맹인 안내견 maeng·in an·nae·gyŏn
guided tour 가이드 투어 ga·i·dŭ t'u·ŏ
guilt 유죄 yu·joé
guitar 기타 gi·t'a
gum (chewing) 껌 ggŏm
gum (of mouth) 잇몸 in·mom
gun 총 ch'ong
gym (gymnasium) 체육관 ch'e·yuk·kwan
gym (health club) 헬스장 hel·sŭ·jang
gymnastics 체조 ch'e·jo
gynaecologist 산부인과 san·bu·in·gwa

H

hair 머리 mŏ·ri
hairbrush 빗 bit
haircut 헤어 커트 he·ŏ·k'ŏ·t'ŭ
hairdressing salon 미용실 mi·yong·shil
halal a 할랄 hal·lal
half n 반 ban
hallucination 환각 hwan·gak
ham 햄 haem
hamburger 햄버거 haem·bŏ·gŏ
hammer n 망치 mang·ch'i
hammock 그물 침대 gŭ·mul ch'im·dae
hand 손 son
handbag 핸드백 haen·dŭ·baek
handball 핸드볼 haen·dŭ·bol
handicraft 수공예품 su·gong·ye·p'um
handkerchief 손수건 son·su·gŏn
handlebars 핸들 haen·dŭl
handmade 수제 su·jé
handsome 잘생긴 jal saeng·gin
happy 행복한 haeng·bo·k'an
harassment 희롱 hi·rong
harbour n 항구 hang·gu
hard (difficult) 어려운 ŏ·ryŏ·un
hard (not soft) 단단한 dan·dan·han
hardware store 철물점 ch'ŏl·mul·jŏm
hat 모자 mo·ja
have 가져요 (갖~) ga·jyŏ·yo (gaj~)
have a cold 감기 걸렸어요 (감기 걸리~) gam·gi gŏl·lyŏss·ŏ·yo (gam·gi gŏl·li~)
have fun 즐거워요 (즐겁~) jŭl·gŏ·wŏ·yo (jŭl·gŏp~)
hay fever 건초열 gŏn·ch'o·yŏl
hazelnut 헤이즐넛 he·i·jŭl·lŏt
he inf 그 gŭ
he pol 그분 gŭ·bun
head 머리 mŏ·ri
headache 두통 du·t'ong
headlights 헤드라이트 he·dŭ·ra·i·t'ŭ
health 건강 gŏn·gang
hear 들어요 (듣~) dŭ·rŏ·yo (dŭt~)
hearing aid 보청기 bo·ch'ŏng·gi
heart 심장 shim·jang
heart attack 심장 마비 shim·jang ma·bi
heart condition 심장 상태 shim·jang sang·t'ae
heat n 열 yŏl
heated 데운 de·un
heater 히터 hi·t'ŏ
heating 난방 nan·bang
heavy (weight) 무거운 mu·gŏ·un
helmet 헬멧 hel·met
help n 도움 do·um

H – I ENGLISH – KOREAN

help v 도와줘요 (도와주~) do·wa·jwŏ·yo (do·wa·ju-)
hepatitis 간염 ga·nyŏm
her (possessive) 그녀의 gŭ·nyŏ·é
herb 허브 hŏ·bŭ
here 여기 yŏ·gi
hermitage 암자 am·ja
herring 청어 ch'ŏng·ŏ
high (height) 높은 no·p'ŭn
highchair 어린이용 높은 의자 ŏ·ri·ni·yong no·p'ŭn ŭi·ja
high school 고등학교 go·dŭng·hak·kyo
high tide 만조 man·jo
highway 고속도로 go·sok·do·ro
hike v 등산해요 (등산하~) dŭng·san·hae·yo (dŭng·san·ha-)
hiking 등산 dŭng·san
hiking boots 등산화 dŭng·san·hwa
hiking route 등산로 dŭng·san·no
hill 언덕 ŏn·dŏk
hire v 고용해요 (고용하~) go·yong·hae·yo (go·yong·ha-)
his 그의 gŭ·é
historical 역사상의 yŏk·sa·sang·é
history 역사 yŏk·sa
HIV 에이즈 바이러스 e·i·jŭ ba·i·rŏ·sŭ
hockey 하키 ha·k'i
holiday n 휴일 hyu·il
home 집 jip
homeless people 노숙자 no·suk·ja
homemaker 가정주부 ga·jŏng·ju·bu
homesick 고향이 그리운 go·hyang·i gŭ·ri·un
homosexual n 동성애자 dong·sŏng·ae·ja
honey 꿀 ggul
honeymoon 신혼여행 shin·hon yŏ·haeng
horoscope 별자리 점 byŏl·cha·ri·jŏm
horse 말 mal
horse racing 경마 byŏng·ma
horse riding 승마 sŭng·ma
hospital 병원 byŏng·won
hospitality 환대 hwan·dae
hostel 호스텔 ho·sŭ·t'el
hot (to the touch) 뜨거운 ddŭ·gŏ·un
hot (weather) 더운 dŏ·un
hot dog 핫도그 hat·to·gŭ
hotel 호텔 ho·t'el
hot spring 온천 on·ch'ŏn
hot water 온수 on·su
hot water bottle 보온병 bo·on·byŏng
hour 시간 shi·gan
house n 집 jip
housework 집안일 ji·ban·nil
how 어떻게 ŏt·tŏ·k'é
how many 몇 개 myŏk·kae
hug n 포옹 p'o·ong
huge 거대한 gŏ·dae·han
human rights 인권 in·gwŏn
hungry 배고픈 bae·go·p'ŭn
hunting 사냥 sa·nyang
hurt v 아파요 (아프~) a·p'a·yo (a·p'ŭ-)
husband 남편 nam·p'yŏn

I

I inf/pol 나/ 저 na/jŏ
ice 얼음 ŏ·rŭm
ice axe 아이스바일 a·i·sŭ·ba·il
ice cream 아이스크림 a·i·sŭ·k'ŭ·rim
identification 신원 확인 shin·wŏn hwa·gin
identification card (ID) 신분증 shin·bun·jŭng
idiot n 바보 ba·bo
if 만약 ma·nyak
ill 아픈 a·p'ŭn
immigration 출입국 ch'u·rip·guk
important 중요한 jung·yo·han
impossible 불가능한 bul·ga·nŭng·han
in ... prep ... 안에 ... a·né
(be) in a hurry v 급해요 (급하~) gŭ·p'ae·yo (gŭ·p'a-)
included 포함된 p'o·ham·doén
income tax 소득세 so·dŭk·sé
independence 독립 dong·nip
India 인도 in·do
indicator 깜빡이 ggamp·pa·gi
indigestion 소화불량 so·hwa bul·lyang
indoor a 실내의 shil·lae·é
industry 산업 sa·nŏp

infection 감염 ga·myŏm
inflammation 염증 yŏm·jŭng
influenza 독감 dok·kam
information 안내 an·nae
in front of ... prep ... 앞에 ... a·p'é
ingredient 재료 jae·ryo
inhaler (for asthma) (천식환자용) 흡입기 (chŏn·shik hwan·ja·yong) hŭ·bip·gi
inject 주사해요 (주사하~) ju·sa·hae·yo (ju·sa·ha~)
injection 주사 ju·sa
injured 다친 da·ch'in
injury 부상 bu·sang
inner tube 튜브 t'yu·bŭ
innocent a 순진한 sun·jin·han
insect 벌레 bŏl·lé
insect repellent 방충제 bang·ch'ung·jé
inside adv 안에 a·né
instructor 강사 gang·sa
insurance 보험 bo·hŏm
interesting 흥미로운 hŭng·mi·ro·un
intermission 휴식 시간 hyu·shik shi·gan
international 국제적인 guk·je·jŏ·gin
internet 인터넷 in·t'ŏ·net
interpreter 통역사 t'ong·yŏk·sa
interview n 면접 myŏn·jŏp
invite 초대해요 (초대하~) ch'o·dae·hae·yo (ch'o·dae·ha~)
Ireland 아일랜드 a·il·laen·dŭ
iron (for clothes) n 다리미질 da·ri·mi·jil
island 섬 sŏm
Israel 이스라엘 i·sŭ·ra·el
it 그것 gŭ·gŏt
Italy 이탈리아 i·t'al·li·a
itchy 가려운 ga·ryŏ·un
itinerary 여행 일정 yŏ·haeng il·jŏng
IUD 자궁내 피임장치 ja·gung·nae p'i·im·jang·ch'i

J

jacket 재킷 jae·k'it
jail n 교도소 gyo·do·so
jam n 잼 jaem
Japan 일본 il·bon
jar 항아리 hang·a·ri
jaw 턱 t'ŏk
jealous 질투하는 jil·t'u·ha·nŭn
jeans 청바지 ch'ŏng·ba·ji
jeep 지프차 ji·p'ŭ·ch'a
jet lag 시차증 shi·ch'a·jŭng
jewellery 보석 bo·sŏk
job 일 il
joke n 농담 nong·dam
journalist 기자 gi·ja
journey n 여행 yŏ·haeng
judge n 판사 p'an·sa
juice n 주스 jus·sŭ
jump v 뛰어올라요 (뛰어오르~) ddwi·ŏ·ol·la·yo (ddwi·ŏ·o·rŭ~)
jumper (sweater) 스웨터 sŭ·we·t'ŏ

K

karaoke 노래방 no·rae·bang
ketchup 케첩 k'e·ch'ŏp
key (door, etc) 열쇠 yŏl·soé
keyboard 키보드 k'i·bo·dŭ
kick v 차요 (차~) ch'a·yo (ch'a~)
kidney 신장 shin·jang
kill 죽여요 (죽이~) ju·gyŏ·yo (ju·gi~)
kilogram 킬로그램 k'il·lo·gŭ·raem
kilometre 킬로미터 k'il·lo·mi·t'ŏ
kind (nice) 친절한 ch'in·jŏl·han
kindergarten 유치원 yu·ch'i·wŏn
king 왕 wang
kiosk (newstand) 신문 가판대 shin·mun ga·p'an·dae
kiss n 키스 k'i·sŭ
kiss v 키스해요 (키스하~) k'i·sŭ·hae·yo (k'i·sŭ·ha~)
kitchen 주방 ju·bang
knee 무릎 mu·rŭp
knife n 칼 k'al
know 알아요 (알~) a·ra·yo (al~)
Korea 한국 han·guk
Korean a 한국의 han·gu·gé
Korean (language) n 한국어 han·gu·gŏ

L

labourer 노동자 no·dong·ja
lace (fabric) n 레이스 re·i·sŭ
lacquerware 칠기 ch'il·gi
lake 호수 ho·su
lamb (meat) 양고기 yang·go·gi
land n 땅 ddang
landlord 집주인 jip·ju·in
language 언어 ŏ·nŏ
laptop 노트북 no·t'ŭ·buk
large 거대한 gŏ·dae·han
last (final) 마지막 ma·ji·mak
last (previous) 지난 ji·nan
late adv 늦게 nŭk·ké
later 나중에 na·jung·é
laugh v 웃어요 (웃~) u·sŏ·yo (us~)
launderette 빨래방 bbal·lae·bang
laundry (clothes) 빨래 bbal·lae
laundry (room) 세탁실 se·t'ak·shil
law (legislation) 법 bŏp
law (profession/study) 법학 bŏ·p'ak
lawyer 변호사 byŏn·ho·sa
laxative 배변촉진제 bae·byŏn·ch'ok·jin·jé
lazy 게으른 gé·ŭ·rŭn
leader 지도자 ji·do·ja
leaf n 잎 ip
learn 배워요 (배우~) bae·wŏ·yo (bae·u~)
leather n 가죽 ga·juk
lecturer 강사 gang·sa
ledge 선반 sŏn·ban
leeks 파 p'a
left (direction) 왼쪽 oén·jjok
left luggage 분실 수하물 bun·shil su·ha·mul
left-luggage office 분실 수하물 보관소 bun·shil su·ha·mul bo·gwan·so
left-wing 좌익 jwa·ik
leg (body) 다리 da·ri
legal 합법의 hap·pŏ·bé
legislation 법률 제정 bŏm·nyul je·jŏng
legume 콩류 k'ong·nyu
lemon 레몬 re·mon
lemonade 레모네이드 re·mo·ne·i·dŭ
lens (camera) 렌즈 ren·jŭ
lentil 렌즈콩 ren·jŭ·k'ong
lesbian n 레즈비언 re·jŭ·bi·ŏn
less 보다 적은 bo·da jŏ·gŭn
letter (mail) 편지 p'yŏn·ji
lettuce 양상추 yang·sang·ch'u
liar 거짓말쟁이 gŏ·jin·mal·jaeng·i
library 도서관 do·sŏ·gwan
lice 이 i
licence n 면허 myŏn·hŏ
licence plate number 자동차번호 ja·dong·ch'a bŏn·ho
lie (not stand) 누워요 (눕~) nu·wŏ·yo (nup~)
lie (not tell the truth) v 거짓말해요 (거짓말하~) gŏ·jin·mal·hae·yo (gŏ·jin·mal·ha~)
life 인생 in·saeng
life jacket 구명 조끼 gu·myŏng·jok·ki
lifeboat 구명선 gu·myŏng·sŏn
lift (elevator) 엘리베이터 el·li·be·i·t'ŏ
light (brightness) n 빛 bit
light (colour) 밝은 bal·gŭn
light (weight) 가벼운 ga·byŏ·un
light bulb 전구 jŏn·gu
lighthouse 등대 dŭng·dae
lighter (cigarette) 라이터 ra·i·t'ŏ
light meter 조명 측정기 jo·myŏng ch'ŭk·jŏng·gi
like v 좋아해요 (좋아하~) jo·a·hae·yo (jo·a·ha~)
lime 라임 ra·im
linen (material) 리넨 ri·nen
linen (sheets) 리넨천 ri·nen·ch'ŏn
linguist 언어학자 ŏ·nŏ·hak·ja
lip balm 립밤 rip·pam
lips 입술 ip·sul
lipstick 립스틱 rip·sŭ·t'ik
liquor store 주류 판매점 ju·ryu p'an·mae·jŏm
listen 들어요 (듣~) dŭ·rŏ·yo (dŭt~)
little (quantity) n 조금 jo·gŭm
little (size) a 작은 ja·gŭn
live v 살아요 (살~) sa·ra·yo (sal~)
liver 간 gan
lizard 도마뱀 do·ma·baem
local a 지방의 ji·bang·é

location 위치 wi·ch'i
lock n 자물쇠 ja·mul·soé
lock v 잠궈요 (잠그~) jam·gwŏ·yo (jam·gŭ~)
locked 잠긴 jam·gin
lollies 막대 사탕 mak·tae sa·t'ang
long 긴 gin
look v 봐요 (보~) bwa·yo (bo~)
look after 돌봐요 (돌보~) dol·bwa·yo (dol·bo~)
look for 찾아요 (찾~) ch'a·ja·yo (ch'aj~)
lookout 전망대 jŏn·mang·dae
loose change 푼돈 p'un·don
lose 잃어버렸어요 (잃어버리~) i·rŏ·bŏ·ryŏss·ŏ·yo (i·rŏ·bŏ·ri~)
lost 잃어버린 i·rŏ·bŏ·rin
lost-property office 분실물 센터 bun·shil·mul sen·t'ŏ
loud 소리가 큰 so·ri·ga k'ŭn
lounge n 휴게실 hyu·ge·shil
love n 사랑 sa·rang
love v 사랑해요 (사랑하~) sa·rang·hae·yo (sa·rang·ha~)
lover 애인 ae·in
low 낮은 na·jŭn
low tide 간조 gan·jo
lubricant 윤활제 yun·hwal·jé
luck 행운 haeng·un
lucky 운 좋은 un jo·ŭn
luggage 짐/수하물 jim/su·ha·mul
luggage locker 짐 보관함 jim bo·gwan·ham
luggage tag 수하물 꼬리표 su·ha·mul ggo·ri·p'yo
lump 혹 hok
Lunar New Year 설날 sŏl·lal
lunch 점심 jŏm·shim
lung 폐 p'yé
luxury 사치 sa·ch'i

M

machine 기계 gi·gyé
magazine 잡지 jap·ji
mail (letters) n 편지 p'yŏn·ji
mail (postal system) n 우편 u·p'yŏn
mail v 부쳐요 (부치~) bu·ch'ŏ·yo (bu·ch'i~)
mailbox 우체통 u·ch'e·t'ong
main a 주된 ju·doén
main road 주요 도로 ju·yo·do·ro
make 만들어요 (만들~) man·dŭ·rŏ·yo (man·dŭl~)
make-up n 화장 hwa·jang
mall (shopping) 쇼핑몰 sho·p'ing·mol
mammography 유방조영술 yu·bang·jo·yŏng·sul
man n 남자 nam·ja
manager 매니저 mae·ni·jŏ
mandarin 귤 gyul
mango 망고 mang·go
manual worker 육체 노동자 yuk·ch'é no·dong·ja
many 많은 ma·nŭn
map (of country) 지도 ji·do
map (of neighbourhood) 약도 yak·do
margarine 마가린 ma·ga·rin
marital status 결혼 상태 gyŏl·hon sang·t'ae
market (outdoor) n 시장 shi·jang
marriage 결혼 gyŏl·hon
married 결혼한 gyŏl·hon·han
marry 결혼해요 (결혼하~) gyŏl·hon·hae·yo (gyŏl·hon·ha~)
martial arts 무술 mu·sul
mask n 탈 t'al
massage n 안마 an·ma
masseur/masseuse 안마사 an·ma·sa
mat (sleeping) 요 yo
match (sport) 경기 gyŏng·gi
matches (for lighting) 성냥 sŏng·nyang
mattress 매트리스 mae·t'ŭ·ri·sŭ
maybe 아마 a·ma
mayonnaise 마요네즈 ma·yo·ne·jŭ
mayor 시장 shi·jang
meal 식사 shik·sa
measles 홍역 hong·yŏk
meat 고기 go·gi
mechanic n 정비사 jŏng·bi·sa
media 미디어 mi·di·ŏ
medicine (medication) 약 yak

medicine (profession/study) 의학 üi·hak
meditation 명상 myŏng·sang
meet 만나요 (만나~) man·na·yo (man·na~)
melon 멜론 mel·lon
member 회원 hoé·wŏn
memorial n 기념물 gi·nyŏm·mul
memory card/stick 메모리 카드/스틱 me·mo·ri k'a·dŭ/sŭ·t'ik
menstruation 생리 saeng·ni
menu 메뉴 me·nyu
message 메시지 me·shi·ji
metal 금속 gŭm·sok
metre 미터 mi·t'ŏ
metro (train) 지하철 ji·ha·ch'ŏl
metro station 지하철역 ji·ha·ch'ŏl·yŏk
microwave oven 전자레인지 jŏn·ja·re·in·ji
midday 정오 jŏng·o
midnight 자정 ja·jŏng
migraine 편두통 p'yŏn·du·t'ong
military n 군대 gun·dae
military police 헌병 hŏn·byŏng
military service 군복무 gun·bong·mu
milk 우유 u·yu
millimetre 밀리미터 mil·li·mi·t'ŏ
mind n 마음 ma·ŭm
mineral water 생수 saeng·su
minute 분 bun
mirror n 거울 gŏ·ul
miscarriage 유산 yu·san
miss (feel absence of) 그리워해요 (그리워하~) gŭ·ri·wŏ·hae·yo (gŭ·ri·wŏ·ha~)
miss (not catch train, etc) 놓쳐요 (놓치~) no·ch'yŏ·yo (no·ch'i~)
mistake n 실수 shil·su
mix v 섞어요 (섞~) sŏk·kŏ·yo (sŏkk~)
mobile phone 휴대폰 hyu·dae·p'on
modem 모뎀 mo·dem
modern 현대의 hyŏn·dae·é
moisturiser 보습제 bo·sŭp·jé
monarchy 군주제 gun·ju·jé
monastery 수도원 su·do·wŏn
money 돈 don
Mongolia 몽골 mong·gol
monk (Buddhist) 스님 sŭ·nim
monk (Catholic) 수사 su·sa
monkey 원숭이 wŏn·sung·i
monsoon 장마 jang·ma
month 달 dal
monument 기념비 gi·nyŏm·bi
moon 달 dal
more 더 많은 dŏ·ma·nŭn
morning 아침 a·ch'im
morning sickness 입덧 ip·dŏt
mosque 이슬람 사원 i·sŭl·lam·sa·wŏn
mosquito 모기 mo·gi
mosquito coil 모기향 mo·gi·hyang
mosquito net 모기장 mo·gi·jang
motel 모텔/여관 mo·t'el/yŏ·gwan
mother 어머니 ŏ·mŏ·ni
mother-in-law (husband's mother) 시어머니 shi·ŏ·mŏ·ni
mother-in-law (wife's mother) 장모님 jang·mo·nim
motorbike 오토바이 o·to·ba·i
motorboat 모터보트 mo·t'ŏ·bo·t'ŭ
motorway (expressway) 고속도로 go·sok·do·ro
mountain 산 san
mountain bike 산악자전거 sa·nak ja·jŏn·gŏ
mountaineering 등산 dŭng·san
mountain pass 산길 san·gil
mountain path 등산로 dŭng·san·no
mountain range 산맥 san·maek
mouse 쥐 jwi
mouth 입 ip
movie 영화 yŏng·hwa
mud 진흙 jin·hŭk
mum 엄마 ŏm·ma
mumps 이하선염 i·ha·sŏ·nyŏm
mural 벽화 byŏ·k'wa
murder n 살인 sa·rin
murder v 살인해요 (살인하~) sa·rin·hae·yo (sa·rin·ha~)
muscle 근육 gŭ·nyuk
museum (art) 미술관 mi·sul·gwan
museum (other) 박물관 bang·mul·gwan

mushroom 버섯 bŏ·sŏt
music 음악 ŭ·mak
musician 음악가 ŭ·mak·ka
music shop 음반 매장 ŭm·ban mae·jang
mussel 홍합 hong·hap
mute a 무언의 mu·ŏn·é
mutton 양고기 yang·go·gi
my inf/pol 나의/저의 na·é/jŏ·é

N

nail clippers 손톱깎이 son·t'op·kkak·ki
(first) name n inf 이름 i·rŭm
(full) name n pol 성명 sŏng·myŏng
napkin 냅킨 naep·k'in
nappy 기저귀 gi·jŏ·gwi
nappy rash 기저귀 발진 gi·jo·gwi bal·jin
nationality (citizenship) 국적 guk·jŏk
nationality (ethnicity) 민족 min·jok
national park 국립 공원 gung·nip·gong·won
nature 자연 ja·yŏn
nature reserve 자연 보호 지역 ja·yŏn bo·ho ji·yŏk
nausea 메스꺼움 me·sŭk·kŏ·um
near ... prep ... 가까이 ... gak·ka·i
nearest 제일 가까운 je·il gak·ka·un
necessary 필요한 p'i·ryo·han
neck 목 mok
necklace 목걸이 mok·kŏ·ri
nectarine 천도 복숭아 ch'ŏn·do bok·sung·a
need v 필요해요 (필요하~) p'i·ryo·hae·yo (p'i·ryo·ha~)
needle (sewing) 바늘 ba·nŭl
needle (syringe) 주사바늘 ju·sa·ba·nŭl
negative a 부정적인 bu·jŏng·jŏ·gin
negatives (photos) 네거티브 ne·gŏ·t'i·bŭ
neighbourhood 동네 dong·né
neither adv 어느 것도 아닌 ŏ·nŭ·gŏt·to a·nin
net 그물 gŭ·mul
Netherlands 네덜란드 ne·dŏl·lan·dŭ
network (phone) 통신사 t'ong·shin·sa
new 새로운 sae·ro·un
news 뉴스 nyu·sŭ
newsagency 통신사 t'ong·shin·sa
newspaper 신문 shin·mun
newsstand 신문가판대 shin·mun·ga·p'an·dae
New Zealand 뉴질랜드 nyu·jil·laen·dŭ
next (following) 다음 da·ŭm
next time 다음에 da·ŭm·é
next to ... ... 다음에 ... da·ŭ·mé
nice 좋은 jo·ŭn
nickname 별명 byŏl·myŏng
night 밤 bam
no 아니요 a·ni·yo
noisy 시끄러운 shik·kŭ·rŏ·un
nonsmoking area 금연 구역 gŭ·myŏn gu·yŏk
noodles 국수 guk·su
noon 정오 jŏng·o
north n 북쪽 buk·jjok
North Korea 북한 bu·k'an
nose 코 k'o
not 안 an
notebook 공책 gong·ch'aek
now 지금 ji·gŭm
nuclear energy 핵 에너지 hae·ge·nŏ·ji
nuclear testing 핵 실험 haek·shil·hŏm
nuclear waste 핵 폐기물 haek·p'ye·gi·mul
number n 숫자 sut·cha
numberplate 번호판 bŏn·ho·p'an
nun (Buddhist) 여승 yŏ·sŭng
nun (Catholic) 수녀 su·nyŏ
nurse n 간호사 gan·ho·sa
nut (food) 견과류 gyŏn·gwa·ryu

O

oats 귀리 gwi·ri
ocean 바다 ba·da
octopus 낙지 nak·ji
off (power) 꺼짐 ggŏ·jim
off (spoilt) 상한 sang·han
offence 위반 wi·ban
office 사무실 sa·mu·shil

office worker 회사원 hoé·sa·wŏn
often 자주 ja·ju
oil (cooking) 기름 gi·rŭm
oil (car) 휘발유 hwi·bal·yu
okay 괜찮아요 (괜찮~) gwaen·cha·na·yo (gwaen·chan)
old (people) 늙은 nŭl·gŭn
old (things) 오래된 o·rae·doén
olive 올리브 ol·li·bŭ
olive oil 올리브유 ol·li·bŭ·yu
on prep 위에 wi·é
on (power) 켜짐 k'yŏ·jim
once 한 번 han·bŏn
one-way (road) 일방통행 il·bang t'ong·haeng
one-way ticket 편도 표 p'yŏn·do p'yo
onion 양파 yang·p'a
only ... ...만 ...·man
on time 정각에 jŏng·ga·gé
open (shop) a 영업 중 yŏng·ŏp·jung
open v 열어요 (열~) yŏ·rŏ·yo (yŏl~)
opening hours 영업 시간 yŏng·ŏp shi·gan
opera house 오페라 극장 o·p'e·ra gŭk·jang
operation (medical) 수술 su·sul
opinion 의견 ŭi·gyŏn
opposite prep 반대편에 ban·dae·p'yŏ·né
optometrist 안경사 an·gyŏng·sa
or 아니면 a·ni·myŏn
orange (fruit) n 오렌지 o·ren·ji
orange (colour) a 주황색 ju·hwang·saek
orchestra 오케스트라 o·k'e·sŭ·t'ŭ·ra
order n 주문 ju·mun
order v 주문해요 (주문하~) ju·mun·hae·yo (ju·mun·ha~)
ordinary 보통 bo·t'ong
organic food 유기농 식품 yu·gi·nong shik·p'um
original a 진짜의 jin·jja·é
other 다른 da·rŭn
our 우리의 u·ri·é
outdoor a 실외 shi·loé
out of order 고장 난 go·jang·nan
outside adv 밖에서 bak·ke·sŏ
ovarian cyst 난소 낭종 nan·so nang·jong
ovary 난소 nan·so
oven 오븐 o·bŭn
overcoat 외투 oé·t'u
overdose n 과량 투여 gwa·ryang t'u·yŏ
overnight adv 밤새 bam·sae
overseas n 해외 hae·oé
owe 빚져요 (빚지~) bit·chyŏ·yo (bit·chi~)
owner 주인 ju·in
ox 황소 hwang·so
oxygen 산소 san·so
oyster 굴 gul

P

pacemaker 심장 박동 조절 장치 shim·jang bak·dong jo·jŏl jang·ch'i
pacifier (dummy) 노리개 젖꼭지 no·ri·gae jŏk·kok·ji
package n 소포 so·p'o
packet (general) 꾸러미 ggu·rŏ·mi
padlock 자물쇠 ja·mul·soé
page n 페이지 p'e·i·ji
pagoda 탑 t'ap
pain n 고통 go·t'ong
painful 괴로운 goé·ro·un
painkiller 진통제 jin·t'ong·jé
painter (artist) 화가 hwa·ga
painting (a work) 그림 gŭ·rim
painting (the art) 회화 hoé·hwa
pair (couple) n 한 쌍 han·ssang
palace 궁 gung
pan 프라이팬 p'ŭ·ra·i·p'aen
pants (trousers) 바지 ba·ji
pantyhose 팬티스타킹 p'aen·t'i·sŭ·t'a·k'ing
panty liners 팬티라이너 p'aen·t'i·ra·i·nŏ
paper n 종이 jong·i
paper lanterns 연등 yŏn·dŭng
papers (documents) 서류 sŏ·ryu
paperwork 문서 업무 mun·sŏ ŏm·mu
paraplegic n 하반신 마비 환자 ha·ban·shin ma·bi hwan·ja

parcel n 소포 so·p'o
parents 부모님 bu·mo·nim
park n 공원 gong·wŏn
park (a car) v 주차해요 (주차하~) ju·ch'a·hae·yo (ju·ch'a·ha~)
parking structure 주차 빌딩 ju·ch'a bil·ding
parliament 국회 gu·k'oé
part (component) n 부분 bu·bun
part-time 시간제의 shi·gan·je·é
party (politics) 정당 jŏng·dang
pass (go by) 지나가요 (지나가~) ji·na·ga·yo (ji·na·ga~)
pass (kick/throw) v 차요 (차~) ch'a·yo (ch'a~)
passenger 승객 sŭng·gaek
passport 여권 yŏ·gwŏn
passport number 여권번호 yŏ·gwŏn·bŏn·ho
past n 과거 gwa·gŏ
path 길 gil
patient n 환자 hwan·ja
pay v 돈 내요 (돈 내~) don·nae·yo (don·nae~)
payment 지불 ji·bul
pea 완두콩 wan·du·k'ong
peace 평화 p'yŏng·hwa
peach 복숭아 bok·sung·a
peak (mountain) 봉우리 bong·u·ri
peanut 땅콩 ddang·k'ong
pear 배 bae
pedal n 페달 p'e·dal
pedestrian n 보행자 bo·haeng·ja
pedestrian crossing 건널목 gŏn·nŏl·mok
pedestrian overpass 육교 yuk·kyo
pedestrian underpass 지하도 ji·ha·do
pen (ballpoint) 볼펜 bol·p'en
pencil 연필 yŏn·p'il
pensioner 연금 생활자 yŏn·gŭm saeng·hwal·ja
people 사람들 sa·ram·dŭl
per (day) (하루)당 (ha·ru)·dang
per cent 퍼센트 p'ŏ·sen·t'ŭ
perfect a 완벽한 wan·byŏ·k'an
performance 공연 gong·yŏn
perfume n 향수 hyang·su
period pain 생리통 saeng·ni·t'ong
permission 허가 hŏ·ga
permit n 허가증 hŏ·ga·jŭng
person 사람 sa·ram
personality 성격 sŏng·gyŏk
petrol 휘발유 hwi·bal·yu
petrol station 주유소 ju·yu·so
pharmacist 약사 yak·sa
pharmacy 약국 yak·kuk
photo 사진 sa·jin
photograph v 사진 찍어요 (사진 찍~) sa·jin jji·gŏ·yo (sa·jin jjig~)
photographer 사진작가 sa·jin jak·ka
photography 사진술 sa·jin·sul
phrasebook 회화책 hoé·hwa·ch'aek
piano 피아노 p'i·a·no
pickled 절인 jŏ·rin
pickles 피클 p'i·k'ŭl
picnic n 소풍 so·p'ung
pie 파이 p'a·i
piece n 조각 jo·gak
pig 돼지 dwae·ji
pilgrimage 성지 순례 sŏng·ji sul·lyé
(the) pill 경구 피임약 gyŏng·gu p'i·im·nyak
pill (medicine) 알약 al·lyak
pillow 베개 be·gae
pillowcase 베갯잇 be·gaen·nit
pineapple 파인애플 p'a·i·nae·p'ŭl
pink 분홍색 bun·hong·saek
pistachio 피스타치오 p'i·sŭ·t'a·ch'i·o
place n 장소 jang·so
place of birth 출생지 ch'ul·saeng·ji
plane 비행기 bi·haeng·gi
planet 행성 haeng·sŏng
plant n 식물 shing·mul
plastic n 플라스틱 p'ŭl·la·sŭ·t'ik
plate 접시 jŏp·shi
plateau 고원 go·wŏn
platform 승강장 sŭng·gang·jang
play (theatre) n 연극 yŏn·gŭk
play (game) 해요 (하~) hae·yo (ha~)
play (instrument) 연주해요 (연주하~) yŏn·ju·hae·yo (yŏn·ju·ha~)
plug (bath) n 마개 ma·gae

plug (electricity) n 플러그 p'ŭl·lŏ·gŭ
plum 자두 ja·du
plumber 배관공 bae·gwan·gong
poaching (illegal hunting) 밀렵 mil·lyŏp
pocket n 주머니 ju·mŏ·ni
pocket knife 주머니칼 ju·mŏ·ni·k'al
poetry 시 shi
point v 가리켜요 (가리키~) ga·ri·k'yŏ·yo (ga·ri·k'i~)
poisonous 유독한 yu·do·k'an
police 경찰 gyŏng·ch'al
police officer 경찰관 gyŏng·ch'al·gwan
police station 경찰서 gyŏng·ch'al·sŏ
policy 정책 jŏng·ch'aek
politician 정치인 jŏng·ch'i·in
politics 정치 jŏng·ch'i
pollen 꽃가루 ggok·ka·ru
pollution 오염 o·yŏm
pool (game) 포켓볼 p'o·k'ep·pol
pool (swimming) 수영장 su·yŏng·jang
poor (wealth) 가난한 ga·nan·han
popular 인기 좋은 in·gi jo·ŭn
pork 돼지고기 dwae·ji·go·gi
port (river/sea) 항구 hang·gu
positive a 긍정적인 gŭng·jŏng·jŏ·gin
possible 가능한 ga·nŭng·han
post (letter) v 편지 부쳐요 (편지 부치~) p'yŏn·ji bu·ch'yŏ·yo (p'yŏn·ji bu·ch'i~)
postcard 엽서 yŏp·sŏ
postcode 우편번호 u·p'yŏn·bŏn·ho
poster 포스터 p'o·sŭ·t'ŏ
post office 우체국 u·ch'e·guk
pot (ceramics) 항아리 hang·a·ri
pot (cooking) 냄비 naem·bi
potato 감자 gam·ja
pottery 도자기 do·ja·gi
pound 파운드 p'a·un·dŭ
poverty 가난 ga·nan
powder n 가루 ga·ru
powdered formula 가루형 이유식 ga·ru·hyŏng i·yu·shik
powdered milk 분유 bu·nyu
power n 힘 him
prawn 대하 dae·ha
prayer 기도 gi·do
prayer book 기도서 gi·do·sŏ
prefer 더 좋아해요 (더 좋아하~) dŏ·jo·a·hae·yo (dŏ·jo·a·ha~)
pregnancy test kit 임신 진단 키트 im·shin jin·dan k'i·t'ŭ
pregnant 임신 중인 im·shin jung·in
premenstrual tension 생리전 증후군 saeng·ni·jŏn jŭng·hu·gun
prepare 준비해요 (준비하~) jun·bi·hae·yo (jun·bi·ha~)
prescription 처방전 ch'ŏ·bang·jŏn
present (gift) n 선물 sŏn·mul
present (time) n 현재 hyŏn·jae
president (company) 사장 sa·jang
president (nation) 대통령 dae·t'ong·nyŏng
pressure (tyre) n 공기압 gong·gi·ap
pretty 예쁜 yep·pŭn
prevent 막아요 (막~) ma·ga·yo (mag~)
price n 가격 ga·gyŏk
priest (Buddhist) 스님 sŭ·nim
priest (Catholic) 신부님 shin·bu·nim
prime minister 수상 su·sang
printer (computer) 프린터 p'ŭ·rin·t'ŏ
prison 교도소 gyo·do·so
prisoner 죄수 joé·su
private 사적인 sa·jŏ·gin
produce v 생산해요 (생산하~) saeng·san·hae·yo (saeng·san·ha~)
profession 직업 ji·gŏp
professor 교수 gyo·su
profit n 이윤 i·yun
projector 프로젝터 p'ŭ·ro·jek·t'ŏ
promise v 약속해요 (약속하~) yak·so·k'ae·yo (yak·so·k'a~)
prostitute n 매춘부 mae·ch'un·bu
protect 보호해요 (보호하~) bo·ho·hae·yo (bo·ho·ha~)
protest n 시위 shi·wi
protest v 항의해요 (항의하~) hang·i·hae·yo (hang·i·ha~)
province 도 do
provisions 식량 shing·nyang
pub 맥주집 maek·ju·jip

public toilet 공중 화장실 gong·jung hwa·jang·shil
pull v 당겨요 (당기~) dang·gyŏ·yo (dang·gi~)
pump n 펌프 p'ŏm·p'ŭ
pumpkin 늙은 호박 nŭl·gŭn ho·bak
puncture n 펑크 p'ŏng·k'u
pure 순수한 sun·su·han
purple 보라색 bo·ra·saek
purse 핸드백 haen·dŭ·baek
push v 밀어요 (밀~) mi·rŏ·yo (mil~)
put 놓아요 (놓~) no·a·yo (no~)
Pyongyang 평양 p'yŏng·yang

Q

quadriplegic n 사지 마비 환자 sa·ji ma·bi hwan·ja
qualifications 자격 ja·gyŏk
quality n 질 jil
quarantine 검역 gŏ·myŏk
quarrel n 말싸움 mal·ssa·um
quarter n 사 분의 일 sa·bu·né·il
queen 여왕 yŏ·wang
question n 질문 jil·mun
queue n 줄 jul
quick 빠른 bba·rŭn
quiet 조용한 jo·yong·han
quilt 퀼트 k'wil·t'ŭ
quit 그만둬요 (그만두~) gŭ·man·dwŏ·yo (gu·man·du~)

R

rabbit 토끼 t'ok·ki
race (sport) n 경주 gyŏng·ju
racetrack 경마장 gyŏng·ma·jang
racing bike 경주용 자전거 gyŏng·ju·yong ja·jŏn·gŏ
racism 인종 차별 주의 in·jong ch'a·byŏl·ju·i
racquet 라켓 ra·k'et
radiator 라디에이터 ra·di·e·i·t'ŏ
radio n 라디오 ra·di·o
radish 무 mu
railway 철도 ch'ŏl·do
railway station 기차역 gi·ch'a·yŏk
rain n 비 bi
raincoat 우비 u·bi
rainy season 장마 jang·ma
raisin 건포도 gŏn·p'o·do
rally (protest) n 집회 ji·p'oé
rape n 강간 gang·gan
rare (uncommon) 희귀한 hi·gwi·han
rash 발진 bal·jin
raspberry 라즈베리 ra·jŭ·be·ri
rat 쥐 jwi
raw 날 nal
razor 면도기 myŏn·do·gi
razor blade 면도날 myŏn·do·nal
read 읽어요 (읽~) il·gŏ·yo (ilg~)
reading 독서 dok·sŏ
ready a 준비된 jun·bi·doén
real estate agency 부동산 bu·dong·san
realistic 현실적인 hyŏn·shil·jŏ·gin
rear (location) a 뒤쪽의 dwi·jjo·gé
reason n 이유 i·yu
receipt n 영수증 yŏng·su·jŭng
receive 받아요 (받~) ba·da·yo (bad~)
recently 요즘 yo·jŭm
recommend 추천해요 (추천하~) ch'u·ch'ŏn·hae·yo (ch'u·ch'ŏn·ha~)
record v 기록해요 (기록하~) gi·ro·k'ae·yo (gi·ro·k'a~)
recording 기록 gi·rok
recycle 재활용해요 (재활용하~) jae·hwa·ryong·hae·yo (jae·hwa·ryong·ha~)
red 빨간 bbal·gan
referee n 심판 shim·p'an
reference n 참조 ch'am·jo
refill n 리필 ri·p'il
refrigerator 냉장고 naeng·jang·go
refugee 난민 nan·min
refund n 환불 hwan·bul
refuse 거절해요 (거절하~) gŏ·jŏl·hae·yo (gŏ·jŏl·ha~)
regional 지방의 ji·bang·é
registered mail 등기우편 dŭng·gi·u·p'yŏn
rehydration salts 수분 보충용 소금 su·bun bo·ch'ung·yong so·gŭm

relationship 관계 gwan·gyé
relax 긴장 풀어요 (긴장 풀~) gin·jang p'ŭ·rŏ·yo (kin·jang p'ul~)
relic 유물 yu·mul
religion 종교 jong·gyo
religious 종교적인 jong·gyo·jŏ·gin
remember 기억해요 (기억하~) gi·ŏ·k'ae·yo (gi·ŏ·k'a~)
remote a 먼 mŏn
remote control 리모컨 ri·mo·k'ŏn
rent n 집세 jip·sé
rent v 빌려요 (빌리~) bil·lyŏ·yo (bil·li~)
repair v 수리해요 (수리하~) su·ri·hae·yo (su·ri·ha~)
repeat v 반복해요 (반복하~) ban·bo·k'ae·yo (ban·bo·k'a~)
republic 공화국 gong·hwa·guk
Republic of Korea 대한민국 dae·han min·guk
reservation (booking) 예약 ye·yak
reserve v 예약해요 (예약하~) ye·ya·k'ae·yo (ye·ya·k'a~)
resort n 휴양지 hyu·yang·ji
rest v 쉬어요 (쉬~) shi·ŏ·yo (shi~)
restaurant 식당 shik·dang
résumé (CV) 이력서 i·ryŏk·sŏ
retired 은퇴한 ŭn·t'oe·han
return (give back) v 돌려줘요 (돌려주~) dol·lyŏ·jwŏ·yo (dol·lyŏ·ju~)
return (go back) v 돌아가요 (돌아가~) do·ra·ga·yo (do·ra·ga~)
return ticket 왕복 표 wang·bok p'yo
review n 비평 bi·p'yŏng
rhythm 박자 bak·ja
rib (body) 갈비뼈 gal·bip·pyŏ
ribs (food) 갈비 gal·bi
rice (as grain) 쌀 ssal
rice (cooked) 밥 bap
rich (wealthy) 부유한 bu·yu·han
ride n 탈 것 t'al·gŏt
ride (bike, horse) v 타요 (타~) t'a·yo (t'a~)
right (correct) 옳은 o·rŭn
right (direction) 오른쪽 o·rŭn·jjok
right-wing 우익 u·ik
ring (jewellery) n 반지 ban·ji
ring (phone) v 전화해요 (전화하~) jŏn·hwa·hae·yo (jŏn·hwa·ha~)
rip-off n 바가지 ba·ga·ji
risk n 위험 wi·hŏm
river 강 gang
riverside n 강변 gang·byŏn
road 도로 do·ro
road map 도로지도 do·ro·ji·do
roasted 구운 gu·un
rob 훔쳐요 (훔치~) hum·ch'yŏ·yo (hum·ch'i~)
rock n 바위 ba·wi
rock (music) 록 음악 ro·gŭ·mak
rock climbing 암벽 등반 am·byŏk dŭng·ban
rock group 록 그룹 rok·kŭ·rup
roll (bread) 롤빵 rolb·bang
romantic a 낭만적인 nang·man·jŏ·gin
room n 방 bang
room number 방 번호 bang·bŏn·ho
rope n 줄 jul
rose 장미 jang·mi
round a 동그란 dong·gŭ·ran
roundabout 원형 교차로 wŏn·hyŏng gyo·ch'a·ro
route n 경로 gyŏng·no
rowing 배 젓기 bae·jŏk·ki
rubbish 쓰레기 ssŭ·re·gi
rubella 풍진 p'ung·jin
rucksack 배낭 bae·nang
rug 깔개 ggal·gae
ruins 옛터 yet·t'ŏ
rule n 규칙 gyu·ch'ik
run v 뛰어요 (뛰~) ddwi·ŏ·yo (ddwi~)
running 달리기 dal·li·gi
runny nose 콧물 k'on·mul
Russia 러시아 rŏ·shi·a

S

sad 슬픈 sŭl·p'ŭn
saddle 안장 an·jang
safe n 안전 an·jŏn
safe a 안전한 an·jŏn·han
safe sex 콘돔 사용하는 섹스 k'on·dom sa·yong·ha·nŭn sek·sŭ
saint n 성인 sŏng·in

salad 샐러드 sael·lŏ·dŭ
salami 살라미 소시지 sal·la·mi so·shi·ji
salary 봉급 bong·gŭp
sale n 세일 se·il
sales assistant 판매원 p'an·mae·wŏn
salmon 연어 yŏ·nŏ
salt n 소금 so·gŭm
salty 짠 jjan
same 같은 ga·t'ŭn
sand 모래 mo·rae
sandals 샌들 saen·dŭl
sandwich 샌드위치 saen·dŭ·wi·ch'i
sanitary napkin 생리대 saeng·ni·dae
sardine 정어리 jŏng·ŏ·ri
sauce n 소스 so·sŭ
saucepan 냄비 naem·bi
sauna 사우나 sa·u·na
sausage 소시지 so·shi·ji
say 말해요 (말하~) mal·hae·yo (mal·ha-)
scalp 두피 du·p'i
scarf 스카프 sŭ·k'a·p'ŭ
school 학교 hak·kyo
science 과학 gwa·hak
scientist 과학자 gwa·hak·ja
scissors 가위 ga·wi
score 득점해요 (득점하~) dŭk·jŏm·hae·yo (dŭk·jŏm·ha-)
scoreboard 득점판 d'ŭk·jŏm·p'an
sculpture 조각 jo·gak
sea 바다 ba·da
seafood 해물 hae·mul
seasick 뱃멀미하는 baen·mŏl·mi·ha·nŭn
seaside n 해변 hae·byŏn
season n 계절 gye·jŏl
seat (place) n 자리 ja·ri
seatbelt 안전벨트 an·jŏn·bel·t'ŭ
second n 초 ch'o
second a 둘째 dul·jjae
second class n 이등 i·dŭng
secondhand 중고의 jung·go·é
secondhand shop 중고품점 jung·go·p'um·jŏm
secretary 비서 bi·sŏ
see 봐요 (보~) bwa·yo (bo-)
self-employed 자영업 하는 ja·yŏng·ŏ·p'a·nŭn
selfish 이기적인 i·gi·jŏ·gin
sell 팔아요 (팔~) p'a·ra·yo (p'al-)
send 보내요 (보내~) bo·nae·yo (bo·nae-)
sensible 현명한 hyŏn·myŏng·han
sensual 관능적인 gwan·nŭng·jŏ·gin
Seoul 서울 sŏ·ul
separate a 따로따로의 dda·ro·dda·ro·é
serious 심각한 shim·ga·k'an
service n 서비스 sŏ·bi·sŭ
service charge 팁 t'ip
service station 주유소 ju·yu·so
serviette 냅킨 naep·k'in
several 몇 개의 myŏk·kae·é
sew 바느질해요 (바느질하~) ba·nŭ·jil·hae·yo (ba·nŭ·jil·ha-)
sex (gender) 성별 sŏng·byŏl
sex (intercourse) 섹스 sek·sŭ
sexism 성 차별 sŏng·ch'a·byŏl
sexy 섹시한 sek·shi·han
shade n 그늘 gŭ·nŭl
shadow n 그림자 gŭ·rim·ja
shaman 무당 mu·dang
shamanism 무속신앙 mu·sok·shi·nang
shampoo 샴푸 sham·p'u
shape n 모양 mo·yang
share (accommodation) v 방 같이 써요 (방 같이 쓰~) bang ga·ch'i ssŏ·yo (bang ga·ch'i ssŭ-)
share (with) v 나눠요 (나누~) na·nwŏ·yo (na·nu-)
shark 상어 sang·ŏ
shave v 면도해요 (면도하~) myŏn·do·hae·yo (myŏn·do·ha-)
shaving cream 면도 크림 myŏn·do k'ŭ·rim
she inf 그녀 gŭ·nyŏ
she pol 그분 gŭ·bun
sheep 양 yang
sheet (bed) 시트 shi·t'ŭ
shelf 선반 sŏn·ban
shiatsu 지압 ji·ap
shingles (illness) 대상포진 dae·sang·p'o·jin

ship n 배 bae
shirt 셔츠 shŏ·ch'ŭ
shoes 신발 shin·bal
shoelace 신발끈 shin·balk·kun
shoe shop 신발 가게 shin·bal ga·gé
shoot 쏴요 (쏘~) sswa·yo (sso~)
shop n 가게 ga·gé
shop v 쇼핑해요 (쇼핑하~) sho·p'ing·hae·yo (sho·p'ing·ha~)
shoplifter 가게 좀도둑 ga·gé jom·do·duk
shopping 쇼핑 sho·p'ing
short (height) 작은 ja·gŭn
short (length) 짧은 jjal·bŭn
shortage 부족 bu·jok
shorts 반바지 ban·ba·ji
shoulder 어깨 ŏk·kae
shout v 소리질러요 (소리지르~) so·ri·jil·lŏ·yo (so·ri ji·rŭ~)
show n 쇼 sho
show v 보여줘요 (보여주~) bo·yŏ·jwŏ·yo (bo·yŏ·ju~)
shower n 샤워 sha·wŏ
shrimp 새우 sae·u
shrine 사당 sa·dang
shut a 닫긴 dak·kin
shy 수줍은 su·ju·bŭn
sick 아픈 a·p'ŭn
sickness 병 byŏng
side n 옆면 yŏm·myŏn
side dish 반찬 ban·ch'an
sign n 간판 gan·p'an
sign v 서명해요 (서명하~) sŏ·myŏng·hae·yo (sŏ·myŏng·ha~)
signature 서명 sŏ·myŏng
sign language 수화 su·hwa
silk n 비단 bi·dan
silver n 은 ŭn
similar 비슷한 bi·sŭ·t'an
simple 간단한 gan·dan·han
since (time) 부터 bu·t'ŏ
sing 노래불러요 (노래부르~) no·rae bul·lŏ·yo (no·rae bu·rŭ~)
singer 가수 ga·su
single (person) 싱글 shing·gŭl
single room 싱글 룸 shing·gŭl·lum
sister 자매 ja·mae
sit 앉아요 (앉~) an·ja·yo (anj~)
size (clothes, shoes) n 치수 ch'i·su
size (general) 크기 k'ŭ·gi
skate v 스케이트 타요 (스케이트 타~) sŭ·k'e·i·t'ŭ t'a·yo (sŭ·k'e·i·t'ŭ t'a~)
ski n 스키 sŭ·k'i
ski v 스키 타요 (스키 타~) sŭ·k'i·t'a·yo (sŭ·k'i·t'a~)
skiing 스키 sŭ·k'i
skin n 피부 p'i·bu
skirt 치마 ch'i·ma
skull 두개골 du·gae·gol
sky 하늘 ha·nŭl
sledding 썰매타기 ssŏl·mae·t'a·gi
sleep n 잠 jam
sleep v 자요 (자~) ja·yo (ja~)
sleeping bag 침낭 ch'im·nang
sleeping car 침대차 ch'im·dae·cha
sleeping pills 수면제 su·myŏn·jé
sleepy 졸린 jol·lin
slice n 조각 jo·gak
slow a 느린 nŭ·rin
slowly 느리게 nŭ·ri·gé
small 작은 cha·gŭn
smaller 더 작은 dŏ ja·gŭn
smallest 제일 작은 je·il ja·gŭn
smell n 냄새 naem·sae
smile v 웃어요 (웃~) u·sŏ·yo (us~)
smoke v 담배 피워요 (담배 피우~) dam·bae p'i·wŏ·yo (dam·bae p'i·u~)
smoking area 흡연 구역 hŭ·byŏn gu·yŏk
snack n 간식 gan·shik
snail 달팽이 dal·p'aeng·i
snake 뱀 baem
snow n 눈 nun
snowstorm 눈보라 nun·bo·ra
soap 비누 bi·nu
soap opera 연속극 yŏn·sok·kŭk
soccer 축구 ch'uk·ku
socialist n 사회주의자 sa·hoé·ju·i·ja
social welfare 사회 복지 sa·hoé bok·ji
socks 양말 yang·mal
soft drink 탄산 음료 t'an·san ŭm·nyo
soldier 군인 gu·nin

some a 어떤 ŏt·tŏn
some (a little) 약간 yak·kan
someone 어떤 사람 ŏt·tŏn sa·ram
something 어떤 것 ŏt·tŏn·gŏt
sometimes 가끔 gak·kŭm
son 아들 a·dŭl
song 노래 no·rae
soon 곧 got
sore a 아픈 a·p'ŭn
sound n 소리 so·ri
soup 수프 su·p'ŭ
south n 남쪽 nam·jjok
South Korea 남한 nam·han
souvenir 기념품 gi·nyŏm·p'um
souvenir shop 기념품 가게 gi·nyŏm·p'um ga·gé
soy milk 두유 du·yu
soy sauce 간장 gan·jang
spa 스파 sŭ·p'a
space (room) n 공간 gong·gan
Spain 스페인 sŭ·p'e·in
speak 말해요 (말하~) mal·hae·yo (mal·ha~)
special a 특별한 t'ŭk·b'yŏl·han
specialist n 전문가 jŏn·mun·ga
speed (travel) n 속도 sok·do
speed limit 제한 속도 je·han·sok·do
speedometer 속도계 sok·do·gyé
spicy (hot) 매운 mae·un
spider 거미 gŏ·mi
spinach 시금치 shi·gŭm·ch'i
spoilt (food) 썩은 ssŏ·gŭn
spoke n 스포크 sŭ·p'o·k'ŭ
spoon n 숟가락 suk·ka·rak
sport 운동 un·dong
sportsperson 운동선수 un·dong·sŏn·su
sports store 운동용품 가게 un·dong·yong·p'um ga·gé
sprain n 염좌 yŏm·jwa
spring (coil) 용수철 yong·su·ch'ŏl
spring (season) 봄 bom
spring onion 파 p'a
square (town) 광장 gwang·jang
squid 오징어 o·jing·ŏ
stadium 경기장 gyŏng·gi·jang
stairway 계단 gye·dan
stale 싱싱하지 못한 shing·shing·ha·ji mo·t'an
stamp (postage) n 우표 u·p'yo
stand-by ticket 대기표 dae·gi·p'yo
star n 별 byŏl
(four-)star (사)성 (sa)·sŏng
start n 시작 shi·jak
start v 시작해요 (시작하~) shi·ja·k'ae·yo (shi·ja·k'a~)
station 역 yŏk
stationery (store) 문방구 mun·bang·gu
statue 조각상 jo·gak·sang
stay (at a hotel) v 묵어요 (묵~) mu·gŏ·yo (mug~)
stay (in one place) v 머물러요 (머무르~) mŏ·mul·lŏ·yo (mŏ·mu·rŭ~)
steal v 훔쳐요 (훔치~) hum·jŏ·yo (hum·ch'i~)
steamed 찐 jjin
steep 가파른 ga·p'a·rŭn
step n 걸음 gŏ·rŭm
stew n 찌개 jji·gae
stock (food) 육수 yuk·su
stockings 스타킹 sŭ·t'a·k'ing
stolen 훔친 hum·ch'in
stomach 위 wi
stomachache 복통 bok·t'ong
stone n 돌 dol
stoned (drugged) 취한 ch'wi·han
stop (bus, tram) n 정류장 jŏng·nyu·jang
stop (cease) 그만해요 (그만하~) gŭ·man·hae·yo (gŭ·man·ha~)
stop (prevent) 막아요 (막~) ma·ga·yo (mag~)
storm n 폭풍 pok·p'ung
story 이야기 i·ya·gi
stove 난로 nal·lo
strange 이상한 i·sang·han
stranger 낯선 사람 nas·sŏn sa·ram
strawberry 딸기 ddal·gi
stream n 개울 gae·ul
street 길 gil
street market 시장 shi·jang

strike (labour) n 파업 p'a·ŏp
string n 끈 ggŭn
stroke (health) n 뇌졸중 noé·jol·jung
stroller 유모차 yu·mo·ch'a
strong 힘센 him·sen
stubborn 완고한 wan·go·han
student n 학생 hak·saeng
studio 스튜디오 sŭ·t'yu·di·o
studio apartment 원룸 wŏn·num
stuffed 속을 채운 so·gŭl ch'ae·un
stupid 바보 같은 ba·bo ka·t'ŭn
style n 스타일 sŭ·t'a·il
subtitles 자막 ja·mak
suburb 교외 gyo·oé
subway (train) 지하철 ji·ha·ch'ŏl
subway entrance 지하철 입구 ji·ha·ch'ŏl ip·gu
subway line 지하철 노선 ji·ha·ch'ŏl no·sŏn
subway station 지하철 역 ji·ha·ch'ŏl·yŏk
sugar 설탕 sŏl·t'ang
suitcase 여행가방 yŏ·haeng·ga·bang
summer 여름 yŏ·rŭm
summit (peak) 정상 jŏng·sang
sun n 해 hae
sunblock 선크림 sŏn k'ŭ·rim
sunburn 햇빛에 탐 haep·pi·ch'é t'am
sunflower 해바라기 hae·ba·ra·gi
sunglasses 선글라스 sŏn·gŭl·la·sŭ
sunny 햇빛이 밝은 haep·pi·ch'i bal·gŭn
sunrise 해돋이 hae·do·ji
sunset 해넘이 hae·nŏ·mi
sunstroke 일사병 il·sa·byŏng
supercenter (big-box store) n 대형 할인점 dae·hyŏng ha·rin·jŏm
supermarket 슈퍼마켓 shu·p'ŏ ma·k'et
superstition 미신 mi·shin
supporter (politics) 지지자 ji·ji·ja
supporter (sport) 서포터 sŏ·p'o·t'ŏ
surf n 파도 p'a·do
surf v 파도 타요 (파도 타~) p'a·do t'a·yo (p'a·do t'a~)
surface mail (sea) 선편 우편 sŏn·p'yŏn u·p'yŏn
surfboard 서핑 보드 sŏ·p'ing·bo·dŭ
surfing 파도 타기 p'a·do t'a·gi
surname 성 sŏng
surprise n 놀람 nol·lam
sushi 생선 초밥 saeng·sŏn ch'o·bap
sweater 스웨터 sŭ·we·t'ŏ
sweet a 단 dan
sweets 사탕 sa·t'ang
swelling 팽창 p'aeng·ch'ang
swim v 수영해요 (수영하~) su·yŏng·hae·yo (su·yŏng·ha~)
swimming 수영 su·yŏng
swimming pool 수영장 su·yŏng·jang
swimsuit 수영복 su·yŏng·bok
Switzerland 스위스 sŭ·wi·sŭ
synthetic a 합성의 hap·sŏng·é
syringe 주사기 ju·sa·gi

T

table 탁자 t'ak·ja
tablecloth 식탁보 shik·t'ak·bo
table tennis 탁구 t'ak·ku
taekwondo 태권도 t'ae·gwŏn·do
t'ai chi 태극권 t'ae·gŭk·kwŏn
tail n 꼬리 ggo·ri
tailor n 재단사 jae·dan·sa
take v 가져가요 (가져가~) ga·jyŏ·ga·yo (ga·jyŏ·ga~)
take a photo 사진 찍어요 (사진 찍~) sa·jin·jji·gŏ·yo (sa·jin·jjig~)
talk v 이야기해요 (이야기하~) i·ya·gi·hae·yo (i·ya·gi·ha~)
tall 키가 큰 ki·ga kŭn
tampon 탐폰 t'am·p'on
tanning lotion 선탠 로션 sŏn·t'aen ro·shŏn
tap n 수도꼭지 su·dok·kok·ji
tap water 수돗물 su·don·mul
tasty 맛있는 ma·shin·nŭn
tax n 세금 se·gŭm
taxi 택시 t'aek·shi
taxi stand 택시 정류장 t'aek·shi jŏng·nyu·jang
tea 차 ch'a
teacher 선생님 sŏn·saeng·nim
teahouse 찻집 ch'at·jip

team 팀 t'im
teaspoon 찻숟가락 ch'as·suk·ka·rak
technique 기술 gi·sul
teeth 이 i
telegram 전보 jŏn·bo
telephone n 전화 jŏn·hwa
telephone v 전화해요 (전화하~) jŏn·hwa·hae·yo (jŏn·hwa·ha~)
telescope 망원경 mang·won·gyŏng
television 텔레비전 t'el·le·bi·jŏn
tell 이야기해요 (이야기하~) i·ya·gi·hae·yo (i·ya·gi·ha~)
temperature (fever) 열 yŏl
temperature (weather) 기온 gi·on
temple (body) 관자놀이 gwan·ja·no·ri
temple (building) 절 jŏl
tennis 테니스 t'e·ni·sŭ
tennis court 테니스 코트 t'e·ni·sŭ ko·tŭ
tent 텐트 t'en·t'ŭ
tent peg 텐트용 말뚝 t'en·t'ŭ·yong malt·tuk
terrible 형편없는 hyŏng·p'yŏ·nŏm·nŭn
test n 시험 shi·hŏm
thank 감사드려요 (감사드리~) gam·sa·dŭ·ryŏ·yo (gam·sa·dŭ·ri~)
that (away from listener) a 저 jŏ
that (near listener) a 그 gŭ
that one (away from listener) pron 저것 jŏ·gŏt
that one (near listener) pron 그것 gŭ·gŏt
theatre (cinema) 영화관 yŏng·hwa·gwan
theatre (plays) 극장 gŭk·jang
their 그들의 gŭ·dŭ·ré
there (away from listener) 저기 jŏ·gi
there (near listener) 거기 gŏ·gi
thermometer 체온계 ch'e·on·gyé
they 그들 gŭ·dŭl
thick 두꺼운 duk·kŏ·un
thief 도둑 do·duk
thin 얇은 yal·bŭn
think 생각해요 (생각하~) saeng·gak·hae·yo (saeng·gak·ha~)
third a 셋째 set·tchae
thirsty 목마른 mong·ma·rŭn
this a 이 i
this (one) pron 이것 i·gŏt
thought 생각 saeng·gak
thread n 실 shil
throat 목 mok
thrush (health) 아구창 a·gu·ch'ang
ticket 표 p'yo
ticket booth 표 파는 곳 p'yo p'a·nŭn·got
ticket machine 표 자판기 p'yo ja·pan·gi
ticket office 매표소 mae·p'yo·so
tide n 조수 jo·su
tiger 호랑이 ho·rang·i
time n 시간 shi·gan
time difference 시차 shi·ch'a
timetable 시간표 shi·gan·p'yo
tin (can) 캔 k'aen
tin opener 캔 오프너 k'ae·no·p'ŭ·nŏ
tip (gratuity) n 팁 t'ip
tire n 타이어 t'a·i·ŏ
tired 피곤한 p'i·gon·han
tissues 티슈 t'i·shyu
to ... prep ...으로/로 ...·ŭ·ro/·ro
tobacco 담배 dam·bae
today 오늘 o·nŭl
toe 발가락 bal·ga·rak
tofu 두부 du·bu
together 같이 ga·ch'i
toilet 화장실 hwa·jang·shil
toilet paper 두루마리 휴지 du·ru·ma·ri hyu·ji
tollbooth 요금 내는 곳 yo·gŭm nae·nŭn·got
tomb 무덤 mu·dŏm
tomorrow 내일 nae·il
tongue 혀 hyŏ
tonight 오늘 밤 o·nŭl·bam
too (also) 또한 ddo·han
too (expensive) 너무 (비싸요) nŏ·mu (bi·ssa·yo)
tooth 이 i
toothache 치통 ch'i·t'ong
toothbrush 칫솔 ch'is·sol
toothpaste 치약 ch'i·yak
toothpick 이쑤시개 iss·u·shi·gae

torch (flashlight) 손전등 son·jŏn·dŭng
touch v 건드려요 (건드리~) gŏn·dŭ·ryŏ·yo (gŏn·dŭ·ri-)
tour n 여행 yŏ·haeng
tourist n 여행자 yŏ·haeng·ja
tourist office 관광안내소 gwan·gwang an·nae·so
towards ... prep ... 쪽으로 ... jjo·gŭ·ro
towel 수건 su·gŏn
tower 타워 t'a·wŏ
town 마을 ma·ŭl
toxic waste 유독성 폐기물 yu·dok·sŏng p'ye·gi·mul
toy shop 장난감 가게 jang·nan·gam ga·gé
track (path) 길 gil
track (sport) 트랙 t'ŭ·raek
trade n 무역 mu·yŏk
tradesperson 상인 sang·in
traffic n 교통 gyo·t'ong
traffic light 신호등 shin·ho·dŭng
trail n 길 gil
train n 기차 gi·ch'a
train station 기차역 gi·ch'a·yŏk
transit lounge 환승 라운지 hwan·sŭng ra·un·ji
translate 번역해요 (번역하~) bŏ·nyŏ·k'ae·yo (bŏ·nyŏ·k'a-)
translator 통역 t'ong·yŏk
transport n 수송 su·song
travel v 여행해요 (여행하~) yŏ·haeng·hae·yo (yŏ·haeng·ha-)
travel agency 여행사 yŏ·haeng·sa
travel (motion) sickness 멀미 mŏl·mi
tree 나무 na·mu
trend 유행 yu·haeng
trip (journey) 여행 yŏ·haeng
trolley (shopping) 카트 k'a·t'ŭ
trousers 바지 ba·ji
truck 트럭 t'ŭ·rŏk
trust v 믿어요 (믿~) mi·dŏ·yo (mid-)
truth 진실 jin·shil
try (sample/test) v 시도해요 (시도하~) shi·do·hae·yo (shi·do·ha-)
try (attempt) v 노력해요 (노력하~) no·ryŏ·k'ae·yo (no·ryŏ·k'a-)
tube (tyre) 튜브 t'yu·bŭ
tumour 종양 jong·yang
tuna 참치 ch'am·ch'i
tune n 선율 sŏ·nyul
turkey 칠면조 ch'il·myŏn·jo
turn v 돌아요 (돌~) do·ra·yo (dol-)
TV 티브이 t'i·bŭ·i
tweezers 족집게 jok·jip·ké
twice 두 번 du·bŏn
twin beds 트윈 베드 t'ŭ·win·be·dŭ
twins 쌍둥이 ssang·dung·i
type n 유형 yu·hyŏng
typhoon 태풍 t'ae·p'ung
typical 전형적인 jŏn·hyŏng·jŏ·gin
tyre 타이어 t'a·i·ŏ

U

ultrasound 초음파 ch'o·ŭm·p'a
umbrella 우산 u·san
uncomfortable 불편한 bul·p'yŏn·han
underground walkway 지하도 ji·ha·do
understand 이해해요 (이해하~) i·hae·hae·yo (i·hae·ha-)
underwear 속옷 so·got
unemployed 직업이 없는 ji·gŏ·bi ŏm·nŭn
unfair 불공평한 bul·gong·p'yŏng·han
uniform n 유니폼 yu·ni·p'om
universe 우주 u·ju
university 대학교 dae·hak·kyo
unleaded petrol 무연 휘발유 mu·yŏn hwi·bal·yu
unmarried 미혼 mi·hon
unsafe 안전하지 않은 an·jŏn·ha·ji a·nŭn
until ... prep ...까지 ...gga·ji
unusual 특이한 t'ŭ·gi·han
up 위로 wi·ro
uphill 오르막 o·rŭ·mak
urgent 급한 gŭ·p'an
urinary infection 요도염 yo·do·yŏm
USA 미국 mi·guk
useful 유용한 yu·yong·han

V

vacant 빈 bin
vacation 휴가 hyu·ga
vaccination 예방주사 ye·bang·ju·sa
validate 확인해요 (확인하~) hwa·gin·hae·yo (hwa·gin·ha~)
valley 계곡 gye·gok
valuable 귀중한 gwi·jung·han
value (price) n 가격 ga·gyŏk
van 미니밴 mi·ni·baen
veal 송아지 고기 song·a·ji go·gi
vegan n 완전 채식주의자 wan·jŏn ch'ae·shik·ju·i·ja
vegetable n 야채/채소 ya·ch'ae/ ch'ae·so
vegetarian n 채식주의자 ch'ae·shik·ju·i·ja
vein 정맥 jŏng·maek
venereal disease 성병 sŏng·byŏng
very 아주 a·ju
view n 전망 jŏn·mang
village 마을 ma·ŭl
vine (grape) 포도나무 p'o·do·na·mu
vinegar 식초 shik·ch'o
virus 바이러스 ba·i·rŏ·sŭ
visa 비자 bi·ja
visit v 방문해요 (방문하~) bang·mun·hae·yo (bang·mun·ha~)
visually impaired 시각 장애의 shi·gak jang·ae·ŭi
vitamins 비타민 bi·t'a·min
voice 목소리 mok·so·ri
volcano 화산 hwa·san
volleyball (sport) 배구 bae·gu
volume 볼륨 bol·lyum
vote v 투표해요 (투표하~) t'u·p'yo·hae·yo (t'u·p'yo·ha~)

W

wage n 임금 im·gŭm
wait v 기다려요 (기다리~) gi·da·ryŏ·yo (gi·da·ri~)
waiter 웨이터 we·i·t'ŏ
waiting room 대기실 dae·gi·shil
wake (someone) up 깨워요 (깨우~) ggae·wŏ·yo (ggae·u~)
walk n 산책 san·ch'aek
walk v 걸어요 (걷~) gŏ·rŏ·yo (gŏt~)
wall (building) 벽 byŏk
walnut 호두 ho·du
want (an object) 원해요 (원하~) wŏn·hae·yo (wŏn·ha~)
war n 전쟁 jŏn·jaeng
wardrobe 옷장 ot·jang
warm a 따뜻한 ddat·tŭt·han
warn 경고해요 (경고하~) gyŏng·go·hae·yo (gyŏng·go·ha~)
wash v 씻어요 (씻~) shi·sŏ·yo (shis~)
wash cloth (flannel) 행주 haeng·ju
washing machine 세탁기 se·t'ak·ki
wasp 말벌 mal·bŏl
watch n 손목시계 son·mok·shi·gyé
watch v 봐요 (보~) bwa·yo (bo~)
water n 물 mul
water bottle 물병 mul·byŏng
(hot) water bottle 보온병 bo·on·byŏng
waterfall 폭포 p'ok·p'o
watermelon 수박 su·bak
waterproof 방수 bang·su
water-skiing 수상 스키 su·sang sŭ·k'i
wave (beach) n 파도 p'a·do
way 길 gil
we 우리 u·ri
weak 힘이 없는 hi·mi ŏm·nŭn
wealthy 부유한 bu·yu·han
wear 입어요 (입~) i·bŏ·yo (ib~)
weather n 날씨 nal·shi
wedding 결혼 gyŏl·hon
week 주 ju
weekend 주말 ju·mal
weigh 무게가 나가요 (무게가 나가~) mu·ge·ga·na·ga·yo (mu·ge·ga·na·ga~)
weight 무게 mu·gé
weights 역기 yŏk·ki
welcome v 환영해요 (환영하~) hwa·nyŏng·hae·yo (hwa·nyŏng·ha~)
well (healthy) 건강한 gŏn·gang·han
well adv 잘 jal
west 서쪽 sŏ·jjok
Western 서양의 sŏ·yang·é

wet a 젖은 jŏ·jŭn
whale 고래 go·rae
what 무엇 mu·ŏt
wheat 밀 mil
wheel n 바퀴 ba·k'wi
wheelchair 휠체어 hwil·ch'é·ŏ
when 언제 ŏn·jé
where 어디 ŏ·di
which 어느 ŏ·nŭ
white 흰 hin
white-water rafting 급류 래프팅 gŭm·nyu rae·p'ŭ·t'ing
who 누구 nu·gu
whole 전부 jŏn·bu
why 왜 wae
wide 폭이 넓은 p'o·gi nŏl·bŭn
wife 아내 a·nae
win v 이겨요 (이기~) i·gyŏ·yo (i·gi~)
wind n 바람 ba·ram
window 창문 ch'ang·mun
windscreen 앞유리 am·nyu·ri
windy 바람이 많이 부는 ba·ra·mi ma·ni bu·nŭn
wine 와인 wa·in
wings 날개 nal·gae
winner 우승자 u·sŭng·ja
winter 겨울 gyŏ·ul
wire n 철사 chŏl·sa
wish v 희망해요 (희망하~) hi·mang·hae·yo (hi·mang·ha~)
with ... (someone) prep ...과/와 함께 ...·gwa/·wa hamk·ké
without ... (someone) prep ... 없이 ... ŏp·shi
wok 중국 냄비 jung·gung·naem·bi
woman 여자 yŏ·ja
wonderful 훌륭한 hul·lyung·han
wood n 나무 na·mu
wool n 모직물 mo·jing·mul
word n 단어 da·nŏ
work n 일 il
work v 일해요 (일하~) il·hae·yo (il·ha~)
workout n 운동 un·dong
work permit 취업 허가증 ch'wi·ŏp hŏ·ga·jŭng
workshop n 워크숍 wŏ·k'ŭ·shop
world n 세계 se·gyé
worms (intestinal) 기생충 gi·saeng·ch'ung
worship n 찬양 ch'a·nyang
wrist 손목 son·mok
write 써요 (쓰~) ssŏ·yo (ssŭ~)
writer 작가 jak·ka
wrong a 틀린 t'ŭl·lin

Y

yacht 요트 yo·t'ŭ
year 해 hae
yellow 노란 no·ran
yes 네/예 né/yé
yesterday 어제 ŏ·jé
(not) yet 아직 (아니에요) a·jik (a·ni·e·yo)
yoghurt 요구르트 yo·gu·rŭ·t'ŭ
you inf sg 너 nŏ
you pol sg 당신 dang·shin
you inf pl 너희들 nŏ·hi·dŭl
you pol pl 여러분 yŏ·rŏ·bun
young a 젊은 jŏl·mŭn
your inf sg 너의 nŏ·é
your pol sg 당신의 dang·shi·né
your inf pl 너희들의 nŏ·hi·dŭ·ré
your pol pl 여러분의 yŏ·rŏ·bu·né
youth hostel 유스호스텔 yu·sŭ·ho·sŭ·t'el

Z

zip/zipper 지퍼 ji·p'ŏ
zoo 동물원 dong·mur·wŏn
zoom lens 줌렌즈 jum·nen·jŭ
zucchini 애호박 ae·ho·bak

DICTIONARY

Korean to English

한국어 - 영어

This dictionary has been ordered according to the consonants in the Korean alphabet (see **pronunciation**, p12). Words are marked as nouns n, verbs v, adjectives a, adverbs adv, pronouns pron or prepositions prep for clarity where required. The abbreviations sg (singular), pl (plural), inf (informal) and pol (polite) are also used where applicable. Korean verbs are given in their polite form (ending in ~yo ~요). The verb stem is repeated between brackets after the verb. For more information, see **grammar** (p18). For any food items, refer to the **menu decoder** (p212).

ㄱ

가게 ga·gé shop n
가게 좀도둑 ga·gé jom·do·duk shoplifter
가격 ga·gyŏk price
가구 ga·gu furniture
가까운 gak·ka·un close a
가까워요 (가깝~) gak·ka·wŏ·yo (gak·kap~) be close v
가득 찬 ga·dŭk·ch'an full
가려운 ga·ryŏ·un itchy
가리켜요 (가리키~) ga·ri·k'yŏ·yo (ga·ri·k'i~) point v
가방 ga·bang bag
가벼운 ga·byŏ·un light (weight) a
가스 ga·sŭ gas (for cooking)
가요 (가~) ga·yo (ga~) go
가위 ga·wi scissors
가이드 ga·i·dŭ guide (person)
가이드 책자 ga·i·dŭ ch'aek·ja guidebook
가이드 투어 ga·i·dŭ t'u·ŏ guided tour
가져요 (갖~) ga·jyŏ·yo (kaj~) have
가족 ga·jok family
가죽 ga·juk leather n
각각의 gak·ka·gé each
간식 gan·shik snack n
간호사 gan·ho·sa nurse n
갈색 gal·saek brown a
감기 gam·gi cold (illness) n
감사해요 (감사하~) gam·sa·hae·yo (gam·sa·ha~) grateful
감염 ga·myŏm infection
강 gang river
강사 gang·sa lecturer
같이 ga·ch'i together
개 gae dog
거기 gŏ·gi there (near listener)
거울 gŏ·ul mirror n
건강한 gŏn·gang·han well (healthy)
건강해요 (건강하~) gŏn·gang·hae·yo (gŏn·gang·ha~) be well v
건초열 gŏn·ch'o·yŏl hay fever

건축 gŏn·ch'uk architecture
건축가 gŏn·ch'uk·ka architect
걸어요 (걷~) gŏ·rŏ·yo (gŏt~) walk v
검은 gŏ·mŭn black
겨울 gyŏ·ul winter
결혼한 gyŏl·hon·han married
경찰 gyŏng·ch'al police
경찰관 gyŏng·ch'al·gwan police officer
경찰서 gyŏng·ch'al·sŏ police station
계단 gye·dan stairway
계산기 gye·san·gi calculator
계산서 gye·san·sŏ bill/check n
계절 gye·jŏl season n
고객 go·gaek client
고속 버스 go·sok bŏ·sŭ express intercity bus
고속도로 go·sok·do·ro highway • motorway • tollway
고용해요 (고용하~) go·yong·hae·yo (go·yong·ha~) hire v
고장 난 go·jang·nan broken down • out of order
고전 go·jŏn classical
고통 go·t'ong pain n
곧 got soon
골동품 gol·dong·p'um antique n
골프 gol·p'ŭ golf
골프장 gol·p'ŭ·jang golf course
공산주의 gong·san·ju·i communism
공연장 gyong·yŏn·jang gig
공예품 gong·ye·p'um crafts
공원 gong·wŏn park n
공중 화장실 gong·jung hwa·jang·shil public toilet
공짜의 gong·jja·é free (gratis)
공책 gong·ch'aek notebook
공항 gong·hang airport
공항세 gong·hang·sé airport tax
과학 gwa·hak science
과학자 gwa·hak·ja scientist
관광 버스 gwan·gwang bŏ·sŭ tourist bus
관광안내소 gwan·gwang an·nae·so tourist office
광장 gwang·jang square (town) n
괜찮은 gwaen·cha·nŭn OK
괴로운 goé·ro·un painful
교통 위반 gyo·t'ong wi·ban traffic violation
교통카드 gyo·t'ong k'a·dŭ prepaid transit pass
교환 gyo·hwan exchange n
교환해요 (교환하~) gyo·hwan·hae·yo (gyo·hwan·ha~) exchange v
구급상자 gu·gŭp·sang·ja first-aid kit
구급차 gu·gŭp·ch'a ambulance
구명조끼 gu·myŏng·jok·ki life jacket
국경 guk·kyŏng border (national) n
귀 gwi ear
귀고리 gwi·go·ri earrings
귀중한 gwi·jung·han valuable
그 gŭ he inf • that (near listener) a
그것 gŭ·gŏt it • that one (near listener) pron
그녀 gŭ·nyŏ she inf
그녀의 gŭ·nyŏ·é her (possessive)
그늘 gŭ·nŭl shade n
그램 gŭ·raem gram
그리고 gŭ·ri·go and
그분 gŭ·bun he pol • she pol
그의 gŭ·é his
그저께 gŭ·jŏk·ké day before yesterday
극장 gŭk·jang theatre (for plays)
금 gŭm gold n
금연 구역 gŭ·myŏn gu·yŏk nonsmoking area
금전 등록기 gŭm·jŏn dŭng·nok·ki cash register
급수대 gŭp·su·dae drinking fountain
급한 gŭ·p'an urgent
급해요 (급하~) gŭ·p'ae·yo (gŭ·p'a~) be in a hurry v
기념품 gi·nyŏm·p'um souvenir
기념품 가게 gi·nyŏm·p'um ga·gé souvenir shop
기다려요 (기다리~) gi·da·ryŏ·yo (gi·da·ri~) wait v
기름 gi·rŭm oil (cooking)
기억해요 (기억하~) gi·ŏ·k'ae·yo (gi·ŏ·k'a~) remember
기온 gi·on temperature (weather)
기저귀 gi·jŏ·gwi diaper • nappy
기차 gi·ch'a train n
기차역 gi·ch'a·yŏk railway station

기침해요 (기침하~) gi·ch'im hae·yo (gi·ch'im ha~) cough v
기침약 gi·ch'im·nyak cough medicine
긴 gin long
길 gil path • street
길어요 (길~) gi·rŏ·yo (gil~) be long v

ㄲ

깨끗한 ggaek·kŭ·t'an clean a
깨워요 (깨우~) ggae·wŏ·yo (ggae·u~) wake (someone) up
깨지기 쉬운 ggae·ji·gi shi·un fragile
깨진 ggae·jin broken
꽃집 ggot·jip florist
꾸러미 ggu·rŏ·mi packet (general)
끝 ggŭt end n

ㄴ

나 na I inf
나가요 (나가~) na·ga·yo (na·ga~) go out
나눠요 (나누~) na·nwŏ·yo (na·nu~) share (with) v
나쁜 nap·pŭn bad
나의 na·é my inf
나이트클럽 na·i·t'ŭ·k'ŭl·lŏb nightclub
나중에 na·jung·é later
낚시 nakk·shi fishing
날아요 (날~) na·ra·yo (nal~) fly v
날짜 nal·jja date (day) n
남자 nam·ja man n
남자 아이 nam·ja·a·i boy
남자 친구 nam·ja ch'in·gu boyfriend
남쪽 nam·jjok south n
남편 nam·p'yŏn husband
남한 nam·han South Korea
낭만적인 nang·man·jŏ·gin romantic a
낮 nat daytime
내려요 (내리~) nae·ryŏ·yo (nae·ri~) get off (bus, train)
내일 nae·il tomorrow
냄비 naem·bi pot (cooking) • saucepan
냄새 naem·sae smell n
냅킨 naep·k'in napkin
냉동 식품 naeng·dong shik·p'um frozen food
냉방 중 naeng·bang·jung air-conditioned
냉장고 naeng·jang·go refrigerator
너 nŏ you inf sg
너무 (비싸요) nŏ·mu (bi·ssa·yo) too (expensive)
너무 많은 nŏ·mu ma·nŭn too many
너무 많이 nŏ·mu ma·ni too much
너의 nŏ·é your inf sg
너희들 nŏ·hi·dŭl you inf pl
너희들의 nŏ·hi·dŭ·ré your inf pl
네 né yes
년 nyŏn year (as a classifier)
노란 no·ran yellow
노력해요 (노력하~) no·ryŏ·k'ae·yo (no·ryŏ·k'a~) try (make an effort) v
노리개 젖꼭지 no·ri·gae jŏk·kok·ji dummy/pacifier
노트북 no·t'ŭ·buk laptop
놓쳐요 (놓치~) no·chyŏ·yo (no·ch'i~) miss (not catch train, etc)
누구 nu·gu who
누나 nu·na older sister (male speaker)
눈 nun eye • snow n
뉴스 nyu·sŭ news
느껴요 (느끼~) nŭk·kyŏ·yo (nŭk·ki~) feel (touch) v
느리게 nŭ·ri·gé slowly
늙은 nŭl·gŭn old (people)
늦게 nŭk·ké late adv

ㄷ

다른 da·rŭn different • other
다리 da·ri bridge n • leg (body)
다리미질 da·ri·mi·jil iron (for clothes) n
다시 da·shi again
다음 da·ŭm next (following)
다음에 da·ŭ·mé next time
다친 da·ch'in injured
단 dan sweet a
단단한 dan·dan·han hard (not soft)
단추 dan·ch'u button n
닫긴 dak·kin shut a
닫아요 (닫~) da·da·yo (dad~) close v

달 dal month
달러 dal·lŏ dollar
닭 dak chicken (animal)
담배 dam·bae cigarette
담배 피워요 (담배 피우~) dam·bae p'i·wŏ·yo (dam·bae p'i·u~) smoke v
담요 dam·nyo blanket
(하루)당 (ha·ru)·dang per (day)
당뇨병 dang·nyo·byŏng diabetes
당신 dang·shin you pol sg
당신의 dang·shi·né your pol sg
대기실 dae·gi·shil waiting room
대기표 dae·gi·p'yo stand-by ticket
대사관 dae·sa·gwan embassy
대학교 dae·hak·kyo university
대한민국 dae·han min·guk Republic of Korea
대형 할인점 dae·hyŏng ha·rin·jŏm big-box store • supercenter n
더 나은 dŏ·na·ŭn better
더 많은 dŏ·ma·nŭn more
더 작은 dŏ ja·gŭn smaller
더 큰 dŏ·k'ŭn bigger
더러운 dŏ·rŏ·un dirty
더블 룸 dŏ·bŭl·lum double room
더블베드 dŏ·bŭl be·dŭ double bed
더운 dŏ·un hot (weather)
더워요 (덥~) dŏ·wŏ·yo (dŏp~) be hot v
데오드란트 de·o·dŭ·ran·t'ŭ deodorant
데운 de·un heated
데이트 de·i·t'ŭ date (romantic) n
도로 do·ro road
도서관 do·sŏ·gwan library
도시 do·shi city
도와줘요 (도와주~) do·wa·jwŏ·yo (do·wa·ju~) help v
도움 do·um help n
도착 do·ch'ak arrivals
독감 dok·kam flu • influenza
돈 don money
돌려줘요 (돌려주~) dol·lyŏ·jwŏ·yo (dol·lyŏ·ju~) return (give back) v
돌아가요 (돌아가~) do·ra·ga·yo (do·ra·ga~) return (go back) v
동네 dong·né neighbourhood
동료 dong·nyo colleague • companion
동물원 dong·mur·wŏn zoo
동생 dong·saeng younger sibling
동전 dong·jŏn coins
동쪽 dong·jjok east n
두 개의 du·gae·é two
두루마리 휴지 du·ru·ma·ri hyu·ji toilet paper
두통 du·t'ong headache
둘 다 dul·da both
뒤쪽의 dwi·jjo·gé rear (location)
드레스 dŭ·re·sŭ dress n
들어가요 (들어가~) dŭ·rŏ·ga·yo (dŭ·rŏ·ga~) enter
들어요 (듣~) dŭ·rŏ·yo (dŭt~) listen
들어요 (들~) dŭ·rŏ·yo (dŭl~) cost v
등기우편 dŭng·gi·u·p'yŏn registered mail
등산 dŭng·san hiking
등산로 dŭng·san·no hiking route
등산해요 (등산하~) dŭng·san·hae·yo (dŭng·san·ha~) hike v

ㄸ

따뜻한 ddat·tŭt·han warm a
따뜻해요 (따뜻하~) ddat·tŭ·t'ae·yo (ddat·tŭ·t'a~) be warm v
딸 ddal daughter
떠나요 (떠나~) ddŏ·na·yo (ddŏ·na~) depart
또 하나의 ddo ha·na·é another
뚱뚱한 ddung·ddung·han fat a
뜨거운 ddŭ·gŏ·un hot (to the touch)

ㄹ

라디오 ra·di·o radio n
라이터 ra·i·t'ŏ cigarette lighter
렌즈 ren·jŭ lens (camera)
렌트카 ren·t'ŭ·k'a car hire
록 음악 ro·gŭ·mak rock (music)
리넨 ri·nen linen (material)
리넨천 ri·nen·ch'ŏn linen (sheets)
리모컨 ri·mo·k'ŏn remote control
리프트 ri·p'ŭ·t'ŭ chairlift (skiing)

ㅁ

마개 ma·gae plug (bath) n
마른 ma·rŭn dry a
마셔요 (마시~) ma·shŏ·yo (ma·shi-) drink v
마약 ma·yak dope (illicit drugs) n
마을 ma·ŭl town
마을 버스 ma·ŭl bŏ·sŭ neighbourhood bus
마지막 ma·ji·mak last (final)
막힌 ma·k'in blocked
말해요 (말하~) mal·hae·yo (mal·ha-) speak
맛있는 ma·shin·nŭn tasty
매니저 mae·ni·jŏ manager
매운 mae·un spicy (hot)
매워요 (맵~) mae·wŏ·yo (maep-) be spicy (hot) v
매일 mae·il daily adv
매트리스 mae·t'ŭ·ri·sŭ mattress
매표소 mae·p'yo·so ticket office
맥주 maek·ju beer
맥주집 maek·ju·jip pub
머리 mŏ·ri head n
먹어요 (먹~) mŏ·gŏ·yo (mŏg-) eat
멀리 mŏl·li far adv
멀미 mŏl·mi travel (motion) sickness
멀어요 (멀~) mŏ·rŏ·yo (mŏl-) be far v
메스꺼움 me·sŭk·kŏ·um nausea
메시지 me·shi·ji message
면 myŏn cotton (fabric) n
면도 크림 myŏn·do k'ŭ·rim shaving cream
면도기 myŏn·do·gi razor
면도날 myŏn·do·nal razor blade
면도해요 (면도하~) myŏn·do·hae·yo (myŏn·do·ha-) shave v
면세 myŏn·sé duty-free n
모뎀 mo·dem modem
모두 mo·du everyone
모든 mo·dŭn all • every a
모레 mo·rae day after tomorrow
모범택시 mo·bŏm·t'aek·shi deluxe taxi
모자 mo·ja hat
모텔 mo·t'el motel
목 mok neck • throat
목걸이 mok·kŏ·ri necklace
목마른 mong·ma·rŭn thirsty
목말라요 (목마르~) mong·mal·la·yo (mong·ma·rŭ-) be thirsty v
목욕 mo·gyok bath n
목적지 mok·jŏk·ji destination
몰라요 (모르~) mol·la·yo (mo·rŭ-) not know
무거운 mu·gŏ·un heavy (weight)
무거워요 (무겁~) mu·gŏ·wŏ·yo (mu·gŏp-) be heavy v
무릎 mu·rŭp knee
문방구 mun·bang·gu stationery
문서 업무 mun·sŏ ŏm·mu paperwork
물 mul water n
물집 mul·jip blister n
미술 mi·sul art
미술관 mi·sul·gwan art gallery • art museum
미용실 mi·yong·shil beauty salon • hairdressing salon
미터 mi·t'ŏ metre
미혼 mi·hon unmarried
민박집 min·bak·jip guesthouse
민속 음악 min·sok ŭ·mak folk music
밀리미터 mil·li·mi·t'ŏ millimetre

ㅂ

바늘 ba·nŭl needle (sewing)
바다 ba·da ocean • sea
바람이 많이 부는 ba·ra·mi ma·ni bu·nŭn windy
바쁜 bap·pŭn busy (person)
바지 ba·ji trousers • pants
박물관 bang·mul·gwan museum
밖에서 bak·ke·sŏ outside adv
반 ban half n
반바지 ban·ba·ji shorts
반복해요 (반복하~) ban·bo·k'ae·yo (ban·bo·k'a-) repeat v
반지 ban·ji ring (jewellery) n
반창고 ban·ch'ang·go plaster • Band-Aid
받아들여요 (받아들이~) ba·da·dŭ·ryŏ·yo (ba·da·dŭ·ri-) accept
받아요 (받~) ba·da·yo (bad-) receive

발 bal foot (body)
발목 bal·mok ankle
발신음 bal·shi·nŭm dial tone
밝은 bal·gŭn light (colour) a
밤 bam night
밤새 bam·sae overnight adv
방 bang room n
방 같이 써요 (방 같이 쓰~) bang ga·ch'i ssŏ·yo (bang ga·ch'i ssŭ~) share (accommodation) v
방 번호 bang·bŏn·ho room number
방향 bang·hyang direction
배 bae boat • ship
배고파요 (배고프~) bae·go·p'a·yo (bae·go·p'ŭ~) be hungry v
배고픈 bae·go·p'ŭn hungry
배낭 bae·nang backpack • rucksack
배달해요 (배달하~) bae·dal·hae·yo (bae·dal·ha~) deliver
배변촉진제 bae·byŏn·ch'ok·jin·jé laxative n
배터리 bae·t'ŏ·ri battery
백 baek hundred
백만 baeng·man million
백화점 bae·k'wa·jŏm department store
밴드 baen·dŭ band (music)
버스 정류장 bŏ·su jŏng·nyu·jang bus stop
버스 터미널 bŏ·su t'ŏ·mi·nŏl bus station
번역해요 (번역하~) bŏ·nyŏ·k'ae·yo (bŏ·nyŏ·k'a~) translate
벌금 bŏl·gŭm fine n
법학 bŏ·p'ak law (profession/study)
베개 be·gae pillow
베갯잇 be·gaen·nit pillowcase
벼룩시장 byŏ·ruk·shi·jang flea market
변비 byŏn·bi constipation
변속 장치 byŏn·sok jang·ch'i derailleur • gearbox
변호사 byŏn·ho·sa lawyer
변화 byŏn·hwa change n
병 byŏng bottle
병따개 byŏngt·ta·gae bottle opener
병원 byŏng·won hospital
보다 적은 bo·da jŏ·gŭn less
보도 bo·do footpath
보라색 bo·ra·saek purple
보석 bo·sŏk jewellery
보여줘요 (보여주~) bo·yŏ·jwŏ·yo (bo·yŏ·ju~) show v
보온병 bo·on·byŏng hot water bottle
보증 bo·jŭng guarantee n
보증금 bo·jŭng·gŭm deposit n
보험 bo·hŏm insurance
복통 bok·t'ong stomachache
볼펜 bol·p'en ballpoint pen
봄 bom spring (season)
봉투 bong·t'u envelope n
부모님 bu·mo·nim parents
부상 bu·sang injury
부유한 bu·yu·han rich
부채 bu·ch'ae fan (hand-held)
북쪽 buk·jjok north n
북한 bu·k'an North Korea
분 bun minute
분수 bun·su fountain
분실 수하물 bun·shil su·ha·mul left luggage
분실 수하물 보관소 bun·shil su·ha·mul bo·gwan·so left-luggage office
분실물 센터 bun·shil·mul sen·t'ŏ lost-property office
분홍색 bun·hong·saek pink
불가능한 bul·ga·nŭng·han impossible
불량인 bul·lyang·in faulty
불편한 pul·p'yŏn·han uncomfortable
불평 bul·p'yŏng complaint
붕대 bung·dae bandage
브래지어 bŭ·rae·ji·ŏ bra
브레이크 bŭ·re·i·kŭ brakes
비 bi rain n
비누 bi·nu soap
비단 bi·dan silk n
비무장지대 bi·mu·jang ji·dae demilitarized zone (DMZ)
비상구 bi·sang·gu emergency exit
비싸요 (비싸~) bi·ssa·yo (bi·ssa~) be expensive v
비싼 bi·ssan expensive
비용 bi·yong cost n
비자 bi·ja visa
비즈니스석 bi·jŭ·ni·sŭ·sŏk business class

비행 bi·haeng flight
비행기 bi·haeng·gi airplane
빈 bin empty a • vacant
빌딩 bil·ding building
빌려요 (빌리~) bil·lyŏ·yo (bil·li~) rent v
빗 bit comb n
빛 bit light (brightness) n

ㅃ

빠른 우편 bba·rŭn u·p'yŏn express mail
빨간 bbal·gan red
빨래 bbal·lae laundry (clothes)
빨래방 bbal·lae·bang launderette
빵 bbang bread
빵집 bbang·jip bakery
빼고 bbae·go without

ㅅ

사고 sa·go accident
사랑 sa·rang love n
사랑해요 (사랑하~) sa·rang·hae·yo (sa·rang·ha~) love v
사발 sa·bal bowl (for food) n
사업 sa·ŏp business n
사요 (사~) sa·yo (sa~) buy
사적인 sa·jŏ·gin private a
사전 sa·jŏn dictionary
사진 sa·jin photo
사진 찍어요 (사진 찍~) sa·jin jji·gŏ·yo (sa·jin jjig~) take a photo
사진술 sa·jin·sul photography
사진작가 sa·jin jak·ka photographer
사치 sa·ch'i luxury
산 san mountain
산책 san·ch'aek walk n
상자 sang·ja box n
상한 sang·han off (spoilt)
새로운 sae·ro·un new
새벽 sae·byŏk dawn
색깔 saek·kal colour n
생년월일 saeng·nyŏn·wŏ·ril date of birth
생리대 saeng·ni·dae sanitary napkin
생선 가게 saeng·sŏn ga·gé fish shop
생수 saeng·su mineral water
생일 saeng·il birthday
샤워 sha·wŏ shower n
서류 sŏ·ryu papers (documents)
서류 가방 sŏ·ryu·ga·bang briefcase
서비스 sŏ·bi·sŭ service n
서비스 sŏ·bi·sŭ free of charge
서양의 sŏ·yang·é Western
서점 sŏ·jŏm book shop
서쪽 sŏ·jjok west
선글라스 sŏn·gŭl·la·sŭ sunglasses
선물 sŏn·mul gift • present n
선생님 sŏn·saeng·nim teacher
선크림 sŏn k'ŭ·rim sunblock
선탠로션 sŏn·t'aen·ro·shŏn tanning lotion
선편 우편 sŏn·p'yŏn u·p'yŏn surface mail (sea)
선풍기 sŏn·p'ung·gi fan (machine)
설사 sŏl·sa diarrhoea
설탕 sŏl·t'ang sugar
섬 sŏm island
성 sŏng family name • surname
성냥 sŏng·nyang matches (for lighting)
성당 sŏng·dang cathedral
성명 sŏng·myŏng name n pol
성별 sŏng·byŏl sex (gender)
세관 se·gwan customs
세탁기 se·t'ak·ki washing machine
섹스 sek·sŭ sex (intercourse)
센티미터 sen·t'i·mi·t'ŏ centimetre
셀프(서비스) sel·p'ŭ(·sŏ·bi·sŭ) self-service a
셔츠 shŏ·ch'ŭ shirt
소금 so·gŭm salt n
소독약 so·dong·nyak antiseptic n
소리 so·ri sound n
소리가 큰 so·ri·ga k'ŭn loud
소책자 so·ch'aek·ja brochure
소포 so·p'o package n • parcel
소풍 so·p'ung picnic n
소화불량 so·hwa bul·lyang indigestion
속옷 so·got underwear
속임수 so·gim·su cheat n
손 son hand
손가락 son·ga·rak finger
손녀 son·nyŏ granddaughter

손목시계 son·mok·shi·gyé watch n
손수건 son·su·gŏn handkerchief
손자 son·ja grandson
손전등 son·jŏn·dŭng torch • flashlight
손톱깎이 son·t'op·kkak·ki nail clippers
솔 sol brush n
쇼 sho show n
쇼핑 sho·p'ing shopping
쇼핑센터 sho·p'ing·sen·t'ŏ shopping centre
쇼핑몰 sho·p'ing·mol shopping mall
쇼핑해요 (쇼핑하~) sho·p'ing·hae·yo (sho·p'ing·ha~) go shopping
수건 su·gŏn towel
수공예품 su·gong·ye·p'um handicraft
수도꼭지 su·dok·kok·ji tap • faucet
수리해요 (수리하~) su·ri·hae·yo (su·ri·ha~) repair v
수수료 su·su·ryo commission
수신자 부담 통화 su·shin·ja bu·dam t'ong·hwa collect call
수영장 su·yŏng·jang swimming pool
수영해요 (수영하~) su·yŏng·hae·yo (su·yŏng·ha~) swim v
수저와 포크 su·jŏ·wa p'o·k'ŭ cutlery • silverware
수제 su·jé handmade
수표 su·p'yo cheque (banking)
수하물 su·ha·mul baggage • luggage
수하물 수취대 su·ha·mul su·ch'wi·dae baggage claim
수하물 허용량 su·ha·mul hŏ·yong·nyang baggage allowance
수화 su·hwa sign language
숙박 suk·bak accommodation
숟가락 suk·ka·rak spoon n
술 sul alcohol • alcoholic drink
술 취한 sul·ch'wi·han drunk a
술 취해요 (술 취하~) sul·ch'wi·hae·yo (sul·ch'wi·ha~) be drunk v
술집 sul·jip bar n
숫자 sut·ja number n
숲 sup forest
슈퍼 shu·p'ŏ food shop • grocery
슈퍼마켓 shu·p'ŏ ma·k'et supermarket
스웨터 sŭ·we·t'ŏ jumper • sweater
스카프 sŭ·k'a·p'ŭ scarf
스키 sŭ·k'i ski n • skiing
스타킹 sŭ·t'a·k'ing stockings
스파 sŭ·p'a spa
승강장 sŭng·gang·jang platform
승객 sŭng·gaek passenger
승마 sŭng·ma horse riding
시가 shi·ga cigar
시간 shi·gan hour • time n
시간표 shi·gan·p'yo timetable
시골 shi·gol countryside
시끄러운 shik·kŭ·rŏ·un noisy
시끄러워요 (시끄럽~) shik·kŭ·rŏ·wŏ·yo (shik·kŭ·rŏp~) be noisy v
시내 shi·nae city centre
시내버스 shi·nae·bŏ·sŭ intracity bus
시도해요 (시도하~) shi·do·hae·yo (shi·do·ha~) try (sample/test) v
시아버지 shi·a·bŏ·ji father-in-law (husband's father)
시어머니 shi·ŏ·mŏ·ni mother-in-law (husband's mother)
시작해요 (시작하~) shi·ja·k'ae·yo (shi·ja·k'a~) begin
시장 shi·jang market (outdoor) n
시차 shi·ch'a time difference
시차증 shi·ch'a·jŭng jet lag
시트 shi·t'ŭ sheet (bed)
식당 shik·dang restaurant
식량 shing·nyang provisions
식사 shik·sa meal
식중독 shik·jung·dok food poisoning
식품점 shik·p'um·jŏm delicatessen
신경 써요 (신경 쓰~) shin·gyŏng ssŏ·yo (shin·gyŏng ssŭ~) care (about something)
신문 shin·mun newspaper
신문 가판대 shin·mun ga·p'an·dae kiosk • newsstand
신발 shin·bal shoes
신발 가게 shin·bal ga·gé shoe shop
신분증 shin·bun·jŭng identification card (ID)
신선한 shin·sŏn·han fresh
신용카드 shi·nyong k'a·dŭ credit card
신원 확인 shin·wŏn hwa·gin identification

신혼여행 shin·hon·yŏ·haeng honeymoon
실외 shi·loé outdoor a
심장 shim·jang heart
심장 상태 shim·jang sang·t'ae heart condition
싱글 shing·gŭl single (person) a
싱글 룸 shing·gŭl·lum single room

ㅆ

싼 ssan cheap
써요 (쓰~) ssŏ·yo (ssŭ-) write
쓰레기통 ssŭ·re·gi·t'ong rubbish bin • garbage can
쓴 ssŭn bitter
씻어요 (씻~) shi·sŏ·yo (shis-) wash v

ㅇ

아기 a·gi baby
아내 a·nae wife
아들 a·dŭl son
아래로 a·rae·ro down
아름다운 a·rŭm·da·un beautiful
아름다워요 (아름답~) a·rŭm·da·wŏ·yo (a·rŭm·dap-) be beautiful v
아버지 a·bŏ·ji father
아스피린 a·sŭ·p'i·rin aspirin
아이 돌보기 a·i·dol·bo·gi child-minding service
아이스크림 a·i·sŭ·k'ŭ·rim ice cream
아저씨 a·jŏ·shi older man
아주머니 a·ju·mŏ·ni older woman
아침 a·ch'im breakfast • morning
아파트 a·p'a·t'ŭ apartment
아픈 a·p'ŭn ill • sick
안 an not
안경 an·gyŏng glasses (spectacles)
안내 an·nae information
안녕히 가세요 an·nyŏng·hi ga·se·yo goodbye (when staying) pol
안녕히 계세요 an·nyŏng·hi gye·se·yo goodbye (when leaving) pol
안마 an·ma massage n
안마사 an·ma·sa masseur/masseuse
안전 an·jŏn safe n
안전벨트 an·jŏn·bel·t'ŭ seatbelt
알람 시계 al·lam shi·gyé alarm clock
알레르기 al·le·rŭ·gi allergy
알약 al·lyak pill (medicine)
애프터쉐이브 ae·p'ŭ·t'ŏ·she·i·bŭ aftershave
야영해요 (야영하~) ya·yŏng·hae·yo (ya·yŏng·ha-) camp v
야채 ya·ch'ae vegetable n
약 yak drug • medication • medicine
약간 yak·kan some (a little)
약국 yak·kuk chemist • pharmacy
약도 yak·do map (of neighbourhood)
약사 yak·sa chemist • pharmacist
약속 yak·sok appointment
약해요 (약하~) ya·k'ae·yo (ya·k'a-) be weak v
약혼 ya·k'on engagement (to marry)
약혼녀 ya·k'on·nyŏ fiancée
약혼자 ya·k'on·ja fiancé
약혼한 ya·k'on·han engaged (to be married)
양말 yang·mal socks
어깨 ŏk·kae shoulder
어느 ŏ·nŭ which
어댑터 ŏ·daep·t'ŏ adaptor
어두운 ŏ·du·un dark
어두워요 (어둡~) ŏ·du·wŏ·yo (ŏ·dup-) be dark v
어디 ŏ·di where
어떤 ŏt·tŏn some a
어린이 ŏ·ri·ni child • children (general)
어린이용 좌석 ŏ·ri·ni·yong jwa·sŏk child seat
어머니 ŏ·mŏ·ni mother
어제 ŏ·jé yesterday
언니 ŏn·ni older sister (female speaker)
언어 ŏ·nŏ language
언제 ŏn·jé when
얼굴 ŏl·gul face n
얼음 ŏ·rŭm ice
없어요 (없~) ŏp·sŏ·yo (ŏps-) not be present • not exist
에스컬레이터 e·sŭ·k'ŏl·le·i·t'ŏ escalator
엔지니어 en·ji·n·i·ŏ engineer n
엔진 en·jin engine
엘리베이터 el·li·be·i·t'ŏ lift • elevator
여관 yŏ·gwan motel

여권 yŏ·gwŏn passport
여권번호 yŏ·gwŏn·bŏn·ho passport number
여기 yŏ·gi here
여러분 yŏ·rŏ·bun you pol pl
여러분의 yŏ·rŏ·bu·né your pol pl
여름 yŏ·rŭm summer
여성의 yŏ·sŏng·é female a
여자 yŏ·ja woman
여자 아이 yŏ·ja·a·i girl
여자 친구 yŏ·ja ch'in·gu girlfriend
여행 yŏ·haeng journey n • tour n
여행 복대 yŏ·haeng·bok·dae bumbag • fanny pack
여행 일정 yŏ·haeng il·jŏng itinerary
여행가방 yŏ·haeng·ga·bang suitcase
여행사 yŏ·haeng·sa travel agency
역 yŏk station
연극 yŏn·gŭk play (theatre) n
연금 생활자 yŏn·gŭm saeng·hwal·ja pensioner
연필 yŏn·p'il pencil
열 yŏl fever • heat n
열쇠 yŏl·soé key (door, etc)
염좌 yŏm·jwa sprain n
엽서 yŏp·sŏ postcard
영사관 yŏng·sa·gwan consulate
영수증 yŏng·su·jŭng receipt n
영어 yŏng·ŏ English (language)
영업 시간 yŏng·ŏp shi·gan opening hours
영화 yŏng·hwa film • movie
영화관 yŏng·hwa·gwan cinema/ theatre
예를 들면 ye·rŭl·dŭl·myŏn for example
예방주사 ye·bang·ju·sa vaccination
예산 ye·san budget n
예약 ye·yak reservation (booking)
예약해요 (예약하~) ye·ya·k'ae·yo (ye·ya·k'a~) make a booking
옛터 yet·t'ŏ ruins
오늘 o·nŭl today
오늘 밤 o·nŭl·bam tonight
오래된 o·rae·doén old (things)
오른쪽 o·rŭn·jjok right (direction)
오빠 op·pa older brother (female speaker)
오후 o·hu afternoon
온천 on·ch'ŏn hot spring
옷 ot clothing
옷가게 ok·ka·gé clothing store
와인 wa·in wine
완전 채식주의자 wan·jŏn ch'ae·shik·ju·i·ja vegan n
왕복 표 wang·bok p'yo return ticket
왜 wae why
외국의 oé·gu·gé foreign
외국인 oé·gu·gin foreigner
왼쪽 oén·jjok left (direction)
요금 yo·gŭm fare n
요금 내는 곳 yo·gŭm nae·nŭn·got tollbooth
요리사 yo·ri·sa chef • cook n
요리해요 (요리하~) yo·ri·hae·yo (yo·ri·ha~) cook v
욕실 yok·shil bathroom
우리의 u·ri·é our
우비 u·bi raincoat
우산 u·san umbrella
우스운 u·sŭ·un funny
우유 u·yu milk n
우체국 u·ch'e·guk post office
우체통 u·ch'e·t'ong mailbox
우편 u·p'yŏn mail (postal system) n
우편번호 u·p'yŏn·bŏn·ho postcode
우표 u·p'yo postage stamp
운동용품 가게 un·dong·yong·p'um ga·gé sports store
운전면허증 un·jŏn myŏn·hŏ·jŭng driver's licence
운전해요 (운전하~) un·jŏn·hae·yo (un·jŏn·ha~) drive v
웨이터 we·i·t'ŏ waiter
위 wi stomach
위로 wi·ro up
위에 wi·é on
위장염 wi·jang·nyŏm gastroenteritis
위치 wi·ch'i location
위험한 wi·hŏm·han dangerous
유기농 식품 yu·gi·nong shik·p'um organic food
유로 yu·ro euro
유료 주차 yu·ryo ju·ch'a paid parking
유모차 yu·mo·ch'a stroller (for child)

유스호스텔 yu·sŭ·ho·sŭ·t'el youth hostel
유아식 yu·a·shik baby food
유제품 yu·je·p'um dairy products
육수 yuk·su stock (food)
육아 도우미 yu·ga do·u·mi babysitter
윤활제 yun·hwal·jé lubricant
은 ŭn silver n
은행 ŭn·haeng bank n
은행 계좌 ŭn·haeng gye·jwa bank account
음료수 ŭm·nyo·su drink n
음반 매장 ŭm·ban mae·jang music shop
음식 ŭm·shik food
음악 ŭ·mak music
응급 상황 ŭng·gŭp sang·hwang emergency
의류 매장 ŭi·ryu mae·jang boutique (fashion) n
의사 ŭi·sa doctor (medical)
의자 ŭi·ja chair n
의학 ŭi·hak medicine (profession)
이 주일 i·ju·il fortnight
이등 i·dŭng second class n
이른 i·rŭn early adv
이름 i·rŭm first name • name inf
이메일 i·me·il email n
이코노미석 i·k'o·no·mi·sŏk economy class
이혼한 i·hon·han divorced
인터넷 in·t'ŏ·net internet
일 il job
일 인당 i·rin·dang per person
일기 il·gi diary
일반 택시 il·ban t'aek·shi regular taxi
일방통행 il·bang t'ong·haeng one-way
잃어버린 i·rŏ·bŏ·rin lost
임신 중인 im·shin jung·in pregnant
입 ip mouth
입구 ip·gu entrance
입장 ip·jang entry n
입장료 ip·jang·nyo admission (price)
있어요 (있~) iss·ŏ·yo (iss~) be present • exist

ㅈ

자녀 ja·nyŏ children (offspring)
자동차 등록증 ja·dong·ch'a dŭng·nok·jŭng car registration
자리 ja·ri seat (place) n
자막 ja·mak subtitles
자매 ja·mae sister
자물쇠 ja·mul·soé padlock
자요 (자~) ja·yo (ja~) sleep v
자전거 ja·jŏn·gŏ bicycle
자정 ja·jŏng midnight
작아요 (작~) ja·ga·yo (jak~) be small v
작은 ja·gŭn short (height) • small
잔 jan glass (drinking)
잔돈 jan·don change (coins) n
잘라요 (자르~) jal·la·yo (ja·rŭ~) cut v
잘생긴 jal saeng·gin handsome
잠궈요 (잠그~) jam·gwŏ·yo (jam·gŭ~) lock v
잠긴 jam·gin locked
장갑 jang·gap gloves (clothing)
장마 jang·ma monsoon • rainy season
장모님 jang·mo·nim mother-in-law (wife's mother)
장애인 jang·ae·in disabled person
장인어른 jang·i·nŏ·rŭn father-in-law (wife's father)
재단사 jae·dan·sa tailor n
재떨이 jaet·tŏ·ri ashtray
재미없는 jae·mi·ŏm·nŭn boring
재미없어요 (재미없~) jae·mi·ŏpsŏ·yo (jae·mi·ŏp~) be boring v
재킷 jae·k'it jacket
저 jŏ I pol • that (away from listener) a
저것 jŏ·gŏt that one (away from listener) pron
저기 jŏ·gi there (away from listener)
저기에 jŏ·gi·é over there
저녁 jŏ·nyŏk dinner • evening
저의 jŏ·é my pol
전기 jŏn·gi electricity
전류 jŏl·lyu current (electricity) n
전망 jŏn·mang view n
전보 jŏn·bo telegram
전부 jŏn·bu everything • whole

전자레인지 jŏn·ja·re·in·ji microwave oven
전자제품 jŏn·ja·je·p'um electronics
전파사 jŏn·p'a·sa electrical store
전화 jŏn·hwa telephone n
전화해요 (전화하~) jŏn·hwa·hae·yo (jŏn·hwa·ha~) telephone v
점심 jŏm·shim lunch n
접시 jŏp·shi dish n • plate
정각에 jŏng·ga·gé on time
정오 jŏng·o midday • noon
정원 jŏng·wŏn garden n
정육점 jŏng·yuk·jŏm butcher's shop
정확히 jŏng·hwa·k'i exactly
제일 가까운 je·il gak·ka·un nearest
제일 작은 je·il ja·gŭn smallest
제일 큰 je·il k'ŭn biggest
제한 속도 je·han·sok·do speed limit
조명 측정기 jo·myŏng ch'ŭk·jŏng·gi light meter
조선인민공화국 jo·sŏn in·min gong·hwa·guk Democratic People's Republic of Korea
조용한 jo·yong·han quiet
족집게 jok·jip·ké tweezers
종이 jong·i paper n
좋아요 (좋~) jo·a·yo (jo~) be good v
좋아해요 (좋아하~) jo·a·hae·yo (jo·a·ha~) like v
좋은 jo·ŭn good • great
좌석 버스 jwa·sŏk bŏ·sŭ deluxe metropolitan bus
주 ju week
주류 판매점 ju·ryu p'an·mae·jŏm liquor store
주말 ju·mal weekend
주방 ju·bang kitchen
주사 ju·sa injection
주사바늘 ju·sa·ba·nŭl needle (syringe)
주소 ju·so address n
주유소 ju·yu·so petrol/gas station
주차 빌딩 ju·ch'a bil·ding parking structure
주차 위반 ju·ch'a wi·ban parking violation
주차해요 (주차하~) ju·ch'a·hae·yo (chu·ch'a·ha~) park (a car) v
주황색 ju·hwang·saek orange a
죽여요 (죽이~) ju·gyŏ·yo (ju·gi~) kill
중앙 jung·ang centre n
중요한 jung·yo·han important
중요해요 (중요하~) jung·yo·hae·yo (jung·yo·ha~) be important v
지금 ji·gŭm now
지난 ji·nan last (previous)
지도 ji·do map (of country)
지방의 ji·bang·é local a
지불 ji·bul payment
지연 ji·yŏn delay n
지퍼 ji·p'ŏ zip/zipper
지폐 ji·p'yé banknote
지프차 ji·p'ŭ·ch'a jeep
지하철 ji·ha·ch'ŏl metro (train)
지하철역 ji·ha·ch'ŏl·yŏk metro station
직업 ji·gŏp profession
직접적인 jik·jŏp·jŏ·gin direct a
진동 jin·dong concussion
진실 jin·shil truth
진통제 jin·t'ong·jé painkiller
짐 보관함 jim bo·gwan·ham luggage locker
짐 jim baggage • luggage
집 jip home • house
집세 jip·sé rent n

ㅉ

짠 jjan salty

ㅊ

차 ch'a car • tea
차가운 ch'a·ga·un cold (to senses) a
찻숟가락 ch'as·suk·ka·rak teaspoon
찻집 ch'at·jip teahouse
창문 ch'ang·mun window
채식주의자 ch'ae·shik·ju·i·ja vegetarian n
책 ch'aek book n
처방전 ch'ŏ·bang·jŏn prescription
처음으로 ch'ŏ·ŭ·mŭ·ro first adv
철도 ch'ŏl·do railway
첫 ch'ŏt first a
청바지 ch'ŏng·ba·ji jeans

청소 ch'ŏng·so cleaning
청소해요 (청소하~) ch'ŏng·so·hae·yo (ch'ŏng·so·ha~) clean v
체육관 ch'e·yuk·kwan gym (gymnasium)
체조 ch'e·jo gymnastics
체크인 ch'e·k'ŭ·in check-in (desk)
초과 수하물 ch'o·gwa su·ha·mul excess baggage
초록색 ch'o·rok·saek green a
초콜릿 ch'o·k'ol·lit chocolate
최고의 ch'oé·go·é best
추운 ch'u·un cold (weather) a
추워요 (춥~) ch'u·wŏ·yo (ch'up~) be cold (weather) v
추천해요 (추천하~) ch'u·ch'ŏn·hae·yo (ch'u·ch'ŏn·ha~) recommend
축구 ch'uk·ku football • soccer
출구 ch'ul·gu exit n
출국장 ch'ul·guk·jang departure hall
출발 ch'ul·bal departure
출장 ch'ul·jang business trip
춤 ch'um dance n
춤 춰요 (춤 추~) ch'um·ch'wŏ·yo (ch'um·ch'u~) dance v
충분한 ch'ung·bun·han enough
충치 ch'ung·ch'i dental cavity
취소해요 (취소하~) ch'wi·so·hae·yo (ch'wi·so·ha~) cancel
층 ch'ŭng floor (storey)
치과의사 ch'i·gwa ŭi·sa dentist
치마 ch'i·ma skirt
치수 ch'is·su size (clothes, shoes) n
치실 ch'i·shil dental floss
치약 ch'i·yak toothpaste
치통 ch'i·t'ong toothache
친구 ch'in·gu friend
친절한 ch'in·jŏl·han kind (nice)
침낭 ch'im·nang sleeping bag
침대 ch'im·dae bed
침대 시트 ch'im·dae shi·t'ŭ bed sheet
침대차 ch'im·dae·ch'a sleeping car
침실 ch'im·shil bedroom
칫솔 ch'is·sol toothbrush

ㅋ

카메라 k'a·me·ra camera
카트 k'a·t'ŭ trolley (shopping)
카페 k'a·pé cafe
칼 k'al knife n
캔 k'aen can • tin
캔 오프너 k'ae·no·p'ŭ·nŏ can opener • tin opener
캠코더 k'aem·k'o·dŏ video camera
커요 (크~) k'ŏ·yo (k'ŭ~) be big v
커피 k'ŏ·p'i coffee
컴퓨터 k'ŏm·p'yu·t'ŏ computer
컵 k'ŏp cup
코 k'o nose
코르크 따개 k'o·rŭ·k'ŭ dda·gae corkscrew
코트 k'ŏ·t'ŭ coat n • court (tennis, sports)
콘돔 k'on·dom condom
콘돔 사용하는 섹스 k'on·dom sa·yong·ha·nŭn sek·sŭ safe sex
콘서트 k'on·sŏ·t'ŭ concert
콘택트 렌즈 k'on·t'aek·t'ŭ ren·jŭ contact lenses
크기 k'ŭ·gi size (general)
큰 k'ŭn big
킬로그램 k'il·lo·gŭ·raem kilogram
킬로미터 k'il·lo·mi·t'ŏ kilometre

ㅌ

타요 (타~) t'a·yo (t'a~) board (plane, ship) v
타이어 t'a·i·ŏ tire • tyre
탈 것 t'al·gŏt ride n
탈의실 t'a·ri·shil changing room
탐폰 t'am·p'on tampon
탑승한 t'ap·sŭng·han aboard
탑승권 t'ap·sŭng·gwŏn boarding pass
태풍 t'ae·p'ung typhoon
택시 정류장 t'aek·shi jŏng·nyu·jang taxi stand
테니스 t'e·ni·sŭ tennis
테니스 경기장 t'e·ni·sŭ gyŏng·gi·jang tennis court
텔레비전 t'el·le·bi·jŏn television
토스터 t'o·sŭ·t'o toaster

통로 t'ong·no aisle (on plane)
통신사 t'ong·shin·sa newsagency
통역사 t'ong·yŏk·sa interpreter
통화 중 t'ong·hwa·jung busy (phone)
튀겨요 (튀기~) t'wi·gyŏ·yo (t'wi·gi~) fry
트윈 베드 t'ŭ·win·be·dŭ twin bed
티브이 t'i·bŭ·i TV
티셔츠 t'i·shŏ·ch'ŭ T-shirt
티슈 t'i·shyu tissues
팁 t'ip cover charge • service charge • tip (gratuity) n

ㅍ

파란 p'a·ran blue
파업 p'a·ŏp strike (labour) n
파티 p'a·t'i party (night out) n
팔 p'al arm (body)
패션 p'ae·shŏn fashion n
팬티라이너 p'aen·t'i·ra·i·nŏ panty liners
팬티스타킹 p'aen·t'i·sŭ·t'a·k'ing pantyhose
퍼스트 클래스 p'ŏ·sŭ·t'ŭ k'ŭl·lae·sŭ first class
페리 p'e·ri ferry n
편도 표 p'yŏn·do p'yo one-way ticket
편안한 p'yŏ·nan·han comfortable
편의점 p'yŏ·ni·jŏm convenience store
편지 p'yŏn·ji letter • mail n
편지 부쳐요 (편지 부치~) p'yŏn·ji bu·ch'yŏ·yo (p'yŏn·ji bu·ch'i~) post (letter) v
평평한 p'yŏng·p'yŏng·han flat a
포크 p'o·k'ŭ fork
포함된 p'o·ham·doén included
표 p'yo ticket
표 자판기 p'yo ja·pan·gi ticket machine
표 파는 곳 p'yo p'a·nŭn·got ticket booth
푸드코트 p'u·dŭ·k'o·t'ŭ food court
푹푹 쪄요 (푹푹 찌~) p'uk·p'uk jjyŏ·yo (p'uk·p'uk jji~) be hot and humid v
풍습 p'ung·sŭp custom
프라이팬 p'ŭ·ra·i·p'aen frying pan
프리마 p'ŭ·ri·ma creamer (for coffee)
프린터 p'ŭ·rin·t'ŏ printer (computer)
플러그 p'ŭl·lŏ·gŭ plug (electricity) n

피곤한 p'i·gon·han tired
피곤해요 (피곤하~) p'i·gon hae·yo (p'i·gon ha~) be tired v

ㅎ

하루 ha·ru day
하숙집 ha·suk·jip boarding house
학생 hak·saeng student n
한가한 han·ga·han free (available) a
한국 han·guk Korea
한국어 han·gu·gŏ Korean (language) n
한국의 han·gu·gé Korean a
할머니 hal·mŏ·ni elderly woman • grandmother
할아버지 ha·ra·bŏ·ji elderly man • grandfather
할인 ha·rin discount n
항공 우편 hang·gong u·p'yŏn airmail
항공사 hang·gong·sa airline
항생제 hang·saeng·jé antibiotics
해 hae sun • year
해넘이 hae·nŏ·mi sunset
해돋이 hae·do·ji sunrise
해변 hae·byŏn beach (seaside)
해수욕장 hae·su·yok·jang beach (for swimming)
해외 hae·oé overseas n
핸드백 haen·dŭ·baek handbag • purse
햇빛에 탐 haep·pi·ch'é t'am sunburn
행복한 haeng·bo·k'an happy
행복해요 (행복하~) haeng·bo·k'ae·yo (haeng·bo·k'a~) be happy v
향수 hyang·su perfume n
허리 hŏ·ri back (body)
헤드라이트 he·dŭ·ra·i·t'ŭ headlights
헤어 커트 he·ŏ·k'ŏ·t'ŭ haircut
헬스장 hel·sŭ·jang gym (health club)
혀 hyŏ tongue
현금 hyŏn·gŭm cash n
현금으로 바꿔요 (현금으로 바꾸~) hyŏn·gŭ·mŭ·ro bak·kwŏ·yo (hyŏn·gŭ·mŭ·ro bak·ku~) cash (a cheque) v
현금인출기 hyŏn·gŭ·min·ch'ul·gi ATM
현대의 hyŏn·dae·é modern
혈액 hyŏ·raek blood

혈액형 hyŏ·rae·k'yŏng blood group
형 hyŏng older brother (male speaker)
형제 hyŏng·jé brother
형편 없는 hyŏng·p'yŏn ŏm·nŭn awful
호수 ho·su lake
호스텔 ho·sŭ·t'el hostel
호텔 ho·t'el hotel
홀로 hol·lo alone
후에 ... hu·é after ...
화상 hwa·sang burn n
화장 hwa·jang make-up n
화장실 hwa·jang·shil toilet
확인해요 (확인하~) hwa·gin·hae·yo (hwa·gin·ha~) confirm (a booking) • validate
환불 hwan·bul refund n
환승 라운지 hwan·sŭng ra·un·ji transit lounge
환율 hwa·nyul exchange rate
환자 hwan·ja patient n
환전해요 (환전하~) hwan·jŏn·hae·yo (hwan·jŏn·ha~) change (money) v
회사 hoé·sa company (firm)
회색의 hoé·sae·gé grey • gray
회의 hoé·i conference
회화책 hoé·hwa·ch'aek phrasebook
훔친 hum·ch'in stolen
휘발유 hwi·bal·yu petrol • gas
휠체어 hwil·ch'é·ŏ wheelchair
휴가 hyu·ga vacation
휴대폰 hyu·dae·p'on cell/mobile phone
휴대품 보관소 hyu·dae·p'um bo·gwan·so cloakroom
휴무 hyu·mu closed
휴식 시간 hyu·shik shi·gan intermission
휴양지 hyu·yang·ji resort n
흡연 구역 hŭ·byŏn ku·yŏk smoking area
희귀한 hi·gwi·han rare (uncommon)
흰 hin white
히치하이크해요 (히치하이크하~) hi·ch'i·ha·i·k'ŭ·hae·yo (hi·ch'i·ha·i·k'ŭ·ha~) hitchhike v
히터 hi·t'ŏ heater

INDEX

For topics that are covered in several sections of this book, we've indicated the most relevant page number in bold.

A

B

C

D

E

F

G

H

I

J

K

L

M

N

O

P

Q

R

S

T

V

W

10 Ways TO START A SENTENCE

When's (the next bus)?	(다음 버스) 언제 있나요?	(da·ŭm bŏ·sŭ) ŏn·jé in·na·yo
Where's (the train/ subway station)?	(역) 어디예요?	(yŏk) ŏ·di·ye·yo
Where do I (buy a ticket)?	어디에서 (표 사나요)?	ŏ·di·e·sŏ (p'yo sa·na·yo)
I'm looking for (a hotel).	(호텔) 찾고 있어요.	(ho·t'el) ch'ak·ko iss·ŏ·yo
Do you have (a map)?	(지도) 가지고 계신가요?	(ji·do) ga·ji·go gye·shin·ga·yo
Is there (a toilet)?	(화장실) 있나요?	(hwa·jang·shil) in·na·yo
I'd like (the menu).	(메뉴) 주세요.	(me·nyu) ju·se·yo
I'd like to (hire a car).	(차 빌리)고 싶어요.	(ch'a bil·li)·go shi·p'ŏ·yo
Do I need (a visa)?	(비자) 필요 한가요?	(bi·ja) p'i·ryo·han·ga·yo
I have (a passport).	(여권) 있어요.	(yŏ·gwŏn) iss·ŏ·yo